Constructive
Social Work

Also by Nigel Parton

The Politics of Child Abuse

Governing the Family: Child Care, Child Protection and the State

Social Theory, Social Change and Social Work (edited)

Child Protection: Risk and the Moral Order (with David Thorpe and Corrine Wattam)

Also by Patrick O'Byrne

Assessment in Social Work (with Judith Milner)

Constructive Social Work

Towards a New Practice

Nigel Parton

and

Patrick O'Byrne

1-23-7

First published in Great Britain 2000 by
MACMILLAN PRESS LTD
Houndmills, Basingstoke, Hampshire RG21 6XS
and London
Companies and representatives throughout the world

A catalogue record for this book is available from the British Library.

ISBN 0-333-92948-9 (hardcover)
ISBN 0-333-74729-1 (paperback)

First published in the United States of America 2000 by
ST. MARTIN'S PRESS, INC.
Scholarly and Reference Division,
175 Fifth Avenue,
New York, N.Y. 10010

ISBN 0-312-23309-4

Library of Congress Cataloging-in-Publication Data

Parton, Nigel.
Constructive social work : towards a new practice
Nigel Parton and Patrick O'Byrne.
p.cm.
Includes bibliographical references and index.
ISBN 0-312-23309-4 (cloth)
1. Social service – Philosophy. 2. Constructivism (Psychology) 3. Schemas
(Psychology) I. O'Byrne, Patrick. II. Title.
HV 40 .P28 2000
361.3′01–dc

99-086556

This book is printed on paper suitable for recycling and made from fully managed and
sustained forest sources.

10 9 8 7 6 5 4 3 2 1
09 08 07 06 05 04 03 02 01 00

Printed in China

Transferred to digital printing 2005

Contents

Acknowledgements

Numerous people have helped and contributed to the project: some by sharing experiences; others by discussing ideas; others by reading and critically commenting on our draft chapters as they emerged; and others by providing both practical and emotional support. We owe a particular gratitude to Trevor Butt, Linda Davies, Brid Featherstone, Linda Halliwell, Sue Hanson, Chris Hall, Bill Jordan, Judith Milner, Trish Morris, Mary O'Byrne, Chris Parton and Barbara Pellymounter. However, we know that some, if not all, of them will not be happy with the product and will feel we have emphasised some issues and themes at the cost of others. As ever, therefore, we take full responsibility for what follows.

NIGEL PARTON
PATRICK O'BYRNE

Introduction

Our motivations for and interest in writing this book are various. A major concern for us is that we are increasingly of the view that social work, particularly in the United Kingdom, has lost its way. In particular we have become concerned that social work both in the way we think about it and practise it has become very defensive, overly proceduralised and narrowly concerned with assessing, managing and insuring against risk. The last twenty-five years, again particularly in the UK, has witnessed a range of criticisms, public inquiries and media opprobrium which has placed both managers and practitioners, primarily in the statutory sectors, in the spotlight. These developments became even more intense during the 1990s when we saw the introduction of sophisticated attempts to make social workers accountable and subject their practice to ever more detailed reviews, inspections, audits and managerial oversight and prescription.

We are not, in principle, against these developments as it is clear they represent serious attempts to improve quality and increase consistency for service users who, by definition, are likely to be some of the most powerless and vulnerable people in society. However, it seems to us the changes are essentially of a top-down nature and are rarely informed by a detailed knowledge of the nature and realities of practice. More particularly we are concerned that the nature of the changes has increased the organisational demands upon both practitioners and users themselves.

The result is that less and less time is spent working directly with the users or clients and in particular listening to their concerns and talking with them about what might be done. It is as if social work is becoming almost *asocial*. The attempts to try and make social work more and more rational and predictable are having the consequence, probably unintended, of deflecting social work from what is distinctive about it and the essential elements of what constitute its main strengths.

Traditionally social workers' expertise has been built on the ability to: know how to establish relationships with a wide variety of people; survey the environment for resources and bring these together on behalf of the client; negotiate with various individuals, groups and organisations and to mobilise their energies; and enter other worlds of meaning in order to offer help. Increasingly, however, social workers have taken on the role of organisational functionaries. In part this arises from the introduction of the purchaser/provider split and the emergence of the role of the care manager. However, this is not the sole reason, for there have been important changes in the overall contexts and rationale of the work. There has also been, however, a failure to develop theoretical approaches which are useful to practitioners and which therefore try to inform practice directly – particularly approaches which are explicitly concerned with language and dialogue and which lie at the core of practice and thus make it distinctive.

This brings us to our second broad area of motivation, for at the same time we have become aware of the growing intellectual interest in social theory and the human sciences more generally of a number of theoretical developments associated with social constructionism, postmodernity and, more specifically, the centrality of language and narrative for understanding both the social world and what it is to be human. While such perspectives have been drawn on to inform research-based analyses *of* social work and social workers, rarely have they been used to develop concepts and insights *for* practice. This is the primary task we have set ourselves here and in the process develop an innovative and challenging approach to practice which we characterise as *constructive social work*.

Constructive social work emphasises process, plurality of both knowledge and voice, possibility and the relational quality of knowledge. It proceeds on the assumption that users, no matter what their circumstances, have significant resources within and around them but that the way these are *storied* is key to opening up new and more positive possibilities. Because social workers are experts in process, they can help people to focus these resources to best assist them in accomplishing their goals and in re-storying their situations. The social worker does not presume to know what is best and what to do, so that an ability to work with ambiguity and uncertainty both in terms of process and outcome is key. The principle of indeterminacy suggests the fluid, recursive and non-determined way that social situations unfold; for the general thrust is that life is replete with possibilities and that the linguistic social bond is more open to alteration and change than is often assumed.

Constructive social work argues that social work is as much, if not more, an art than a science and proceeds on the basis that practice is better characterised as a *practical-moral activity* rather than a *rational-technical* one, and that attempts to increase realism and objectivism are likely to be misguided. However, we do not fall into an ethical abyss or sink into moral nihilism but rather make even more explicit the moral choices and responsibilities that are central to social work practice.

The *constructive* approach we develop is affirmative and reflexive and focuses on dialogue, listening to and talking with the other. It aims to reveal by paradox, myth and enigma and persuades by showing, reminding, hinting and evoking rather than applying knowledge and approximating truth. The focus is narrative and different stories, so that social work at times may take on the guise of persuasive fiction or poetry. In outlining such an approach we recognise it has relevance in all contexts, roles and tasks that social workers are engaged with. It suggests quite new ways of presenting the professional self to managers, courts, other agencies, community groups and social networks of every sort. Such an approach challenges many of our taken-for-granted assumptions, the way we think and the way we operate in all spheres. It is thus part of a much wider project which is trying to develop constructionist and narrative approaches to practice. However, our prime focus here is upon the direct face-to-face interactions and work with clients and users. We do so for a number of reasons.

First, it is our view that the last twenty years have seen something of a neglect in developing and refining our detailed knowledge of what to do and how to relate to and with clients. Yet it is our view that even though a declining proportion of social workers' time is spent in direct face-to-face work with clients this is still the core of the work. It is the core which makes practice *practice* and which distinguishes practitioners from others. It is our view therefore that if we can demonstrate the relevance and creativity of *constructive social work* on the terrain of direct practice with users it will provide the catalyst for encouraging others to develop its use in other but very related spheres.

But second, it also reflects our own interests and experiences. One of us (Nigel Parton) originally worked as a social worker in a local authority social services department, and during the 1980s continued to work as a social services duty officer, on an honorary part-time basis. In more recent years he has worked with a number of small community-based voluntary organisations and has been a foster-carer. He thus has direct experience of being on the receiving end of social work. During the past twenty years he has written and researched in the broad areas of child welfare and child protection and has always had an interest in the use of and application of ideas from social theory to social work. In contrast, Patrick O'Byrne came into social work much later after having spent eleven years as a priest in the North East of England, having been brought up in Southern Ireland. He then joined the Probation Service where he worked for ten years. Over the last twenty years he has also developed an interest and ongoing practice in family therapy and, more recently, mediation. His particular interests are trying to develop empowering ways to bring change about with service users, drawing on ideas from solution-focused and narrative practice.

Over the past twenty years we have worked together at Huddersfield University primarily in relation to the professional training of social workers – initially via the CQSW and more recently the DipSW. While coming from different professional backgrounds and having different interests, it is this relationship between theory and practice which has been an ongoing mutual interest. More particularly it is the mutual interest in constructionism, narrative and postmodern approaches, and developing and demonstrating their relevance to social work practice at the start of the new millennium, which has spurred us on.

The book is organised in such a way that while theoretically grounded our overall aim of articulating creative and innovative approaches to practice is explicit. Chapter 1 outlines what we mean by *constructive social work* and critically discusses perspectives associated with social constructionism and which we see as providing some important theoretical frameworks for such an approach. Chapter 2 is concerned with debates about the nature of social work theory and in particular the theory/practice relationship. It argues that such debates and the form they take are crucially influenced by changing social and political contexts and that our current times point to the importance of developing constructionist and narrative approaches to practice. Chapters 3 and 4 set out in some detail the key theoretical orientations we see informing *constructive social work* and its future refinement.

Chapters 5 and 6 are explicitly concerned with demonstrating how such approaches can be *used* in practice. Chapter 5 draws on and develops approaches familiar in therapy and counselling associated with narrative ideas. The work of White, Epston and O'Hanlon is particularly drawn upon. Chapter 6 critically discusses the solution-focused work of de Shazer, Berg and others. Chapter 7 then provides two lengthy case studies from practice to illustrate how such approaches can be drawn upon in mainstream social work. Chapter 8 then critically discusses the way assessment, which is so central to much social work activity, might be approached from a *constructive point of view*.

Chapter 9 has two main aims: firstly to summarise and critically discuss a number of research studies which have been carried out on narrative and solution-focused practice; and secondly to consider how far such approaches can be gender sensitive. The final chapter attempts to summarise what we see as the key characteristics of *constructive social work*, but in a way which addresses some fundamental issues which its critical commentators are likely to voice in terms of its failure to recognise the importance of objectivity and reality and its inherent moral relativising and nihilism. We argue that on none of these points can the approach be found culpable and in fact it helps to rediscover the central values and strengths of social work which in recent years have been lost.

1

What Do We Mean by 'Constructive Social Work'?

Curiosity. To me it evokes 'concern'; it evokes the care one takes for what exists and could exist; a readiness to find strange what surrounds us; a certain relentlessness to break up our familiarities; a fervor to grasp what is happening and what passes; a casualness in regard to the traditional hierarchies of the important and the essential. (Foucault, 1989, p. 198)

Introduction

The central purpose of this opening chapter is two-fold: first to outline what we mean by *constructive social work* and what we see as some of its central elements; and second to discuss the perspectives associated with *constructionism* which we see as providing important theoretical frameworks for developing such an approach to practice. Before doing so, however, we outline why we feel it is important to engage in such a task at the present time. Why do we need a *constructive* approach to social work practice now?

While we believe it is an exaggeration to say that social work in the United Kingdom is currently in 'crisis' (Clarke, 1993), there can be little doubt that over recent years social work has been subject to considerable criticism and is currently undergoing major change and reconfiguration (Parton, 1996; Parton, 1998a) which is likely to continue well into the new millennium following the publication of the White Paper (1998) *Modernising Social Services*. In particular it seems that practitioners are subject to a range of increasingly detailed procedures, targets, outcome measures and managerial oversights which have the effect of undermining both their professional skills and morale. As one of us has argued elsewhere: 'Increasingly it feels as if social work does not have a core theoretical knowledge base, and that there is a hole at the centre of the enterprise' (Parton, 1994b, p. 30). There has been a failure to articulate and develop concepts and theories *for* practice in recent years which has done a considerable disservice not only to practitioners but, more crucially, the people with whom they work. In particular we have not built on a range of insights and concepts which had previously been derived from detailed analysis of what goes on between social worker and service user. Our central aim in this book is to help both practitioners and those in the social work academy to *(re)value* the importance of developing detailed and critical analysis of the meaningfulness of language and narrative between social worker and service user and to offer social workers ways of using narrative to construct change. Such a (re)orientation is of real urgency in that while there are various calls, for example in the White Paper (1998) *Modernising Social Services*, for practitioners to be 'user-centred', for partnership, empowerment and promoting independence, practitioners are given few clues as to the skills they require and the knowledge and theory they can use to do this.

The significance of such a task has recently been underlined by Olive Stevenson in her reflections on fifty years of child welfare practice in England and Wales since the Children Act 1948. While we have some major reservations with her analysis we do feel the issues to which she draws attention are important.

The reorganisation of social services, the expansion of training, the growing influence of sociological critiques and the increased awareness of broader social policy issues are all seen by Stevenson to have contributed to the demise of enthusiasm for psycho-dynamic theory on social work courses: 'The 1960s saw the beginning of a decline; not only were there "too many" ways of understanding on offer to the intending social worker, they were often inadequately applied to the day-to-day work and sometimes taught from a position of hostility, masquerading as rational criti-cism, to the business of social work' (Stevenson, 1998b, pp. 84–5).

She argues that the marginalising and general undermining of psychodynamic theory led to a major problem which has dogged both training and practice ever since – 'the failure to develop an indigenous, coherent body of practice theory *for* social work' (Stevenson, 1998a, p. 156, our emphasis). More particularly, and of direct relevance for our purposes here, she argues that 'it is not an exaggeration to see in the 1960s the beginning of a decline in the search for *meaning* which dogs us today, when *comprehensive assessments* may be devoid of theoretical substance' (Stevenson, 1998b, p. 84, original emphasis).While there has since been a proliferation of theories available (see, for example, Howe, 1987; Payne, 1997; Adams, Dominelli and Payne, 1998), according to Stevenson the problem 'remains the same as in the 1960s and 1970s: how to enable social workers to select, apply and integrate theory so that they address their work in child welfare more purposefully' (Stevenson, 1998b, p. 93).

We would argue, however, that the explanations for the changes in social work, particularly how it is practised in state agencies, are much more complex than Stevenson allows for, nor is it adequate to hark back to a 'golden age' in the post-war period. What is significant, however, is that the failure to develop theory *for* practice in recent years that she points to is somehow emblematic of the situation social work finds itself in. It is as if social workers are deployed to process *needs* in an essentially bureaucratic way and slot human misery into categories of *risk* and vulnerability. As David Howe has argued (1992, 1996), social work has become legalised and proceduralised where manuals, guidelines and lines of accountability are carried out in a functional way almost to the exclusion of any creativity or skill in dealing with human relationships. As we will argue in the next chapter, there has been a failure to recognise the complex nature of social work. We would suggest, however, these failures to develop helpful and relevant theories *for* practice are as much a consequence as they are a cause of the changing nature of social work.

Recent years have witnessed something of a re-emergence of interest in trying to build on the earlier psychodynamic and ego psychological approaches in terms of the development of psychosocial relationship-based theories and an understanding of attachment for social work (Howe, 1995a; Howe, 1997; Howe, 1998; Howe and Hinings, 1995; Howe, Brandon, Hinings and Schofield, 1999). That is not our purpose here, however, for in many respects Stevenson is over-dismissive of certain developments particularly in the 1970s and early 1980s in terms of various writers' attempts to move beyond the psychodynamic approach. Far from being negative and hostile to social work we can see the impact of ideas associated with interactionism, labelling and deviancy theory, particularly the work of Erving Goffman (1968a, 1968b, 1971), Howard Becker (1963, 1964) and Ronald Laing (1965, 1971; Laing and Esterson, 1970) – as well as the neo-Marxism of the radical social work movement (Bailey and Brake, 1975) – as helping practitioners see that not only were their interventions influenced by a variety of social and political factors but that social work interventions were not necessarily in the interests of the client. Similarly, the 1980s and 1990s saw a growing awareness of the importance of sexuality, gender, race, disability and age as well as social class as key factors in increasing exclusion, oppression and discrimination, and of the fact that social workers can play a key role in developing anti-discriminatory and empowering practice (see Thompson, 1997 and 1998, for a discussion of these issues).

There was also evidence in the 1970s and 1980s of others writing about what happened at the interpersonal, detailed level of exchanges between client and worker and in the process moved beyond the problems associated with adopting the traditional casework model based on the psychodynamic approach. They emphasised the importance of trying to make sense of how people understand their day-to-day experiences and how this affects how they act and feel towards other people. There was the development of an explicitly 'client-centred' approach which tried to articulate the art of helping in social work (Jordan, 1970, 1972, 1979; Brandon and Jordan, 1979; Wilkes, 1981; England, 1986) and which emphasised the use of self, the nature of and quality of the relationship, the understanding of experience, the search for meaning, the importance of communication and the transactional nature of the relationship between the social worker and the client and that an understanding of and use of language was central. The nature of this writing was such that neat and clear-cut theoretical models were not developed. However, it was on this terrain that the potential for developing theory *for* practice could have been developed and in many respects it is from this tradition that we can see the clearest connections and roots of what we are trying to develop here. Unfortunately since the mid-1980s such a tradition has been all but lost from the literature. At the heart of such an approach was the attempt to help the service-user recognise and understand themselves and bring about change both of meaning and the perception of experiences. To do so, however, required the worker to engage in detailed awareness and use of the social work process and sensitive acknowledgement of the nature, limitations and potentials of their own role and authority. Crucially it saw social work as more than the application of either science or technique and that the skills required were qualitatively different from those needed to be an organisational functionary.

Constructive social work

What, therefore, do we understand by *constructive social work*? We have chosen the term for two reasons. First, we are drawing on what have come to be called constructionist and narrative approaches for both analysing and understanding social work and more particularly for developing our theoretical insights *for* practice. In many respects this can be seen as our major task.

Second, however, we have chosen the term *constructive* to reflect our wish to try and provide a perspective which is explicitly positive and tries to build on what is distinctive about social work and what we see as its major strengths – but which are in danger of being lost in the current climate. While we are using the term metaphorically we do not want to lose its literal meaning, for the core idea of *construction*, from the Latin to the present day, is that of *building* or of *putting together*. The *Oxford Dictionary* defines *construction* as 'the action or manner of constructing' while *constructive* is defined as 'having a useful purpose; helpful'. These are ideas which we want to articulate and capture. The term *constructive* as we use it here is thus theoretical and metaphorical – both are important.

We are also clear that, while social work is an increasingly complex activity which has a range of allegiances and accountabilities, for us here the key focus is work *with* the service user, and it is the failure, over recent years, to address how we can make sense of the face-to-face encounters of the work that has been missing and which we see as in urgent need of attention.

While we feel the approach we are developing here has wide potential for the way practitioners think about their work for example within the agency, with other agencies, organisations and professionals, work with communities and the wider society it is work with individuals and their immediate relationships that we concentrate on in this book. We do so for two reasons. First, because it is work with individuals and their immediate environment which, certainly in the United Kingdom, continues to be the focus of most social work; and second, because we feel this is an area which, in recent years, has received little attention. What is it that clients and users find most useful and helpful in their contact with social workers?

There are now numerous studies available which have attempted to identify what those on the receiving end of social work and the human services more generally have found most useful and helpful. David Howe (1993) has reviewed a wide cross-section of studies covering a sixty-year period which includes more traditional evaluations, studies which asked consumers about their experiences, and the work of those who have written personally about their experiences. A similar task has been carried out by Seligman (1995) in the United States. The central message that comes across time and time again is that it is not the particular model or techniques used by the social worker or counsellor which are significant but the quality and value of the experience. The key themes which users identify for success are summarised by Howe as 'accept me, understand me and talk with me'. This is not simply saying that good social work is about establishing a 'relationship', important though this is, but that the way we understand and come to terms with difficult and painful experiences is through talk. *Talk* and *language* are key to making sense and taking control. It is the 'making sense' which is important, no matter what it looks like and where it comes from. A client who wishes to re-form the self and make sense of what is going on needs to immerse himself or herself in talk, for it is via *language* that the individual self is formed. As Howe demonstrates, it is less the specific procedures and techniques and more the opportunity to engage in an active *conversation* about oneself that brings about understanding and change. Users say clearly that what they value is the experience of talking which helps them to make sense of their experience and which gives them the opportunity to better control and cope with their life and try and change it accordingly. Howe concludes his study by arguing:

If one distils and distils the messages that are contained in the accounts given by clients of their experiences of counselling and therapy – the need for acceptance and regard, and the search for understanding and meaning – it might be possible to claim that one is left with one very condensed but none the less quintessential observation: *clients seek to control the meaning of their own experience and the meanings that others give to that experience*. Control helps clients to cope, and it empowers. It boosts self-esteem and personal confidence, and ultimately it encourages people to believe that they are valued and worthwhile human beings. (Howe, 1993, p. 195, original emphasis)

Similarly, studies of successful family therapy demonstrate that it is the strength of the therapeutic alliance with someone whom the recipients perceive as warm, trustworthy, non-judgmental and empathic which is key. It seems that telling one's story in one's own terms and having it heard respectfully is a very necessary ingredient for change to begin to occur. It may be that the psychodynamic approach's greatest contribution had little to do with providing an understanding of the functioning of the ego, the superego and the id but the importance of the validation that a person receives simply in telling their story to an attentive listener. The idea of careful listening is a relatively new theme in family therapy and counselling (Anderson, 1987; Hoffman, 1993) but traditionally has been seen as central to the social work process for it has been recognised that listening creates a space for thinking and reflection (Rees and Wallace, 1982; Fisher, 1983). For example, the traditional 'principles of social work' espoused by Biestek (1961) include good individualised listening, as well as: availability; being non-judgmental and non-directive; and working on the basis of trust and confidentiality.

While these issues have always been central to writers who have tried to develop the 'client-centred' approaches, an explicit recognition, theoretically, of the importance of language and narrative has not been recognised. Yet ironically back in 1968 Noel Timms (1968) was arguing that it was vital that social work recognise the centrality of language to its practice. He wrote that 'it is surprising that social workers, who are largely dependent on language, should have given such little attention to words and to what it means to speak a language' (Timms, 1968, p. 1), particularly as at the time the activity was often characterised as an attempt to 'cure through talk', and their case records contained in summary or verbatim form accounts of innumerable conversations with their clients. He felt there was a major incongruity which needed to be rectified – social work's lack of any systematic critical attention to language when words play such a crucial role in both social work education and practice.

He went beyond identifying this incongruity, however, and located language in a theoretical framework which in many respects can be seen to prefigure versions of constructionism which were to emerge some years later. He argued that language plays a critical part in the constitution of our social life, not simply in its description. This was true whether we are concerned with public relationships, with those of a more intimate nature, or, with what he described as 'man's *[sic]* relationship with himself' (p. 4). He saw language as key in the creation and maintenance of human relations. For 'language is the medium through which man becomes conscious of his inner self and at the same time it is the key to the understanding of his outer relationships. It unites him with, but also differentiates him from, others' (p. 4). Unfortunately the issue and challenge which Timms identified has rarely been addressed since.

It seems we have become so concerned about assessing, managing, planning, monitoring and accounting that we have lost the core of what social workers and social work has to offer in terms of the narrative and interactional processes involved. We need a way of bringing language, listening and talking back in but in a way which is theoretically informed and usable so that we recognise it for what it is – central to social work. As we will demonstrate, understanding as a collaborative process is a core idea in constructionism. Here meaning and understanding are matters of negotiation between the participants in conversation and thus the understanding of and use of language is seen as central to the helping process. What, however, do we understand by constructionism for the purposes of informing theory *for* practice?

Some central themes in constructionism

While constructionist perspectives have only recently begun to enter social work in any explicit sense (Rodwell, 1990, 1998; Witkin, 1991; Atherton, 1993; Laird, 1993; Dean, 1993; Rodwell and Wood, 1994; Thyer, 1994; Franklin, 1995; Jokinen *et al.*, 1999), it is important to recognise that they have become increasingly widespread in various areas of Western intellectual life over a number of years. They have been central to some of the most important developments and heated debates in literary studies, philosophy, history, socio-legal studies, anthropology, sociology and psychology. It would be incorrect, however, to assume that there is one single stance or position that can exemplify the work of those that it would be reasonable to include under the umbrella term 'constructionism'.

However, while Mike Lynch is critical of attempts to assert that there is something deeper and more coherent to the various writers and approaches which are happy to use the term he does assert that 'nothing could be more definitive of constructionism than the thesis that social identities depend on audience ascriptions' (1998, p. 14). This is perhaps well illustrated by telling a story related by Sarbin and Kitsuse (1994, p. 2) about three baseball umpires who are reflecting on their professional practice of calling balls and strikes. The first, a self-confident realist says, 'I call 'em the way they are', to which the second, who leans towards phenomenological analysis, says, 'I call 'em as I see 'em', and the third closes the discussion with 'They ain't nothin' until I call 'em', thus alluding to her/his constructionist sympathies. The contrast between the realist umpire and the social constructionist umpire illustrates Lynch's point that audience, or as in this case umpire, ascription is key to social identity. Similar stories can be told about all games; for example in soccer is a foul always a foul or does it depend on whether the referee calls something a foul? Constructionist umpires or referees would argue that it doesn't exist until they call it and, in calling it, assign meaning to it. While such stories may seem inappropriately 'playful' they do illustrate what is distinctive about constructionism.

A little closer to our concerns, constructionist perspectives have become increasingly common in the sociological study of social problems in the United States and are particularly associated with the work of Spector and Kitsuse (1987) which has itself led to considerable theoretical debate (Holstein and Miller, 1993; Miller and Holstein, 1993). However, such an approach has a much longer heritage (see Waller, 1936) and in 1941 Fuller and Myers argued that:

A social problem is a condition which is defined by a considerable number of persons as a deviation from some social norm which they cherish. Every social problem thus consists of an *objective condition* and a *subjective definition*. The objective condition is a verifiable situation which can be checked as to existence and magnitude (proportions) by impartial and trained observers. The subjective definition is the awareness of certain individuals that the condition is a threat to certain cherished values. (Fuller and Myers, 1941, p. 320, original emphasis)

However, while Fuller and Myers suggested that objective conditions are not sufficient on their own to explain why something should become a social problem, they stopped short of arguing that objective conditions are neither necessary nor sufficient. Yet as Blumer (1971) and Spector and Kitsuse (1973) subsequently argued, it is the *assertion* that a problem exists that is key. The focus for analysing the emergence and maintenance of issues as social problems thus becomes the way that claims-makers *construct* certain areas of social life as problematic. Such an approach informed a study that one of us carried out in the early 1980s into the problem of child abuse (Parton, 1985). There are also studies which analyse the way practitioners – whether these be police, doctors or whoever – actively construct aspects of everyday life as problems in the micro-sense by doing *social problems work* (see, for example, Miller, 1992; Holstein and Miller, 1997).

There are now a number of research studies which explicitly use constructionist methodologies for analysing and trying to make transparent what is going on in social work encounters with clients and in social work practice more generally (see Hall, 1997; Jokinen *et al.*, 1999; Karvinen *et al.*, 1999; Parton, Thorpe and Wattam, 1997; Pithouse, 1998, for example). The central message of this research tends to be that, far from being neutral, rational and scientific, social work practice is not only variable but is inherently moral and manipulative and invariably not in the interests of the service users. The emphasis in such research tends to be to *deconstruct* practice and thus demonstrate it is not nearly as benign as may be assumed. However the practical contributions of such research to developing *constructive* practice is rarely made apparent.

Perhaps the key event in introducing the notion of 'social constructionism' to a much wider academic audience was the publication in 1967 of Berger and Luckman's *The Social Con-struction of Reality*, and while a number of commentators have argued that they developed a particular version of social constructionism, the choice of 'social constructionist' in the title was to prove a useful hook for subsequent writers to hang their own ideas on to. Berger and Luckman took issue with images of society which were dominant in social theory in the post-war period and which they saw as excessively rationalistic and functional, giving little room for individual freedom and agency. They were concerned that something had gone terribly wrong with the Enlightenment project such that, probably unintentionally, most social theories had become antihumanistic and were overly concerned with the impersonal laws of social order rather than how order was an outcome of human action, choice and creativity.

They set themselves two tasks. First, to specify the main premises and concepts that clarify the nature of everyday life. Drawing from the phenomenological philosophy of Edmund Husserl (1975) and Alfred Schutz (1962–6), they introduced a range of concepts such as intentional consciousness, multiple realities, the practical attitude, intersubjectivity and so on, in order to frame everyday life as a fluid, multiple, precariously negotiated achievement in interaction. Their second and perhaps prime aim was to offer a general theory of the social origins and maintenance of social institutions. Their principal thesis was that individuals in interaction create social worlds through their linguistic, symbolic activity for the purpose of providing coherence and purpose to an essentially open-ended, unformed human existence. Society is neither a system, a mechanism, nor an organism; it is a symbolic construct composed of ideas, meanings and language which is all the time changing through human action and imposing constraints and possibilities on human actors themselves.

What such an approach does is to emphasise the *processes* through which people define themselves (their identities) and their environments. People do so by participating in their social worlds, interacting with others, and assigning *meaning* to aspects of their experience. *Constructing* social realities is seen as an ongoing aspect of people's everyday lives and relationships.

In more recent years, such approaches have increasingly recog-nised the *rhetorical* aspects of construction, in that it is partly a process of *persuading* one's self and others that one rendering of social reality is more legitimate or credible than any other.

While constructionism made a relatively late entry into psychology there are now numerous examples where such thinking is making a direct impact. Michael Billig (1987) and more recently John Shotter (1993) have, for example, analysed thinking as a rhetorical process where conversation and language are key to understanding identity. Thinking is seen not as a private or personal activity, but as a micropolitical and interactional process concerned with and categorising everyday life and developing arguments that justify preferred realities and courses of action. Similarly, Potter and Wetherell (1987) argue that language orders our perceptions and makes things happen. They suggest that what they call social texts do not merely reflect or mirror objects, events and categories existing in the social and natural world, they actively *construct* a version of those things. They do not just describe things, they *do* things and thus have social and political implications. Therefore relating this back to our earlier analysis, social problems and personal troubles are versions of events or situations which people use to justify some courses of action and to undermine others. Constructions thus have real implications for all concerned both practically and politically.

John Shotter's work in social psychology is of particular interest, especially when he argues that 'our talk (and our writing) about talk is beginning to take a dialogical or a conversational turn' (Shotter, 1993, p. 1). His basic premise is that it is within the dynamically sustained context of actively constructed relations that what is talked about gets its meaning. Thus, instead of focusing upon how individuals come to know the objects and entities in the world around them, we should be more interested in how people first develop and sustain ways of relating themselves to each other in their talk, and then, from within these ways of talking, make sense of their surroundings. He calls his approach a *rhetorical-responsive* version of social constructionism because the account of language he offers is a communicational, conversational or dialogical account in which people's responsive understanding of each other is primary. A part of what we must learn in growing up, if we want to be perceived as speaking (and writing) authoritatively about so-called factual matters, is how to *respond* to the others around us should they challenge our claims. This includes *conversations* with ourselves. We must *speak* with an awareness of the possibility of such challenges, and be able to reply to them by justifying our claims. This is a *rhetorical* rather than a referential or representational form of language because rather than merely claiming to depict or reflect a state of affairs or an external reality, talk and language can have the effect of *moving* people to action and changing their views and perceptions. Language can be seen as not just constituting reality but actively changing it.

Shotter calls the approach *rhetorical* because rhetoric makes use of metaphors which otherwise can seem unconnected. Rhetoric gives intelligible linguistic form to otherwise merely sensed feelings or tendencies shared between speakers (and writers) and their audiences.

This version of constructionism argues that we need to understand language as a communicational, conversational or dialogical process in which people's responsive understanding of each other is primary. What matters is not so much the conclusions arrived at as the terms within which arguments are conducted. For to talk in new ways is to *construct* new forms of social relations, and to *construct* new forms of social relations is to *construct* new ways of being for ourselves.

The 'postmodern' turn

More recently the interest in constructionism has been further stimulated by the emergence in both North America and Britain of a variety of perspectives which have been termed 'postmodern' and which have again only begun to enter the social work domain in recent years (Aldridge, 1996; Dominelli, 1996; Fawcett *et al.*, 2000; Featherstone and Fawcett, 1995; Gorman, 1993; Healy, 1999; Howe, 1994; Leonard, 1994, 1995, 1996, 1997; Lloyd, 1998; McBeath and Webb, 1991; Meinert, Pardeck and Murphy, 1998; Pardeck, Murphy and Chung, 1994; Parton, 1994a, 1994b; Peese and Fook, 1999; Pietroni, 1995; Pozatek, 1994; Rojek, Peacock and Collins, 1988; Sands and Nuccio, 1992). While it is not our intention to discuss how we see developments and debates associated with constructionism relating, conceptually and theoretically, to those associated with 'postmodernism', it is important to note that there are a number of similar themes. This is not surprising when we recognise that numerous theorists are bracketed under both headings and a number of writers seem to use the terms almost interchangeably. For us, however, we see social constructionism as being concerned with a more particular methodological stance, whereas 'postmodernity' is, potentially, much more fundamental in its implications – theoretically, politically' and practically. However, concerns related to 'postmodernity' have provided a fertile context in which an interest in constructionism can flourish. Similarly, constructionist perspectives themselves can be seen to make a significant contribution to underlining the concerns to which debates about 'postmodernity' themselves draw attention (for two interesting parallel texts on these issues, see Good and Velody, 1998; Velody and Williams, 1998).

The term 'postmodernity' was first used in the 1930s but became increasingly common in the areas of literature, architecture, philosophy and the arts more generally from the 1960s onwards (Turner, 1990; Featherstone, 1988) and came to particular prominence with the publication of Jean-François Lyotard's *The Postmodern Condition* in 1984. While perhaps 'postmodern' perspectives are united by a number of cultural projects which proclaim a commitment to heterogeneity, fragmentation and difference, it is perhaps their critiques of modernity which have proved most influential and contentious.

Modernity as a summary term is seen to refer to the cluster of social, economic and political systems which emerged in the West with the Enlightenment in the late eighteenth century. Unlike the pre-modern, modernity assumed that human order is neither natural nor God-given, but is vulnerable and contingent. However, by the development and application of science, nature could be subject to human control. The distinguishing features of modernity are seen to be: the understanding of history as having a definite and progressive direction; the attempt to develop universal categories of experience; the idea that reason can provide a basis for all activities; and that the nation state could coordinate and advance such developments for the whole society. The guiding principle of modernity is the search to establish reliable foundations for knowledge. It aims to identify the central truths about the world but also assumes that truth does not reside on the surface of things but is hidden by appearances. The two crucial elements of modernity in the post-Enlightenment period were thus seen as the progressive union of scientific *objectivity* and politico-economic *rationality* (our emphasis, Parton, 1994a).

In the modern 'frame' the goal is to produce knowledge about a chosen aspect of the physical or social world by which we can claim *greater certainty*. At that point we can confer a sense of truth about that knowledge, and also confer on the people producing knowledge (for example, scientists or professionals) the status of holder-of-truth and expert about that aspect of the world. 'In short, the modernist equation is: *external reality – objective knowledge – certainty about that knowledge – claim to truth – expert status given to holder-of-truth knowledge*. Modernist truth is indeed bound to certainty, external reality and objective knowledge. And modernism both relies on (and produces) a clear splitting of the subject who wants to know, and the object which is being observed for knowledge and truth' (Flaskas, 1997, p. 5, original emphasis).

Increasingly, however, there is a recognition that we now inhabit a world which has become disorientated, disturbed and subject to doubt. The pursuit of order and control, the promotion of calculability, belief in progress, science and rationality and other features which were so intrinsic to modernity are being undermined by a simultaneous range of unsettling conditions and experiences. In part this is related to the major social, economic and cultural transformations that have characterised recent times in terms of globalisation, the increasing significance of media and the widening networks of information technology which transform and transmit knowledge, the changes in modes of consumption and production and the increased awareness of risk and uncertainty. More fundamentally, however, it is related to changing notions of ontology (who we are and our sense of being) and epistemology (how we know what we know).

It is argued that modernism's promise to deliver order, certainty and security has been unfulfilled and increasingly it is felt there are no transcendental and universal criteria of truth (science), judgment (ethics) and taste (aesthetics). The overriding belief in reason and rationality is disappearing as there is a collapse of consensus related to any 'grand narratives' (overarching theories or explanations) and their articulation of progress, emancipation and perfection and what constitutes the centres of authority and truth. The rejection of the idea that any one theory or system of belief can ever reveal the truth, and the emphasis on the plurality of truth and 'the will to truth', captures some of the essential elements associated with 'postmodernity'. While contemporary times have been called variously 'late modern', 'post-industrial', and 'post-traditional' as well as 'postmodern', there is wide agreement on the key elements of social transformation under discussion in terms of: the increasing *pace* of change; the growing significance of *difference, plurality* and the growth of various new political movements and strategies; and the pervasive awareness of *relativities*, the opening up of individual 'choice' and 'freedom' and, which will become central for our purposes, the *increasing awareness of the socially constructed nature of reality*. Following Smart, 'postmodern' means 'living without guarantee, without security and order and with contingency and ambivalence. To put it another way, it means living without illusions and with uncertainty' (Smart, 1999, p. 16).

'Postmodernity' is thus characterised by the fragmentation of modernity into forms of institutional pluralism, marked by increasing awareness of difference, contingency, relativism and ambivalence – all of which modernity sought (and claimed) to have overcome. It is this constant and growing questioning of modern approaches and modern resolutions that has been diag-nosed as symptomatic of the 'postmodern' condition (Parton, 1994a); and it is the conception of 'postmodernity' as the con-dition of modernity coming to its senses, emancipated from false consciousness which is seen as key (Bauman, 1992). Truth thus now takes the guise of 'truth' and is centred neither in God's word (as in the pre-modern) nor human reason (as in the modern) but is decentred and localised so that many 'truths' are possible, dependent on different times and different places.

In many respects the modern, because of its reliance on allegedly universal categories and neutral rationality, is not seen as necessarily humanitarian, progressive or emancipatory as was often assumed, but can be exploitative and repressive because of its failure to recognise difference. There is a failure to recognise the nature, consequences and implications of relying on totalising belief systems whether these be capitalist, socialist, patriarchal, ablist, colonial, or whatever. The views, experiences and interests of white, middle-class, able-bodied males have invariably been embedded in ideas, theories and approaches but presented as if they were universal, objective and neutral.

In the 'postmodern' there is thus a considerable destabilisation of a core assumption of modernism – that the way something is represented closely reflects its underlying reality. For if nothing is inherently or immutably true nothing is inherently or immutably real. In a world where everything is increasingly mediated and relayed via complex systems of representation, the symbols that are used have a life of their own and take on their meaning, not on the basis of what reality they are meant to represent, but the context in which they are used. It is in this sense that Baudrillard (1983, 1990) argues that the distinctions between concepts and objects, representations and reality, and theory and practice no longer hold – if they ever did. Perhaps most crucially 'the way things are said is more important than the possession of truths' (Rorty, 1979, p. 359).

An understanding of language is thus central to approaches which are sympathetic to the 'postmodern'. This is the thesis, originally advanced by Wittgenstein (1963) and developed by Lyotard (1984), that knowledge can only be derived from 'language games'. Instead of merely being a tool that points to objects, language mediates everything that is known. Far from having a separate existence, reality is embedded in interpretation so that 'truth' is a product of language not reality. We cannot transcend interrogation and assume that reality is simply waiting to be discovered; it emerges from the linguistic acts of persons. An understanding of the part that language plays in the formation of human selves, human thought and human subjectivity thus underpins 'postmodern' perspectives.

Questions about knowledge, difference, power and subjectivity have also been central preoccupations of feminism and other theoretical and political movements which, in more recent years, have tried to give voice to the marginalised and excluded sections of society. Feminists, for example, have contested what counts as *knowledge* and *truth* and have demonstrated how language constructs sexism and have elaborated notions of power which locate it within the everyday and the local. The importance of *difference* has been further recognised via the recognition of the range of experiences amongst women, particularly arising from their ethnicity and social class (Butler and Scott, 1992; Lewis, 1996; Williams, 1996). Theoretical developments in different areas have thus helped underline some of the central themes in 'postmodernism'.

However, because there are probably as many forms of 'postmodernism' as there are 'postmodernists' there are many divergent and even contradictory possibilities that are opened up. Within this diversity, as far as the social sciences are concerned, Rosenau (1992) has delineated two broad orientations which we feel are helpful in taking our thinking forward: the *sceptical* 'postmodernists' and the *affirmative* 'postmodernists'.

She argues that *sceptical* 'postmodernists' offer a distrustful, pessimistic, negative, gloomy assessment of contemporary times characterised by fragmentation, disintegration, meaninglessness, an absence of moral parameters and social chaos. She calls this the dark side of 'postmodernism', the 'postmodernism' of despair that speaks of the demise of the subject, the end of the author, the impossibility of truth and the abrogation of the order of representation. It is concerned about the destructive character of modernity and points to unsurpassable uncertainty where everything is alienating, hopeless and ambiguous and where no social, political or practical project is worthy of commitment. If, as the sceptics claim, there is no truth then all we are left with is parody and play – the play of words and meaning.

While the *affirmative* 'postmodernists' agree with the sceptics' critique of modernity, particularly in terms of science and rationality, they have a more hopeful, optimistic view of the possibilities of the 'postmodern' age and are positively oriented towards the importance of *process*. They are much more open to the potential for practical actions and are not just concerned with *deconstruction* but with *reconstruction*. While they seek a tentative approach to practice there is a central recognition that normative choices and trying to *build* practical and political coalitions and collaboration lies at the heart of everyday life. In recognising that subject(s) can only be understood in context(s) it recognises the importance of interdependence and the social and political cultures in which we live. It is not the death of the subject that is of greatest interest so much as the recognition of the diverse nature of subjectivities which is the focus. Following Bauman (1992, 1993), there is a recognition that in opening up individuals to the possibilities of choice and responsibility they are truly made up as moral. Rather than seeing the disappearance of the subject it is argued there has been a widening in the constructibility of identities from ascriptive and natural (in the pre-modern), to socially acquired and quasi-natural (in the modern), to chosen and socially negotiated (in the 'postmodern') (Hollis, 1985). Because of the intimate relationship between language and reality, persons are seen as placed in positions where they can create their own destiny. They are given agency, for through the exercise of will persons are able to invent reality.

It is not so much that persons have to struggle to find meaning within a melange of meaningless, but they are placed at the centre of reality. Instead of making sense out of events, persons invent options and make them real. Persons are deemed to have the possibilities of positive freedoms and positive choices and the ability to re-moralise and re-invent their personal and social worlds.

While it is clearly difficult to accommodate *sceptical postmodernism* with social work, perspectives offered by *affirmative postmodernism* are much more suggestive in helping us to think about and open up *constructive* approaches to practice – particularly the emphasis on 'truth re-definition'. It is interpretative and prioritises receptivity, dialogue, listening to and talking with the other. It reveals paradox, myth and story, and persuades by questions, hints, metaphors and invitations to the possible rather than by relying on science and trying to approximate truth.

Conclusions

So what are some of the key themes of constructionism which we are looking to build on in the following chapters? Viv Burr (1995) has usefully summarised what she identifies as the key characteristics of social constructionist approaches. While we will return to some of the dilemmas that such an approach poses for social workers, and how we feel they can be addressed and taken forward towards the end of the book, they provide a helpful provisional statement for us at this point in our argument and help us bring together some of the ideas we have been discussing in this chapter.

Firstly, constructionism insists that we develop a critical stance towards our taken-for-granted ways of understanding the world including ourselves. It suggests we should be critical of the idea that our observations of the world unproblematically reveal its nature to us in any straightforward way. It *problematises* 'the obvious', the 'real' and, crucially, the 'taken-for-granted'.

It challenges the view that conventional knowledge is based upon unbiased observation and that we can therefore easily separate subject and object, the perceived and the real. It is therefore highly suspicious of what is referred to as positivism and empiricism in traditional science – the assumption that the nature of the world can be revealed simply by observation and that what exists is what we perceive to exist. Constructionism cautions us to be ever suspicious of our assumptions about how the world appears and the categories that we use to divide and interpret it.

Secondly, such categories and concepts are seen as historically and culturally specific and therefore vary over time and place. Particular forms of knowledge are not only the products of their history and culture and are therefore artefacts of it but there are thus numerous forms of knowledge available. We cannot assume that *our* ways of understanding are necessarily the same as others' and are any nearer the truth.

Thirdly, knowledge of the world is developed between people in their daily *interactions* such that we should be centrally concerned with the *social processes* whereby this comes about and can be changed. These *negotiated* understandings can take a variety of different forms which thereby invite different kinds of action. However, while constructions of the world sustain some patterns of action they also exclude others. Thus rather than being able to separate knowledge and action they are intimately interrelated.

Fourthly, because the social world, including ourselves as people, is the product of social processes, it follows that there cannot be any given, determined nature to the world 'out there'. There are no essences inside things or people which are hidden and which make them what they are. Constructionism is not just saying that one's culture has an impact on our nature nor even that our nature is a product of the environment or social context. It is not simply a question of 'nature' or 'nurture', as both see the person as having some definable and discoverable essence – this is not consistent with constructionism.

Ian Hacking (1999) has recently argued that while there are various approaches to and forms of social constructionism there are some central underlying assumptions that are held to. Social constructionists, when considering *x* – which may be a problem, a category, a trouble or whatever – take the view that: (1) in the present state of affairs, x is taken for granted, so that x *appears* inevitable; but that (2) x need not have existed or need not be as it is, it is not determined by the nature of things and is thus not inevitable; and further (3) that x is quite bad as it is and therefore (4) we would be much better off if x were done away with or at least radically changed. While it is not necessarily the case that if you hold with (1) and (2) then (3) and (4) should follow, it is our view that problematising and criticising with a view to change and transformation are central to the approach we take here and are key elements to *constructive social work*. The four underlying assumptions of social constructionism outlined by Hacking very much inform our approach.

2

The Nature of Contemporary Social Work and Its Knowledge Base

> Contemporary philosophers look at how we have ordered the world in our language and how our language has ordered our world. Therefore . . . we need to study language in order to study anything at all. (de Shazer, 1993b, p. 84)

Having initially outlined some of the perspectives we will develop in our theories *for* practice, the focus in this chapter is to outline our views of the nature and purposes of social work and thus why we see such perspectives as particularly relevant. Michael Sheppard (1995a and 1995b 1998) has argued that when considering knowledge for social work we need to be concerned not only with *theoretical validity*, whether in epistemological and methodological terms a form of knowledge is valid, but also, what he calls, *practice validity*. By practice validity Sheppard is referring to the extent to which it takes a form which is consistent with the nature and purpose of social work, and it is with this issue we are primarily concerned here. What is it about social work that makes it distinctive from other professional practices, for example, law, medicine, therapy, counselling? And is there something about practice knowledge which differentiates it from attempts simply to apply knowledge from other disciplines, for example, the social sciences, to a particular area of social and professional activity? In order to address these issues it is important to locate social work in the United Kingdom in its particular social, political and historical contexts and identify some of the key factors which have not only influenced its development but its form.

While in the UK there have been significant moves to legalise, proceduralise, scientise and rationalise practice it is important to recognise that many of the earliest impulses for social work in the nineteenth century were fed by religious convictions about the nature of human struggles derived from the tremendous social and economic changes of the period. At the centre of much of this early social work were beliefs about the capacity of human beings for personal transformation and the opportunities that were required for meeting human needs. Such sentiments were central to the 'client-centred' approaches we discussed in Chapter 1 and are central to the development of *constructive social work*. However, as Weick and Saleebey (1998) have argued, 'the early moral and social orientations of the profession run deep in memory but they have become part of an increasingly silent language as the weight of the scientific world view suppressed these appreciations' (p. 22). A central part of our argument is thus that social work is a moral enterprise which has particular relevance to contemporary times and that constructionist and narrative approaches can make a significant contribution for articulating these ideas in usable theories *for* practice. These issues are nicely illustrated in a debate carried in the *British Journal of Social Work* in the late 1970s, before constructionism started to have a significant impact on intellectual debates and long before the possible implications of constructionism for social work began to emerge.

In 1978 Brian Sheldon articulated what he saw as major problems in the relationship between theory and practice in social work and produced suggestions about how these might be overcome (Sheldon, 1978). Essentially he argued that the relationship between theory and practice was inconsistent and muddled and needed to be put on a much firmer footing. However, this was difficult in the context of: the social work education curriculum which was seen as eclectic; the negative attitudes by many in the profession towards science as a means of evaluating competing concepts; and the lack of any rigorous evaluation of practice itself. Drawing an analogy with the work of a pharmacist, his main suggestion for improvement was that some of the essential principles of science, particularly bio-medical science, should be drawn on as a model to improve the situation. His aim was to show that *modern* conceptions of the scientific process do not necessarily clash (either at a philosophical or a methodological level) with many of the accepted practices of social work; secondly, that science provides us with the key to the development of a cumulative evaluation of its different theoretical components. Thirdly, there are important similarities between the work of the researcher and that of the social work practitioner: both erect hypotheses about the possible relationships between events, and both ought to be required to pay attention to phrasing these so that they are placed at risk of refutation by subsequent work. (Sheldon, 1978, p. 17, our emphasis)

His solution to the problems of fit he identified between social work theory and practice resided with an injection of knowledge for practice derived from positivistic science. For

> if we wish to retain the advantages of personal evaluation (the immediacy and believability of the findings to those who gather them, for example) then something needs to be done to improve its reliability. My own solution involves a small injection of positivism – counterbalancing emphasis on what can actually be seen to have changed, rather than impressions of change inferred from conversation alone. (Sheldon, 1978, p. 18).

What Sheldon was alluding to was a development which in recent years has gathered apace and can be seen as one of the major developments for trying to legitimate, defend and develop social work – the increasing attractions of evidence-based practice, where it is argued social work should primarily be grounded in research which demonstrates which strategies are beneficial to which clients, when and why. The conceptual framework emphasises a scientific base where predictive techniques about 'what works' are introduced to both the individual case and the planning of services. The value of empirical findings about the circumstances of clients and outcomes from different interventions is seen as central, neutral, and to apply across the situations, contexts and problems faced by practitioners.

In the same issue of the *British Journal of Social Work*, Bill Jordan provided a critical commentary on Brian Sheldon's paper (Jordan, 1978). While sympathising with Sheldon's concerns about the way theory and practice in social work were interrelated, Jordan had major criticisms of Sheldon's analysis of the problems and his suggestions for their resolution. He felt that the analogy with pharmacy grossly simplified the way such occupations operated and exaggerated the positive impact of drugs on social and health well-being. More particularly Sheldon seemed to have a very benign view of the nature and role of science in society and the way such knowledge, particularly the social sciences, can usefully be applied to and drawn on in social work, for Jordan felt that 'literature and poetry afford far more penetrating and meaningful insight into the human heart than psychological texts' (Jordan, 1978, p. 25). Crucially it fails to understand the nature of 'helping' in social work, for many of the 'problems' that come the way of social work cannot be 'solved' in any clear, measurable or calculative way.

Jordan argued that helping in social work has as much to do with caring and sharing as it is with changing things, which in some situations may deteriorate. Social work practice is influenced by far more complex and remote forces than 'a precise scientific knowledge for use' can encompass, and it is vitally important that social workers understand some of these forces if they are to work effectively. He concluded by arguing that 'of course it is important for social work to try to evolve precise, testable theories. But it is also essential that it remains open to real moral, social and political dilemmas, and that it *learns to live with inevitable uncertainty, confusion and doubt*' (Jordan, 1978, p. 25, our emphasis).

As will be already evident, we are very sympathetic to Jordan's view that 'uncertainty, confusion and doubt' are key elements in characterising the nature of social work. Rather than be embarrassed by this and try to define them out via increasingly scientised and rationalised approaches, it is our view that we should recognise they are at the core of what it is to do social work and are significant factors in what makes it distinctive. They should form an essential part of any theoretical approaches which are serious about being usable in practice.

Social work as a 'practical-moral' activity

What the debate between Sheldon and Jordan points to, amongst other things, is how we can best understand and conceptualise the nature of day-to-day social work practice. Is it primarily a *rational-technical* activity or a *practical-moral* one? While the growth of managerialism, systems of audit, procedures, legalism and an emphasis on outcomes and evidence-based practice suggest it is the former, it is a central argument of this book that it is the latter. While the proliferation of procedures and so on in most areas of social work aim to make practice more accountable and transparent, they render the social work *process* and the tacit assumptions upon which 'thinking as usual' takes place in practice immune from analysis. For even prescriptive assessment and monitoring schedules require interpretation and judgment to be made practical (White, 1998). These developments, however, are only the most recent example of the dominance of the *rational-technical* approach to understanding the theory practice relationship.

The work of Donald Schön (1983, 1987) is instructive in this respect. While he is concerned with the nature of professional practice beyond social work he argues that the technical-rational model has been embedded in the institutional context of professional life for many years. He sees it as implicit in the institutionalised relations of research and practice and in the normative curricula of professional education, so that even when practitioners, educators and researchers question the model they have considerable difficulty challenging it as they are a party to the institutions that perpetuate it. Such an approach can be seen to epitomise what has come to be associated with *modernity*.

According to Schön, the epistemology of professional practice which has dominated most thinking and writing about the professions treats rigorous professional practice as an exercise of technical rationality, that is as an application of research-based knowledge to the solution of problems of instrumental choice. Rigorous professional practice is conceived as deriving its rigour from the use of describable, testable, replicable techniques derived from scientific research and which is based on knowledge that is objective, consensual, cumulative and convergent. On this view social work becomes the *application* of rigorous social science in the same way as engineering becomes the *application* of engineering science.

However, Schön argues that such a model fails to capture how professionals operate and how they 'know' in practice, for problems are not presented in a way where such rational-technical approaches easily fit. Real-world problems do not come well-formed but, on the contrary, present themselves as messy and indeterminate. Knowing in such situations is *tacit* and *implicit* in the practitioners' patterns of action and feel for what they are dealing with. It develops from dialogue with people about the situation, through which the practitioner can come to understand the uniqueness, uncertainty and potential value conflicts that must be addressed and thereby reaches 'a new theory of the unique case' that informs action. Practice-knowledge is thus derived from 'reflection-in-action' and emphasises interaction. Knowledge of this sort, Schön argues, not only provides a more accurate reflection of the theory/practice relationship but is more flexible and adaptable than technical rationality. Such an approach recognises that social work practitioners are not so much theoretical as they are practical, concrete and intuitive and incorporate elements of art and craft as well as disciplined reasoning. Social work characterised as art rather than science is a theme which has been lost in many recent discussions of social work, yet art has the virtue of being able to accommodate notions of ambiguity and uncertainty in ways which pose major problems for rational-technical approaches (Goldstein, 1990, 1992).

Schön's approach, while suggestive, is a *generic* theory of professional activity developed primarily from the experiences of private practice in the fields of architecture and design, as well as the human services, where the concern is the inappropriate way theory/practice are traditionally conceptualised. His introduction of the 'reflective practitioner' idea never seriously questions that practitioners, let alone those with whom they work, would not agree about the most appropriate way of reflecting and what would constitute the most appropriate outcome. While seriously trying to engage with the way practitioners operate, he never questions that this could ever be anything other than based on rational processes which can be understood and explained. A major problem with Schön's work is that it is not derived directly from observing practitioners in practice but from sessions where experienced practitioners in a tutorial role are attempting to explicate and pass on their knowledge to 'novices'. However, what people do and what people say they do, and how people think in action and how people reflect on the way they think in action, are not necessarily the same things (Fook, 1996). It is important, therefore, to be much more specific about the nature of social work.

There are clearly important, sometimes quite divergent, even contradictory, dimensions to social work in that the practitioner, particularly in a statutory agency, has to combine the roles of practical helper, counsellor, protector, supervisor, advocate, and general provider of support and maintenance (Reid, 1978). At its crudest, social work practice involves both care *and* control. However, the attempt to try and categorise and separate these roles is in great danger of missing the essential nature and characteristics of social work.

In order to develop these insights further we will return to the work of Jordan, who in various publications since 1978 (1979, 1984, 1987 and 1990, together with Jordan and Parton 1983) has taken forward his ideas in much greater detail. He argues that while social work, like medicine, the law, education or social security, is organised through a system of formal roles, linked to each other in a complex, hierarchical organisation which in turn is linked with others to form a network of social services under central and local government oversight, what is different about social work is not that it tries to influence individuals, families or communities – clearly it does – but that it goes about this in a certain way – through informal *negotiation*. Social workers are differentiated from workers in other services mainly by their willingness to forsake the formality of their roles, and to work *with* ordinary people in their 'natural' settings, using the informality of their methods as a means of *negotiating solutions to problems* rather than imposing them. Imposed, formal solutions are a last resort in social work, whereas they are the norm in other settings. The further social work moves from this situation the more it loses what is distinctive about it. Jordan argues that the uniqueness of social work is derived from the way it addresses issues of welfare that pays close attention to individuals' own understandings of their needs, and to the informal processes by which they cooperate together. He suggests that the success of a social work intervention should always be measured in terms of the *meanings* attached to behaviour by actors in their social context. 'This does not mean that social workers must become moralistic and judgmental – exactly the reverse. It means that they must become more sensitive to the significance attached to *words* and *actions* by clients and others, and to the subtleties of the *processes* by which people *co-exist* and *cooperate* in communities' (Jordan, 1987, p. 143, our emphasis).

This involves searching for solutions that take into account people's 'idiosyncratic ideas about their needs' (p. 141); it involves paying close attention to people's understandings and to their process of cooperating. It is about providing services that take into account people's individuality rather than providing standardised or imposed solutions via rigid procedures. This involves entering people's own worlds where the person's standards are as relevant as the worker's. Social workers thus need to be as (or more) skilled at working with uncertainty, creating possible meanings and cooperation at various levels as in the use of any specific techniques – creativity and imagination are crucial characteristics to respond to the inherent complexity and ambiguity (Fook *et al.*, 1997).

Like many forms of social interaction, social work consists of improvised performances in which people achieve more-or-less convincing performances of themselves. These allow exchanges of value and support, for some approximately agreed purpose. While what is exchanged, and with what results, is always complex and often contested, the aim of social work is usually to help bring about some change, including trying to stop or cushion a deterioration in the social environment and or the service user's behaviour.

Social constructionism is particularly strong at drawing attention to the ways in which activities and communication are fundamentally ambiguous and open to various interpretations. Social constructionism thus lends itself well to providing a useful and very relevant theory *for* practice – but rarely has this been done.

It is now fairly commonplace to draw upon social constructionism to provide a conceptual framework for understanding and explaining the changing nature *of* social work, but there has been much less serious effort at using constructionism for developing theory *for* practice.

For example, while Malcolm Payne (1991, 1996, and 1997) argues that 'social work is a socially constructed activity' (1991, p. 7), the major section of his widely used text on social work theory makes no attempt to outline what a constructionist approach to practice might look like. While there are chapters on psychodynamic, crisis intervention and task-centred behavioural systems, and ecological, social psychological and communication, humanist and existential, cognitive, radical and Marxist approaches – there is no discussion of a constructionist approach to practice. This is not meant to be a criticism of Malcolm Payne's work but it is meant as a critical comment on the current state of social work theory and its failure to engage with constructionism as providing a relevant and productive approach *for* practice. Increasingly, however, the changing political-social contexts point to the need to develop constructionist approaches *for* practice.

The changing nature and context of social work

In trying to capture the nature of modern social work, particularly as it is practised under the auspices of the state, we can usefully return to the work of Michael Sheppard, who argues that:

> State social work may, then, be considered a socially constructed profession, in the sense that it has been created as a means for working with certain individuals who have been defined as socially problematic. Its focus is one on individual–environment interaction and its orientation is towards these individuals as subjects. It is in the combinations of these elements of concern, focus and orientation that social work may be most clearly 'marked out'. This formulation helps both define social work and to distinguish it from other activities. (Sheppard, 1995a, p. 52)

While we sympathise with Sheppard's characterisation, it is important to recognise that the notion of 'state' social work is not straightforward. For while many social workers are employed in state agencies this is currently changing significantly and an increasing number are employed in large and small voluntary organisations with a growing number in the private sector. While the role of both voluntary and private organisations has become increasingly significant in recent years, particularly as they have taken on a growing profile as 'service providers', it is important to recognise that the state not only provides many of the resources for funding such services but that it has a growing and significant role in terms of inspection and regulation. In this respect the introduction of more and more audits, inspections, regulations, procedures and monitoring systems has not so much reduced the role of the state, but reconfigured it in important ways such that in some respects its significance has increased. As we will argue, it is this relationship between the individual and the environment, as Sheppard calls it, or the relationship between the individual and society, as we prefer to call it, that is key to understanding the nature of social work, and it is the role of the state which is the major influence on the way this relationship is mediated and articulated.

The emergence of modern social work is associated with the transformations that took place from the mid nineteenth century onwards in response to a number of interrelated anxieties about the family and the community more generally. It developed as a hybrid in the space, the 'social' (Donzelot, 1988), between the private sphere of the household and the public sphere of the state and society. It operated in an intermediary zone. It produced and was reproduced by new relations between the law, administration, medicine, the school and the family. The emergence of the 'social' and the practices of social workers, who were to become its major technologists, was seen as a positive solution to a major problem for the liberal state (Hirst, 1981). Namely – how can the state establish the health and development of family members who are weak and dependent, while promoting the family as the 'natural' sphere for caring for those individuals and thus not intervening in all families? Social work developed at a midway point between individual initiative and the all-encompassing state. It provided a compromise between the liberal vision of unhindered private philanthropy and the socialist vision of the all-pervasive state which would take responsibility for everyone's needs and hence undermine individual initiative and family responsibility.

Issues in relation to the child exemplify these tensions: for children to develop their full health and sensibilities, they could not be left to the vagaries of the market and the autonomous patriarchal family (Dingwall and Eekelaar, 1988). The emergence of the 'social' was seen as the most appropriate way for the state to maintain its legitimacy while protecting individual children. For liberalism, 'the unresolved problem is how child rearing can be made into a matter of public concern and its qualities monitored without destroying the ideal of the family as a counterweight to state power, a domain of voluntary, self-regulating actions' (Dingwall, Eekelaar and Murray, 1983, pp. 214–15).

Originally, with the emergence of modern industrial society, this activity was carried out by voluntary philanthropic organisations, and Donzelot (1980) argues that two techniques were of significance in their relationship with families, particularly on behalf of children – moralisation and normalisation. *Moralisation* involved the use of financial and material assistance which was used as a leverage to encourage poor families to overcome their moral failure. It was used primarily for the deserving poor who could demonstrate that their problems arose for reasons beyond their control. *Normalisation* applied to attempts to spread specific norms of living via education, legislation or health, and involved a response to complaints, invariably from women about men, and hence provided a means of entry into the home. In return for this guidance, and moral and minimal material support, philanthropic workers were given an insight into what was happening inside the home and leverage to bring about changes in behaviour and lifestyle. Clearly, however, there were problems if individuals did not cooperate or did not approach the worker in the first place, so that children were left to unbridled parental devices.

In the late nineteenth century and early twentieth century in Britain, such philanthropic activities were increasingly absorbed into the formal institutions of the state. This process continued through to the early 1970s with the introduction of local authority social service departments as the 'fifth social service' (Townsend, 1970), to operate alongside the other main state welfare services of education, health, housing and social security. While moralisation and normalisation were to be the primary forms of contact by social workers, this was increasingly framed in legislation which would also give the possibility for coercive intervention. *Tutelage*, as Donzelot (1980) calls it, based on the notion of preventive intervention, would combine a number of elements, though coercive intervention would be used only for the exceptional circumstances where the techniques of moralisation and normalisation had failed.

One of social work's enduring characteristics seems to be its essentially contested and ambiguous nature (Martinez-Brawley and Zorita, 1998). Most crucially, this ambiguity arises from its commitment to individuals and families and their needs on the one hand and its allegiances to and legitimation by the state in the guise of the court and its 'statutory' responsibilities on the other. This ambiguity captures the central but often submerged nature of modern social work as it emerged from the late nineteenth century onwards. Social work occupied the space between the respectable and the dangerous classes, and between those with access to political and speaking rights and those who are excluded (Philp, 1979; Stenson, 1993). Social work fulfilled an essentially mediating role between those who are actually or potentially excluded and the mainstream of society. Part of what social workers seek to do is strengthen the bonds of inclusive membership by trying to nurture reciprocity, sharing and small-scale redistribution between individuals, in households, groups, communities and so on. But part of it is also concerned with the compulsory enforcement of social obligations, rules, laws and regulations. The two are intertwined and invariably the latter provides the ultimate mandate for the former – it is in this context that social work involves *both* care *and* control. While it has always been concerned to liberate and emancipate those with whom it works, it is also concerned with working on behalf of the state and the wider society to maintain social order.

However, the latter increasingly became its dominating rationale so that the essential ambiguity which lies at its core appeared to become submerged and lost. For as the twentieth century proceeded the growth of modern social work in Britain became increasingly dependent on the development of what came to be called 'the welfare state' which became its primary sponsor and which provided its primary rationale and legitimacy. As a result it mediated not only between other diverse state, voluntary and private agencies but also the diverse and overlapping interests and discourses which informed and constituted them.

Thus the essential ambiguities of social work were increasingly modified and became closely associated with the new forms of social regulation associated with the welfare state (Garland, 1985). The central focus of modern systems of regulation was the classification of the population based on the *scientific* claims of different experts. Increasingly, modern societies regulated the population by sanctioning the knowledge claims of the new human *sciences,* particularly medicine, psychiatry, psychology and social work – the 'psy complex' (Ingleby, 1985; Rose, 1985).

The 'psy complex' refers to the network of ideas about the nature of human beings, their perfectibility, the reasons for their behaviour and the way they may be classified, selected and controlled. It aimed to manage and improve individuals by the manipulation of their qualities and attributes and was dependent upon scientific knowledge and professional interventions and expertise. Human qualities were seen as measurable and calculable and thereby could be changed, improved and rehabilitated. The new human sciences had as their central aim the prediction of future behaviour.

The birth and development of social work was thus very much aligned with *modern* ways of thinking and dealing with social problems – but with its own very distinctive characteristics and rationale.

For social work to operate quietly and in an uncontested way, it required a supportive social mandate together with an internal professional confidence and coherence. The latter, particularly in the period following the Second World War, was provided, as we have seen, from psycho-dynamic theory, while the professional aspirations veered towards medicine and psychiatry (Payne, 1992). Similarly, the growth of social work from the late nineteenth century onwards in the United Kingdom ran in parallel with, and was interrelated with, the development of social interventions associated with the establishment of the welfare state in the post-war period – what Rose and Miller (1992) refer to as 'welfarism'.

The key innovations of 'welfarism' lay in the attempts to link the fiscal, calculative and bureaucratic capacities of the apparatus of the state to the government of social life. As a political rationality, 'welfarism' was structured by the wish to encourage national growth and well-being through the promotion of *social* responsibility and the mutuality of *social* risk, and was premised on notions of *social* solidarity (Donzelot, 1988).

As Olive Stevenson (1998a, 1998b) has indicated, during the post-war period, social work was imbued with a degree of optimism which believed that measured and significant improvements could be made in the lives of children and families via judicious professional interventions. In the context of the institutional framework of the other universal state welfare services, while social work was constituted as a residual service, it was based on a relatively positive and optimistic view of those it was working with and of what could be achieved.

However, just at the point when social work emerged to play an important role in the welfarist project in the late 1960s and early 1970s in Britain, 'welfarism' itself was experiencing considerable strains in both its political rationality and technological utility. As a consequence, the rationale and activities of state social work as it developed in the post-war period was particularly vulnerable to criticism and reconstitution as they could be seen to personify all that was problematic with welfarism. In the UK these criticisms have been as evident under New Labour as under the previous Conservative administration (Driver and Martell, 1998; Jordan, 1998a) and was clearly evidence of much wider social transformations.

The welfare state had little in common with the liberal state of the mid nineteenth century which was little more than a 'night-watchman state'. What emerged with the welfare state was a set of authorities, practices and knowledges whose task was the calculated supervision and administration of all, under the guise, ultimately, of the state and a series of experts. Such developments were programmatic in the sense that they were characterised by an optimism that society could be improved and that reality was in some sense identifiable and programmable.

Such an approach rested on a strong set of assumptions about the nature of the state and the social sciences as well as about the entire social formation in which both were embedded. The state was regarded as unitary, coherent and capable of action; social science was seen as methodologically and epistemologically secure and providing objective knowledge; and society was characterised as having an identifiable structure. It was assumed that a cognitive mastery of society could be pursued in the service of the welfare state so that the focus of social science was in analysing the laws and the predictable character of social reality in the same way as the natural sciences were concerned with identifying the under-lying laws and realities of nature. The dominant forms of social science were positivistic and functionalist.

Peter Wagner (1994) refers to this social configuration as *organised modernity*, and argues that it achieved something of a coherence or closure during the 1960s – in terms of the various institutions, their specific embodiments of collective agency, their interlinkages and respective reaches into society. It appeared as a 'naturally interlocking order'.

What, in retrospect, was largely neglected was a recognition that this social configuration had been constructed over a long period and through a series of intense struggles. By the 1950s and 1960s a series of conventions and assumptions had become so embedded and institutionalised that their socially constructed nature had been lost and had disappeared from consciousness.

The classifications and processes which had been set up to increase intelligibility and manageability gave the appearance of representing some natural order of reality.

However, since the late 1960s there has been a gradual demolishing of these arrangements, mostly without being replaced by any analogous arrangements that might be more adequate for the new problems and situations. Increasingly it seemed that there was no alternative notion of collectivity offering itself in the same way as the nation-state did from the late nineteenth century, when the first steps were being taken towards organised modernity. From the late 1960s many of the social conventions that characterised organised modernity have increasingly broken down: the disappearance of the socio-economic regularities; the reconsideration of the contours of most post-war organisational forms; the bursting of representations and expectations and increasing uncertainties about the future and how to act. What Wagner calls the crisis of organised modernity, is characterised by a de-conventionalisation and pluralisation of practices, knowledge and authorities: the agreement to set the terms of industrial relations on the national level was broken; the Keynesian consensus to develop a national consumption based economy eroded; the organisational rules that fixed and secured position and task were reshaped; and technical innovations whose applications tended to break existing conventions were no longer upheld.

At the height of organised modernity the state was regarded as strong and coherent. In principle it was assumed it could acquire all the necessary knowledge about society and had the ability to intervene in a harmonious and consensual way. By the 1990s this image of the state has changed dramatically as has faith in developing any incontestable science of society to guide policies and practices.

From posing as the omniscient regulator and leader the state is now, at most, represented as partner or moderator. The clarity of the model of the all-pervasive interventionist state has disappeared and given way to a new diffuseness of the boundaries between the spheres of public and private regulation. This blurring of boundaries raises important issues of legitimacy and sovereignty.

The crisis of organised modernity was also evident in terms of its mode of representation, for its achievements were bought at the price of strict boundaries and conventions. Critiques of organised modernity were thus directed at the *constraining* effects of these boundaries and conventions. Intellectually, the recognition of the *social construction* of conventions and their alternatives becomes central to such critiques (Fuchs and Ward, 1994). Politically the right to be different is a claim which interrelates with such reasoning and which has been central to the growth of most political and social movements over the last twenty-five years, particularly those around gender, sexuality, disability and ethnicity (Williams, 1996). This cultural revolution has introduced a strong, almost unlimited, attempt at de-conventionalising and the recreation of ambivalence in a social order that was regarded as over-conventionalised and closed to any freedom of action beyond pre-established channels. This questioning of the order of practices quickly extended to a questioning of the order of representation to the point where the very possibility of representation has itself come under serious doubt.

It is in this intellectual and social context that debates about 'postmodernity' emerge and which in its strong versions postulates the end of modernity, the subject , social science and much, much more. While it has often been argued that 'postmodernist' claims are exaggerated, contradictory, and demonstrably wrong (for example, Norris, 1990; O'Neill, 1995; Simons and Billig, 1994), its significance lies with the way it has contributed to reopening questions which the social sciences of organised modernity had effectively closed off (Parton, 1998a). The discourse on 'post-modernity' sees most social science as being founded on the assumptions, *a priori*, of the intelligibility of the social world, of the coherence of social practices, and of the rationality of action. Increasingly it is accepted that, whether one characterises the contemporary as 'postmodern' or not, the notion of the *contingency* of all social phenomena is evident and needs to inform all social research and conceptions of both community and self-hood. In the process there has been a general shift in our conceptions of the nature of human beings in the Western world from a social subject of solidarity and citizenship rights to, in more recent years, the autonomous subject of choice, self-realisation and self-agency.

One of the considerable achievements of organised modernity was to make practices appear fairly coherent and to make social arrangements appear quasi-natural. This naturalisation of the social order closed off discussion about foundational issues and precluded strong doubts about their viability or thoughts about alternatives. The more widely diffused awareness of the constructiveness and constructability of the social world has strengthened doubts about the possibility of valid, natural and incontestable knowledge. The current condition is marked by doubts about both intelligibility and shapeability, for the increased awareness of the plurality and diversity of social practices makes it difficult to imagine a collective actor who can intervene in the name of any self-evident universalist ideas. As Wagner (1994, p. 33) has argued, 'the increase in social constructiveness as well as the awareness of such constructedness, thus make the political issue of justification highly problematic'. Risk, uncertainty and reflexivity are increasingly seen as characterising contemporary times (Beck, 1992; Beck, Giddens and Lash, 1994; Lash, Szerszynski and Wynne, 1996). More and more social conflicts are characterised as having no unambiguous solutions. They are distinguished by a fundamental ambivalence which might be grasped by calculations of probability, but not removed by them. These are clearly major challenges for social work to address and which are central when looking to develop theories *for* practice.

So long as traditions and customs were widely sustained, experts were people who could be turned to in order to make key decisions and, in the public eye at least, science was, during organised modernity, imbued with some sense of monolithic and generic authority. In effect science and experts were invested with the authority of a final sovereign court of appeal. But increasingly shorn of formulaic truth, all claims to knowledge have become corrigible. We are now living in a world of multiple authorities and wide-ranging knowledge. While modernity had the effect of condemning tradition, a collaboration between modernity and tradition was crucial to the establishment of organised modernity – the period during which risk was thought calculable in relation to external influences. However, this has now become uncertain, contestable and fluid, such that the basis for professional practice and the nature of its knowledge base is placed under the microscope.

Uncertainty and ambiguity in social work

The predominant response to the changes and challenges since the early 1970s has been to construct ever more sophisticated systems of accountability and thereby attempt to rationalise and scientise increasing areas of social work activity via the introduction of increasingly complex procedures and systems of audit – whereby it is assumed the world can be subject to prediction and calculation. As we have argued throughout, however, social work is much better characterised in terms of indeterminacy, uncertainty and ambiguity (Parton, 1998b). As a consequence, systems and organisational frameworks which operate *as if* issues are resolvable in any kind of scientific or calculative probabilistic sense are in great danger of missing the point. The rehabilitation of the idea of uncertainty, and the permission to talk about an indeterminacy which is not amenable to or reducible to authoritative definition or measurement, is an important step, we would suggest, for recognising and beginning to theorise the contemporary complexities of practice. We would argue that notions of ambiguity, indeterminacy and uncertainty are at the core of social work and should be built upon and not defined out and thereby open up the potential for creativity and novel ways of thinking and acting. As David Howe has argued, 'uncertainty is the domain of the educated professional' (1995b, p. 11).

Noel Timms suggested in 1968 in his discussion of the centrality of language to social work, that such an approach not only sees the nature of social work in terms of 'art' as much as 'science', but that more questions are raised than questions answered, and some of the uncertainties exposed are not capable of ready solution. Timms argued further that 'nor would a ready-made solution necessarily be the most helpful, since a recognition of the uncertainty and its patient exploration is more likely to help us understand the nature of social work' (Timms, 1968, p. vii).

Similarly, in the area of social theory Steven Seidman has argued that 'postmodernity may renounce the dream of one reason and one humanity marching forward along one path towards absolute freedom, but it offers its own ideal of a society that tolerates human differences, accepts ambiguity and uncertainty, and values choice, diversity, and democratisation' (1998, p. 347). It is in this context that we are arguing that constructionist and narrative approaches can make a valuable contribution to developing useful theories *for* social work practice.

We are encouraged to think much more creatively and imaginatively about the relationship between theory and practice.

Rather than seeing the relationship in terms of the *application* of theory to practice we are recognising that theory can be *generative*. Theory can offer new insights and perspectives such that practitioners can think and act differently. Ironically there is nothing as practical as a good theory. Many years ago Kenneth Burke (1937) spoke of critical theory as a civic discourse. Burke never separated action from contemplation, willing from imagining, or poetry from power. Instead he argued that all intellectual activity (even the most theoretical sort that disdains politics and practice) is itself a kind of *practice*, first and foremost an *act* (Lentricchia, 1983). In doing so, Burke helped recover the classical relationship between *theoria* and *praxis* through a realisation of theory's practical power. By concerning itself with the ways we make and change allegiances to key symbols, theory participates in the ongoing moral and practical recreation of individuals and society. It is in this sense that we feel constructionist insights can make a positive contribution to developing social work theory *for* practice. It is ironic and perhaps sad that an essential part of our argument is that social work needs to (re)discover its traditional strengths in working with ambiguity, uncertainty and complexity – issues which are more central now than ever.

The constructionist approaches are not founded on the psy complex and do not rely on the 'new sciences' or on scientific knowledge of personal and social problems and interventions, but on an understanding of the power of language and talking together with people to construct change.

3 Some Theoretical Orientations of Constructive Social Work

> In any conversation, it is not so much truth as the phenom-
> enological experience that we respond to. If we only moved
> forward when we build one truth on top of another we would
> get very little done. (G. Cooper in O'Leary, 1998, p. 33)

The theoretical orientations of *constructive social work* include beliefs and assumptions flowing from our underlying construc-tionism, ideas about the implications of the power of language, about human potential and agency, about the nature of problems and change. Its orientations include the values of anti-oppressive practice, a commitment to social justice, empowerment, practical caring, helping and choice as well as embracing the principles underlying the codes of ethics for professional practice developed by national bodies in various countries.

In developing these ideas *for* practice we have drawn on the work of a number of writers whose work is well known in areas associated with social work, such as therapy, family therapy and counselling, but which are little known and used in social work, particularly in the UK. The work of White in Australia and Epston in New Zealand in the area of narrative, de Shazer in the USA in solution-focused work and O'Hanlon in possibility thinking, and several others, have all been important in helping us develop our own ideas. We discuss these in greater detail, and how they can inform practice directly, in Chapters 5 and 6. What we do in this chapter and the next is set out what we identify as the key themes, assumptions and principles which we see as informing *constructive social work* in practice.

Narrative and spin

The scientific mode of thought uses empirical tests and hypotheses, seeks general application and avoids contradiction at all cost. The narrative mode of thought, however, seeks to gain credence by lifelike stories, and is not interested in general principles with wide application but in local knowledge. Miller (1987) explains 'local' as intrinsically linked to the persons and circumstances within which they are produced and not claiming wider application. For E. Bruner (1986), the logico-scientific mode is in the indicative mood of 'is', 'does' and 'causes', while the narrative mode is in the subjunctive mood of 'maybe', 'might', 'could', 'as if' and 'suppose'.

Narrative triggers presupposition and implicit meanings; it allows for interpretation. 'Truths' are suggested by the consciousness of the characters in the story and the world is viewed through several different lenses. Possibilities abound, rather than certainties, and reality is 'subjunctivised', softened with words like 'suppose' or 'perhaps'. The logico-scientific mode is interested in classification rather than individual experiences, in general laws and facts that hold across time and in all places rather than the unique and temporal or the unfolding of events over time. Stories have beginnings, middles and ends; they accept uncertainty, complexity and flux and they listen to every voice – consistency is not the issue and contradictions are lived with, as are alternative meanings and qualitative assessments. The meanings of words are not pre-defined and can be determined by context; the range of possible realities is widened. People are active creative, not just passive towards the given. They are protagonists in their lives, authoring their stories and their very selves.

J. Bruner (1986) discusses what he calls the two components of narrative, 'landscapes of action' and 'landscapes of consciousness'. The former includes events, linked in sequence over time and following a plot, a 'thematic unfolding of events across time' (p. 37), what is happening and being done. The latter includes interpretations, meanings, reflections on events, thoughts, realisations and conclusions drawn by the characters and by the reader. These may concern relationships, desires, qualities, intentions, values and beliefs. The stories that we live our lives by in can be examined under these headings and we will usually find gaps and contradictions that invite us to further meaning making.

Practice that is described as narrative work, therefore, has high regard for individuals' lived experience, for looking at life over time, for using presuppositional questions and 'just suppose . . .', for metaphors, implied meanings and possible new and different stories. It is reflexive regarding itself and seeks to empower personal authorships, constantly returning to the pronouns 'I' and 'you'. It invites people to reflect, ponder, re-examine, try out, dream and construct differently. Later on we will present the 'how?' of this practice.

Central to contemporary thought on representation and ideas associated with narrative are challenges to the 'realist' epistemology which sees representation as a mirror of a reality that lies outside it. Homo Narrans (humans made by/of narratives) offers an alternative to what has been Western thought since Decartes' time. This 'crisis of representation', in Mumby's (1993) view, is 'a tremendous opportunity to explore alternative ways of making knowledge claims' and of viewing life. It relieves us from the obligation to seek 'essential truths' and it opens up the possibility of new 'unthought' social and political ideas. These are necessary to maintain the debate with powerful political forces who would otherwise dominate orthodoxy. For example, as oppressed social groups or defenders of the environment begin to make challenges that shift life towards greater fairness, the status quo supporters are quick to counter with constructions like 'political correctness' and 'free enterprise'. The 'spin' of language has been with us since language was invented and nowadays the importance of narratives (talking, writing and video productions) is being recognised in life at large and also in therapeutic and helping work and other human change efforts. As the major theories of science were challenged by ideas of relativity, attempts to impose scientific laws on human behaviour, which were based on a belief in pre-existing structures, are being challenged by a view that holds that these very structures are created by the words used to describe them. 'An incredulity towards meta-narratives' (Lyotard, 1984, p. xxiv) marks 'postmodernism', and grand narratives are replaced by little, personal (local) narratives that form the 'shifting terrain of meaning that makes up the social world' (Mumby, 1993, p. 3).

We have already made the point that total objectivity becomes impossible since we are all involved in the construction of narratives. Here we add that this is well exemplified in some ethnographic research where discourse is privileged over text and dialogue over monologue. In the cooperative and collaborative nature of this ethnographic research the distinction between observer and observed is rejected, as story is created in mutual dialogue. If we consider the notion of 'our family and its qualities', for example, it is easy to see that prior to its construction by various narratives among its members it would be difficult to say it had these qualities.

Narrative is social in that it only takes on meaning in a social ground and the social context is itself, at least in part, constructed by it and is therefore 'tenuous, precarious, and open to negotiation' (Mumby, 1993, p. 5) in a constant struggle for meanings. The politically powerful however seek ways to 'fix' meanings and it is important to be aware of the process of domination involved in 'hegemony at work'. But the oppressed can also use language to create liberating truth, since the process of truth-finding is no longer one of scientifically unveiling the given.

Stories are a particular type of narrative but like all narrative they construct reality rather than simply represent it – words *do* things, as well as having meaning. The teller demands that the audience pays attention – 'Listen to this . . .'. Family stories are 'ways of doing family' (Langellier and Peterson, 1993, p. 73). These narratives are a most powerful way of creating beliefs in that they impose a coherence as the elements join to form the story (Witten, 1993) and they have a unique power for 'setting forth truth claims' (Witten, 1993, p. 106) that are persuasive, memorable and difficult to debate or test. They include an implicit proposition that they are true and moral. They depart from or suspend the taking-turns of conversation; their knowledge is ready-made to be listened to, needing no proof and capable of creating an obedience that makes reframing or reinterpretation difficult later. They are particularly powerful in covertly creating values. They are designed to be interesting for the audience and the values they convey create can range from racism to religion, to political dogma, to love and generosity; all values are easily storied for the silent audience.

Human beings are interpreting beings, active in giving meaning to life, but some are more influential than others in affecting the wider culture. As it is not possible to interpret experience in a vacuum, a frame of intelligibility is needed to provide a context for attributing meaning, and our personal story (self-narrative) provides this frame. The meanings that we make during our interpretations have a powerful effect in constructing our lives and in influencing the steps we take. Such meanings are not passive but constitutive of life. Our personal stories however are not just invented inside our heads – they are to a large extent developed and promulgated within communities and cultures. As our stories structure our lives they determine also which aspects are expressed. In time our lives are multi-storied as no single edition can cover all the twists and contingencies of living. Among these stories there will be dominant stories and sub-stories; some will be constitutive of a problem-saturated life – we need therefore to develop narratives that are constitutive of life without domination by problems.

However, the processes are not straightforward. For example, while selves and families are to a great extent constructed and maintained by stories, 'family is always gerry-built and has to be reconstructed and re-imagined every generation' (Stone, 1988, p. 4) and 'what blood does not provide narrative can'. Storytelling produces and reforms the family 'by legitimising means and power relations that privilege parents over children, men over women, and middle class over lower class'. But just as the story telling 'participates in social control of the family' it can also 'foster resistance and tactics that contest dominant meanings and power relations' (Langellier and Peterson 1993, p. 50). In discussing family stories however, Stone (1988, p. 7) remarks that 'attention to the stories' truth is never the family's most compelling consideration. Encouraging belief is.' Stone adds that stories lead to 'discursive closure' that restricts interpretation. They have an 'I'm telling you' feel, and this introduces the element of power to which we will return shortly.

The next problem is, if society is already constructed in certain ways and people's minds so filled with certain views, how can people know what they really want? If we are shaped by powerful 'knowledges' that not only keep us in order but control our very wants in getting us to control ourselves – if power can get us to want what power wants, are our desires our own? Who can say what our real interests are? And if knowledge is socially constructed, can we rely on it? Lukes (1974) argues that the best we can do is get a better appreciation of the complexity of social structures and the power structures we encounter. But can narrative theory take the narratives of everyday life seriously as an object of analysis and not treat them as the reflexes of dupes and fools? Clegg (1993) suggests that in listening to everyday narratives we need to enquire into how it is possible for people to say what they say and, with Wittgenstein (1968), study the meanings of language *in use*, since that is all we have. We need collaborative conversations in which both parties share 'where they are coming from', given that their insights will always be partial, if we are to avoid the endless spaghetti process of meanings analysis which may deflect us from fully listening.

Some suspicion of narratives therefore seems sensible in any research into situations, but the suspicion, in our view, probably needs to be aimed more at the theoretic narratives that seek to overwhelm the day-to-day narratives that work in peoples' lives. Clegg (1993) recommends a wariness of the grand narratives that organise people's experiences and more respect for the stories of daily living, although these too should not be taken at face value. One needs to question what language game is used and how it serves a power game. This returns us to the issue of power.

Power

In addressing power, the narrative approach to practice is strongly attracted to the ideas of Foucault. He occupies a central position in the thinking of White and his colleagues. White and Epston (1990) write that an important part of any story is the wider sociological context and how the part played by that context is often omitted from stories. They go on to say how in Foucault's analysis lives are shaped by the 'normalising truths' that prevail in a culture, and these 'truths' are 'produced in the exercise of power' (p. 19). Power constructs ideas concerning gender, age, class, race, colour, ability and so on, and gives these ideas the status of truth and therefore they are able to construct norms around which we are invited to build our lives, in such a way that our lives are subjugated by them. We become conscripted into activities that support these 'truths' and we criticise ourselves if we fail to do so! (The inverted commas on 'truths' are used to suggest that these are not necessarily true – they are ideas that are given the *status* of truth by the powerful.) For Foucault, power and knowledge are linked. There is no exercise of power without a discourse of truth, and knowledge can become a problem when used by the powerful for their purposes. We are all caught in the web and in using it in relation to other people – we are subjugated and we subjugate others.

It is in the granting of the status of 'objective reality' to certain knowledges that moves them up in the hierarchy of power. But power does not rely on top-down enforcement but on 'local' or ground-up policing of ourselves and of others. We are recruited into actively subjugating ourselves and into the surveillance and evaluation of ourselves. It is the society of the ever present 'gaze'. In this society, Foucault claims, there are marginalised and disqualified knowledges at local level that need to be encouraged to rise up against institutions and challenge the power of the dominant. Feminism has empowered women to make many such challenges, for example, and provides possibilities for certain forms of resistance.

People's lives are dependent on language in that it is through language that they ascribe meanings and in using it they are drawing on a stock of available discourses. Understandings of experience are based on meanings that are mediated through language and this is influenced by the dominant 'truths' of our time. When we experience problems and our lives do not fit our stories, we would do well to remember that these stories are not all of our own making and that wider powers press us to do things that subjugate us in line with powerful wider 'truth discourses'.

This power is difficult to deal with. There are several reasons – the source of power is invisible to those who feel it the most; subjugated people become isolated from the experience of subjugation; people feel they are subject to the normalising gaze constantly, even when they may not be; people are incited to criticise and police themselves and power is taken up by those at the bottom and is exercised in local taken-for-granted knowledge and practice.

Power operates through and in the cultural context and social workers need to keep in mind how it might be operating in the culture of social work itself. This culture does not have a privileged position outside of culture at large; it is not free from the influences of the ideologies and structures of the wider culture or from the politics relating to the hierarchies of knowledge and the marginalisation of groups and their local narratives. The culture of social work is linked to practices of the wider dominant culture.

The text analogy

Behaviour always happens at a point in time and by the time it is reported it is in the past, but the telling and the meaning we attach to it is still in the present. Interpreting an event therefore can be likened to *reading* a text and each interpretation or reading makes for a new text, a different writing.

What we know of life is learned by 'lived experience' (White and Epston, 1990, p. 9). It matters then how we store these experiences and how we express them. This process is called 'storying' – it gives meaning to and organises experiences in a linear 'sequence across time' (p. 10). One's life becomes self-narrative, in which the way the present is viewed is influenced by the past and by future expectations.

Our stories however are edited and pruned – bits that do not fit the dominant theme are cut out; stories are never complete accounts – they cannot contain all the emotions and reflections of daily living. They present only selected parts of lived experience, and this applies to our own stories of ourselves. In expressing the story, therefore, the account that is lived is a selective account and the 'performance' (J. Bruner, 1986, p. 11) of our selective narrative contributes to the construction of its development and goes on to shape weave life and relationships for the next 'writing' in an ambiguous and indeterminate way. The process can be compared to a spider weaving spinning a web – sometimes taking apparently random directions, sometimes responding to the constraints of the context and sometimes making mysterious choices. While earlier versions are copied, each copy is different! But also for Bruner, 'narrative emphasises order and sequence' (p. 153) and is therefore appropriate for the study of change. It is the meaning we, for example in a family, attribute to events that determines our behaviour; our meanings therefore keep our problems alive and determine their 'careers' – inadvertently we support the life of the problem by our responses and how we talk about them.

Gaps in stories are filled partly by new lived experiences and so lives evolve in ways similar to the re-writing of texts; we enter the story and re-story it daily. While we give meaning to life by developing a story it does not freeze there; we go on shaping our life by living reliving the story daily. So one's problems can be seen as situated in one's story and in the stories of others about one. Then, as White and Epston (1990) say, dominant stories make it difficult for one to perform one's preferred story. Being unhappy could be re-described as lived experience not living up to one's story or as important aspects of one's story being contradicted by experience, or having problems and needing help could be simply performing a story 'written' by others, either in society at large or in a particular welfare organisation. Helpers could also assume that successful outcomes would require the generation of a new story containing more helpful meanings and 'desired possibilities' (p. 15).

White (1993) says that people are rich in lived experiences and that only a fraction of them are storied. He claims that the many parts of forgotten, ignored and unstoried unstored experiences provide a rich source of alternative stories and options for change. Some experiences may be one-offs, or 'unique outcomes' and bringing these into the story makes a new situation with new possibilities. Such 'unique outcomes' can relate to the past and to the present and can influence the future.

Understanding and misunderstanding

If meaning is made up of ideas (the 'signified') contained in words ('signifiers'), what happens when meaning changes from context to context ? How can we rely on words? We cannot rely on dictionaries; they only give us more words to look up. Derrida (1978) has proposed that meaning is in the difference between words, rather than each word telling us what is meant. What words do not say is probably more important than what they say. Words therefore are two-sided; they mean both what is and what is not; we need to hold on to both – to hold to both and. Furthermore Derrida maintains that the user's mind has no priority over the meaning of words. As de Shazer (1993a, p. 113) adds, 'it is the word that is master, not its user. A word always means both more and less than we, as users, as authors, mean it to mean.' For

Derrida, the 'text' can stand on its own, independent of any external verifying reality.

In his 1921 *Tractatus–Logico–Philosophicus* Wittgenstein first wrote that language gives us a picture of the world and language consists of pictures of reality. But what is the relationship between language and reality? Later, his *Philosophical Investigations*, published posthumously (see Wittgenstein, 1963 and 1968), maintained that language was not a picture of the world but more like a net, or many pieces of interconnected string. The misuse of words gets us 'knotted up' and they need to be unravelled if we are to relate to each other. Language therefore is a way of relating, like a handshake. With it we can include or exclude people. But when it comes to understanding the meanings of words, this is ever changing and we rely greatly on the context in which they are used. In each context they, as it were, overrule and dominate meaning. For example, if we read something we wrote some time ago we often wonder what meaning was *sent* by a word; we are just left with the meaning we receive it with. So if words are *sent* with one meaning and *received* with another, perhaps the meaning is better thought to be *between* words, or better still, *between sender and receiver*. The meaning of a word is greatly, if not totally, determined by the *use* we make of it.

Ever since the influence of Freudian thought, people in the caring professions have distrusted words and seen them as of less value than what lay hidden behind them. The thrust of much practice has been a sort of detective work to uncover hidden truths. Wittgenstein has questioned this enterprise and said (1968, p. 126) that everything already 'lies open to view', and if things are hidden it is because they are there in the surface word, rather than buried beneath the surface – 'aspects of things that are most important to us are hidden because of their simplicity and familiarity; one is unable to notice something because it is always before one's eyes' (p. 129). However, language is both the problem and the solution, in the sense that 'language is what bewitches but language is what we must remain within in order to cure the bewitchment' (Staten, 1984, paraphrasing Wittgenstein).

Such ideas, however, leave us with the question – how can we understand another person? If we can only 'read' them with the meaning we have as 'receivers', we will always be 'misreading' them. There is no way we can understand exactly what they or their words mean. At any particular moment, *misunderstanding is more likely than understanding*, but de Shazer (1994) argues that this is what makes conversation possible in that we ask questions because we know we do not understand. When people talk to us *they* know what they mean and they may know that their words do not say it very clearly, so we may ask them what they mean by 'fed up'; if they say 'I can't get a job' we may pursue what that means too. Seeking to understand the problem is therefore a futile endless game; far better to accept and use our joint misunderstanding to begin constructing ways of solving the problem. Rather than say 'let me try to understand' we can say 'let me try to misunderstand less'. What the problem *is not*, or what is happening when the problem is not, leads us to think of exceptions to the problem, and these exceptions help us to see possibilities for change.

Mind your language

We need to 'mind our language' because not all talking is constructive. Weiner-Davis (1993), and O'Hanlon and Weiner-Davis (1989), have reported on some interesting studies of the power of words to create bias, on how workers' expectations affect outcome and on how the assumptions implied in words and questions affect people for good or ill. These studies alert us to the potential for 'iatrogenic injury' (treatment-caused harm) which is used to describe harm done by assessments and interventions that discourage, invalidate or close down possibilities. O'Hanlon (1993) has coined the phrase 'iatrogenic healing' to refer to practice that encourages, respects, validates and opens up possibilities for change.

In 1983 Weiner-Davis, with de Shazer and Gingrich, studied the difference between clients who reported change and those who did not. She found that if a worker actively elicited 'change talk' they were four times more likely to get 'change talk'. When people were asked to elaborate further ('Tell me what you do differently to make this happen?') in most cases they were able to do so to the extent that change talk dominated the discussion. Prior to doing this, they thought that people continued to talk about problems because no change had happened, or if it had happened it had gone unnoticed, that is they assumed that 'problem talk' was due to factors pertaining to the clients. But the study showed that whether people talked in the same old way about their problems, or not, had more to do with the questions they were asked. Furthermore, people who reported more changes changed more. The conclusion was that the powerful message in the question created an assumption that change was possible – it created a bias for change. It is as if we only know what we know when we say it. People will sometimes say 'let me see if I know this' as they proceed to express what they know.

In a more recent study Weiner-Davis and McKeel (reported in Weiner-Davis, 1993, p. 155) found that in interviewing new service users and asking about change that might have happened since the appointment was made, 67 per cent report change if the question suggests that change is likely; 67 per cent also report no change if the question suggests that their situation would have remained the same. Note that in both cases they go on to give concrete evidence of change or sameness.

Fazio, Effrein and Falender (1981) found that if people rated themselves as introvert or extrovert in a test they were more likely to behave in a more introverted or extroverted way after the test had finished, and in a further study by Swann, Giuliano and Wegner (1982) it was found that even if people were made aware that the questions are leading questions the effect of the questions still stands; people seem to ignore the information and assume that their behaviour warrants being asked the questions they are asked. Presuppositional questions have a most powerful effect in creating what is presupposed.

The implications for social workers will be clear. What we choose to talk about is crucial. If we ask about problems there will be more problems. If we choose to talk about solutions there will be more solutions. For example, if someone reports having a bad argument last night, we can wait for an opportunity to ask 'How did you end it?' Even if they can't tell how it was ended the question conveys that they were capable of ending it. When questions about solutions are used consistently in a session the messages about the potential for change is more powerful still. All questions contain assumptions so that we cannot ask something without telling people something about themselves also. How we need to mind our language! Not only do we need to watch what we say but also how we say it. Even very subtle suggestions embedded in our tone can make a difference. Since we cannot avoid leading, we need to consider where is the most helpful place to lead to – we have a responsibility to lead towards change because that results in 'iatrogenic health', so called because such interventions not only help but encourage optimism and 'open up possibilities for change' (O'Hanlon, 1993, p. 4).

This does not mean that we have to develop 'a problem-avoidance personality' (Weiner-Davis, 1993, p. 157) or that we should drive negative feelings underground. Nor does it mean that we must be gung-ho about people being able to do anything they put their minds to. Nor is it 'a new-age Pollyanna view' (O'Hanlon, ibid) or just 'positive thinking' that minimises hardships in people's lives and the very difficult experiences they have to deal with. But nor is it 'negative thinking' that says nothing can be done and nothing works with some problems or some people. O'Hanlon labels his work 'possibility' work, which neither claims that everything can be successful or perfect, nor that nothing works; it recognises that people's situations are serious, that it is possible that they will not change, but it is an approach that works to make possible change happen and to maximise any potential for change that may be unrecognised. He tells the story of a Fire Officer who was attending a burning building and was asked if he thought the building could be saved – his reply was 'Yes, if there's a shift in the wind, otherwise no'. 'Possibility' work can be described as promoting that 'shift in the wind' in people's problematic lives. Perhaps we should aim at being neither a pessimist nor a blind optimist, but an experienced optimist, when working with service users. We should acknowledge the existence of violence, economic problems, oppression, but hold that even in such situations there are possibilities.

Conversations: for good or ill?

Our conversations with service users can easily and unwittingly become creative of more failure and depression, especially if we are now aware of the power of what Gergen and Gergen (1986), call 'digressive narratives'. They describe three types of conversations: *progressive narratives* that imply that service users and situations are moving towards their goals; *stability narratives* that imply that life is unchanging; *digressive narratives* that imply that they are moving away from the goals, or backwards. A conversation could be said to be constructive *only* if one party is working with the other to bring about a state wanted by the other *and* it is moving in that direction.

Change is the conversational creation of a new narrative. We even live through, or co-construct, our lives with the conversations we have with people. This is how we build our meanings, our understandings and our social systems. This is how we search for new meanings with people that 'dis-solve' problems, as McNamee and Gergen (1992) put it, and open up many new possibilities. De Shazer says that our expertise needs to shift, from being providers of solutions and meanings, to expert conversationalists who can help people to demolish the old destructive stories that oppress and disempower them *by moving towards a co-authored new story*.

Change, difference and agency

Like talk, change is endless, constant and inevitable. Nothing stays the same; Buddhists compare life to a flowing river – one can never put one's foot into the same water twice. Each moment, each day, is different; we are different each day. But change is not just happening to us; we have some agency over it and the more sense of personal agency we have the more empowered we are. In practice this means that *knowing what we do that makes a difference* is important. Therefore talking about what is different, about whether what is happening is different or not, about what people do to make a difference, is central to empowerment. Bateson's (1972, p. 453) well-used phrase about this is 'the elementary unit of information is a difference that makes a difference'. But de Shazer (1991) reminds us that a difference that is not recognised makes no difference (p. 156). By recognising differences however, he adds, 'they can then be put to work to make a difference'. So talking about things that happen that are new for service users, especially when that newness is brought about by them, develops a recognition that can make important differences in their life. Helping to point out differences not only empowers but increases strengths, potential and confidence, so that people can say they have improved some aspect of their lives.

This becomes a listening, validating, humble, collaborative actitvity, based on regard for the service user and their capacity to make a difference. It involves using words to build change. Like interlinking bricks in a wall, the words of both worker and user join in a language game, where the meaning depends greatly on the use made of words. The worker may use the service user's words, and because he or she cannot be sure what meaning is 'sent' in them, there will be muddle at times, but it is this muddle that keeps the conversation going because it causes them to negotiate mutual meanings which will be different.

The identification and amplification of personal agency is central to *constructive social work*. Establishing an 'internal locus of control' is essential for the empowerment especially of those who are victims in various ways, be it of bullies, of violence, of abuse of power by teachers or other professionals. It also opens the door to multiple possibilities of change for the future and for more control of many aspects of one's life. Indeed, it is key to the building of all solutions, to full participation in goal development, for example.

Past, present or future?

Traditionally there has been great emphasis in much social work theory on 'the past', on seeing 'the present' as the result of the past and on looking at the past to explain the present. In *constructive social work* the past is regarded as past, while it is accepted that its construction does *restrain* people's ability to change. The past can be discussed also in terms of learning from it, learning how one was influenced by ideas to allow the problem into one's life. This look at the past is not so much a looking for the cause as a taking into account of the restraints, and perhaps learning useful lessons from errors. The most important use of the past however is the search for *successes* and for *exceptions* to the problem, and an examination of how that was done. Michael White's approach will show some interest in the past in terms of gaining an understanding of how a person was 'recruited' into the problem or into submission to it and whether the person had any influence on that event or not. De Shazer's approach, on the other hand, is primarily future focused. It sets about building change without seeking to understand the problem; it constructs change in the future by talking about a changed future – changed as the service user wants it.

Resistance

We have two views on resistance that differ from the traditional. Firstly there is the worker-error view. Since service users already have the seeds of the solutions they need, once they have decided on the goals, workers can help to locate these seeds along with the user. By cooperating with service users in a joint project, resistance dies. Resistance had no place in Maturana's (1988) thinking and perhaps resistance has more to do with the puzzlement of the worker than with the obduracy of the service user. Bandler and Grinder (1979) wrote that 'there are no resistant clients, only inflexible therapists'. For de Shazer, there is no such thing as resistance, only different ways of cooperating, and it is for workers to act accordingly and work in a way that fits the service user's views. When people seem to be not cooperating they are showing us how they think change happens and it is for us to understand their ideas and respond appropriately. They are letting us know how not to help them; that is, they are telling us how to help them. It is also for workers to avoid creating resistance by not pushing for the change they think is required and by not deciding for people which problem they should tackle first. It certainly is not primarily a persuasion game where we sell our goals; it is a possibility game of opening up options for what the person or family wants. We say 'primarily' because there can be situations where our professional anti-oppression stance will call for persuasion, especially when we are in a protective role. But mainly, it is developing a conversation that will facilitate getting on track towards achieving their goals. Tasks (invitations to experiment with new ways of doing) are part of that conversation, as are invitations to new ways of thinking and talking.

The notion of resistance is therefore redefined as worker error. The error is in not listening to the service user's goals and negotiating agreed goals. When people do not engage in constructive conversations this can be seen as the worker's problem, not the person's. Where the worker cooperates with the user, the user cooperates with the worker. When users are complimented for what they are doing that is good for them, they sense that the worker is on their side and then the worker can suggest something else that might be useful. What the user decides to do is up to them; the only question asked is 'was it useful?' If it was, if it helped to make things better, it is to be applauded; if it didn't, it is plain that something different needs to be done. So the notion of 'resistance' is replaced by cooperation; resistance is seen as the service user's unique way of cooperating and it is the worker's job to cooperate with the user's way of changing. By working with service users, rather than against them, cooperation becomes inevitable.

There will be those who can only think of reasons why change will not happen and they will reply 'yes, but ...' to new ideas. Walter and Peller (1992) suggest 'Well, without any real hope that things will change, I'm really wondering why you want to keep trying.' They maintain that if people want to solve the situation they will be able to answer – there will be something that is motivating them to come. The suggestion is not based on any paradoxical intent – the intent is respectfully to accept their mood; if they feel we understand where they are they will be more able to respond to our invitations. It is about mutual cooperation and that includes going with their pessimism. It is suggested that the same principle can apply with those considering suicide, for example. That however is not the same as saying that the approach leads to goals being attained in every case – it sometimes does not work. As service users experience acceptance and affirmation from workers, the likelihood of their being willing to engage in productive efforts increases.

There is however a second and more exciting notion of resistance – undermining the 'enemy'. This is the narrative-based view that by building stories of heroism in standing up to problems and their influence we can re-write our lives. In this sense our work is to promote resistance to problems, working alongside service users to defeat them. Exceptions can be talked of as the beginning of resistance or as signs that it is possible and service users can be invited to use their ingenuity and cunning to trick and deceive the enemy problem, circumvent it or escape from its grasp, outflank it. Thought of in this way, it is to be encouraged, as we will show in Chapter 5. Next, however, we will present some further ideas and themes which inform both our thinking and orientations to practice.

4 Further Orientations Towards Constructive Practice

Life is understood backwards but lived forwards. (Soren Kierkegaard in Gilligan and Price, 1993, p. 287)

We have discussed how the role of language is central to the notion of meaning and to making meaning. Ben Furman (1998), discussing traumatic events such as rape, says that what happens to us is not as important as how we react to it; how we react is not as important as how we think we react; how we think we react is not as important as what others think about how we react; and that is not as important as what we think about what they think. In rape counselling, for example, people have found it helpful to discuss their responses to the attack, more than the attack itself. When the focus is on what the person did, rather than on what was done to them, there is empowerment, in a conversation in which their resistance is honoured. Even our identity is shaped by how we see significant others seeing us; this 'seeing' comes about mainly by talking. As Insoo Kim Berg (Berg, 1995) has said, language does not merely mirror reality, but is our major means of constructing what we perceive as reality. Therefore what is talked about and how problems or solutions are talked about is central to *constructive social work*. Of course if two or more people are to talk, so that there is a conversation, listening is equally important.

Because of the importance attached to words, there is great attention paid to *what people actually say*, that is to the actual words used, rather than to any hidden meaning. It is felt that the words are all we get and there may be nothing between the lines anyway. The 'local' narrative of service users is as important to constructing change as the wider narratives of professionals, if work is to be collaborative and co-constructive. Therefore, surface reading of the words is preferred to looking below the surface. If we see something below the surface we may well be only reading our own theories. Sometimes, of course, people give non-verbal clues as to what they mean, but even then we need to draw on words and ask about what we think we have seen. However, if it is clear that something is taking place that our professional code or value commitments requires us to challenge (violence for example), we 'encourage [our service users] to reinterpret their options in life [and] to identify personal and social resources that [they] might use to take greater control of their lives' (Miller and de Shazer, 1998). In other words, facts of life are not ignored; injustices and deprivations are not denied. They are talked about in ways that get beyond them, in ways that encourage hopefulness and power, in ways that do not create victims but heroes and heroines.

How problems happen

For Michael White (1990 and 1993) problems are caused by 'invitations' that the person was seduced into accepting, or sometimes by the person welcoming the problem into their life in some way. People's responses to such invitations are 'constrained' by oppressive wider narratives (for example, that children are property, or that women are sex objects, or that young people must drink great quantities of alcohol to be popular). On the other hand, for de Shazer, problems just happen! The cause of problems is of little concern in his approach; searching for the 'true' cause is seen as a waste of time and understanding problems in this way is not seen as useful to the building of solutions. Solutions do not require an understanding of the problem. There is an acceptance that problems simply happen and that the causation is usually circular/ interactional in any case. He writes that in practice, however, 'problem' holds a privileged position and the understanding of the aetiology of problems has been the traditional focus of study, in a way similar to the drive to understand medical problems. Problems have been seen as diseases, and diseases have causes. Similarly, families with problems have been described as dysfunctional; dysfunction leads to symptoms. We do not say that there are no such things as causes. Indeed, we believe oppression of one sort or another causes many of the problems we encounter, but in human affairs specific causes are virtually impossible to prove and therefore can often be set aside when searching for them is not very useful. Wittgenstein (1968, p. 654) wrote that 'our mistake is to look for an explanation where we ought to look at what happens'. When there is a problem we can look at what is happening or not happening and, without asking 'why?' discuss what needs to not happen or happen – in other words, set goals and start building solutions. Problems can be defined as situations where something is not working and what is being done makes no difference, so that it becomes a case of the 'same damn thing' happening over and over again. If there is a cause it is the inability to do something different, something small perhaps, that could set off a ripple effect of solution or interrupt the pattern.

De Shazer (see, for example, Miller and de Shazer, 1998, p. 366) seems to be disinterested in the question 'why is the problem present?' and he argues that answering that question does not necessarily help construct a solution. He quotes Wittgenstein (1968, p. 471) as saying 'It often happens that we only become aware of important facts if we suppress the question "why?"; and then in the course of investigations these facts lead us to an answer.' He suggests that in seeking to answer 'Why?' we are likely to pay more attention to our own theories than to what the service user is saying. Better to listen to that, and to use what the person brings, especially any exceptions to the problem, so as to build solutions. He goes further, maintaining that solutions have only a nominal relationship with problems and they may not consist of the absence of the problem.

What we have is the words and that is all we have, and that is what we need to attend to and work with, adding our words and our questions to generate more words to do the constructing of change. The solution does not need to beautifully deconstruct the problem. A solution is a solution, that is it is only called a solution if it works in attaining the desired goal, and any dirty little solution will do. Understanding the times when a person overcomes their problem is far more useful than discovering some so-called cause. 'Problems are solved, not by new information, but by arranging what we have always known. [It] is a battle against the bewitchment of our intelligence by means of language' (Wittgenstein, 1968, p. 109). As de Shazer adds, 'With the concept of causality held in abeyance and surrounded by doubt, solution-determined conversations help clients describe and orient their lives in new ways. Therapists and clients together enter into the language game of goal definition, thereby creating the social and interactional conditions for producing progressive narratives focused on change and goal achievement' (1991, p. 124). Learning more about a problem involves more talk about it and, as we have seen, that is risky. Wittgenstein has said that 'All the facts belong to the problem, not to its solution' (1972, p. 4321), so it is important to stop searching in the problem cupboard (as Milner, (2000) likes to say) and, either by problem-free talk or exception talk, start searching in the solution cupboard, to start constructing the future.

Consequently, we go about our practice in a very pragmatic manner. What do people want? How will they know when they have it (what will be evident)? How can this happen as quickly as possible? As we have argued, however, in social work, issues of fairness, discrimination and the abuse of power must be addressed. To this extent social workers must have an understanding of how such abuses operate, they must challenge abuse, ensure it is not condoned by silence and must model appropriate behaviour in the face of abuses. Like Miller and de Shazer (1998) we are concerned that our talk does not worsen victimisation and are keen to locate resources that will enable people to take control of their lives and to talk themselves out of trouble *by* talking themselves into solutions. Where there has been oppression of some kind we seek to underline what the person *did*, what self-agency they held on to, *in spite of* what was happening.

Frequently social workers see 'clients' as problems. They were depressed, or feckless or irresponsible and something has to be done with them. The person is the problem or the problem is in the person. In contrast , in *constructive social work* the problem is *the problem*, not the person. So the problem is seen as outside the person, or the person may be seen as in the problem. But the whole person is not in the problem because much of the person's life is OK. Part of the person is stuck in what is an external problem.

Not knowing

Constructive workers do not assume that they know the answer to any person's problem, nor that they know what the best or better solution might be. This is partly because they do not profess to understand the person's life or the nature of their difficulties. They are 'atheoretical' in the sense that they respect the service user's theory as much as any other and they do not believe that there is a theory that can explain the situation with which they are faced. They feel they are in the happy position of not needing such an explanation, since explanations of problems are not seen as necessarily linked to the understanding of solutions. However there is a difficulty where oppression is operating or there is a serious risk of harm – then the worker has a duty to care, to state their view and to use their knowledge of such dangers and of the resources needed to deal with them.

Maintaining curiosity, while not asking 'why?'

Rather than developing hypotheses based on one's preferred theory, the worker remains neutral over theory and tries to clearly obtain the service user's thoughts and accounts, not of the problem but much more of the exceptions to the problem, or those occasions when the problem was less a problem. The worker is simply curious about when things were better, how that happened, and especially what the person was doing differently that made that possible. 'How did you do that?' is a key question therefore, key in two important respects: firstly in that the 'how' tells us about the person's abilities; but, secondly, because if we emphasise the 'do' we are developing or enhancing the person's sense of personal agency. If that question can prompt a person to figure out how he or she copes better sometimes, for example, then the person is empowered to repeat that behaviour more readily next time. Rather than seeking to describe and explain, which may cause one to become instructive or attached to our hypotheses, one maintains a neutrality as to whether an explanation is 'true' or not. One accepts that people are doing what they do and 'that this doing is the it that does it' (Cecchin, 1987, p. 408). Whereas belief in having found the true explanation makes us busy labelling what is wrong and trying to control it, curiosity continues to look for resources within the person or family. In statutory work, where we are expected to take on the role of social controller, we are in a position in which it is difficult to remain neutral and in which it is easy to lose the sense of curiosity. In statutory settings there are social constructions imposed by law and by wider society, which cannot be ignored – we have the responsibility of preventing harm. In these settings we need to co-develop with others 'a sense of curiosity that is different from a sense of linear morality' (Cecchin, 1987, p. 409) so as to be able to act for positive change, as well as legally. If we have team colleagues, reflecting on the situation with them helps us to retain the openness of mind that keeps curiosity alive.

Being expert/non-expert

The worker is not seen as the expert on the problem, or as having professional insights that shed light on it; the service user is the expert on the problem and is the person who has the experience of the problem and of the exceptions to it. However, this approach does not say that the worker has no expertise; workers have expertise in asking helpful questions and in co-constructing new stories/reframes of situations that make solution-building possible. They are also trained to challenge self-defeating attitudes, injustice and oppression and have knowledge of how such oppressions operate. But, as Cade (1992) writes, 'the role of expert can be taken in a way that does not disempower' (p. 30). He takes the view that he is an expert mainly in what does *not work*, and that what *does work* is 'infinitely more varied and personal than anyone could possibly imagine'. Examples of what we know does not work are lecturing service users, nagging, 'why don't you', punishment, appeals to logic, pleading, taking the moral high ground, 'after all I've done for you', or self-sacrifice such as 'walking on eggshells' to keep the peace, putting your own life on hold or protecting people from the consequences of their actions. We also know that asking people to want to do something they don't want is not likely to have much effect; 'you ought to want to go to school'!

In all of this, as readers may have picked up, there is a constant tension between wishing to respect people's views and being open about one's own views, for example on an injustice, modelling appropriate behaviour. Where there is an issue over which one cannot be neutral, one is obliged to convey one's own view and respectfully invite the service user to consider it. Challenges are strong though often indirect in approach.

Goals

We will discuss the significance of goals in practice in more detail in Chapter 6. Here, however, it is important to note goals bring us back to the start, which is 'what does the service user want?'. What will be happening when they can stop meeting with the worker? Service users often do not know the answer to this question, and that may explain why they are service users in the first place. The start of *constructive social work* therefore is clear, well-formed goals that are pertinent to the service user. Most writers on this point agree that well-formed goals are realistic, achievable, time-limited; they consist of the presence of something, not the absence of something; they consist of the start of something, not the end of something (for example, the start of dry beds can be established easily, but the end of wet beds can never be established). Ideally, the service user's goals will be in keeping with the agency's goals, but often they are not, especially in statutory work. As statutory agents, social workers have two main roles, helping and controlling. They have to be aware of both and there is debate as to whether one can get in the way of the other. In statutory work it is important that service users are as clear as possible about whose side we are on and what role we are playing at various times or what 'hat' we are wearing. We maintain that most service users in statutory agencies are aware that social workers are wearing helping and controlling hats. De Shazer, however, has argued that the two roles need to be clearly separated, not only in the mind of the service user but in the mind of the worker. He has suggested the use of different rooms, or at least different chairs. In any case there needs to be frank openness about our roles at all times. The type of service user, whether they are voluntary users or non-voluntary, affects this issue and we will be returning to it later.

Goals are of their nature belonging to the future, and conversations about that future when they are achieved is in itself a major step towards achieving them. Picturing life when the problem is overcome, helps to overcome it. When people can talk of the solution in clear practical terms, including what difference it will make to various significant others, and what they and others will notice and will say, and the difference that will make, and so on, they will have a greater chance of achieving their goals. Such talk can generate not only confidence and optimism but also actually move the person forward without having ever analysed the problem or its causes, or without giving great attention to the very process of getting from 'problem land' to 'solution land'. Exceptions can then be those occasions when a little bit of the solution is already happening. Talk of how this is happening sometimes makes it happen more and more until the service user or the social worker can see that the meetings can end.

Goals can be difficult to negotiate even with willing people, but in statutory work many are unwilling since they are meeting the worker only because they have to. In their case the goal, at least to begin with, is to end the contact. However, if that situation is addressed openly, with frank acknowledgement of the legal position and the consequences of various options, the worker can still get on their side. This is possible in a conversation in which they are asked whose idea it was that contact was necessary, what is expected to be different as a result, and what needs to happen to convince the referrer that the contact can end. 'What will you be doing that's different when they are convinced?' 'What is the first small step that can be taken to get that started?' 'What difference will it make to your life (or your child's life)?' 'How will we know when we have done enough?'

De Shazer has been criticised for being too goal-orientated. Critics ask what of those who do not want change but some adjustment or coming to terms with their situation, or some support for staying as they are, or support in the face of things inevitably getting worse. De Shazer would probably say these are goals. Some people have no vision of or faith in change or even in a future. There is no reason why the worker cannot question this pessimism or begin to talk about life without this view, provided the service user wants to talk. If they do not, one needs to ask what it is they want. If the worker sees some oppression they need to say so and discuss resources and so on.

Goals are negotiated. The service user will have his or her goals to begin with, even if they are often unclear and as yet not well articulated or thought out. However, workers do not simply go with any goal; they have the right to refuse to work on certain 'projects' or to refer the person to another agency. Even so, they can say what they will or will not work on, and so a negotiation takes place to work out what the 'joint project' is going to be.

Workers cannot ethically go along with harmful, illegal or immoral goals. Where there is danger even in the process of the work, one has to ensure that the risks are less than the risks of doing nothing – domestic violence is an example of such a situation. So it is not a question of 'anything goes' in goal setting.

Building solutions

The foundation stones for building solutions are the 'exceptions' to the problem (de Shazer, 1988, 1991 and 1994, among others). White (1993) talks of 'unique outcomes'. These sound as if they are the same as de Shazer's 'exceptions' but they are not . White's 'unique outcomes' are occasions when the problem was resisted in some way. De Shazer's 'exceptions' are occasions when the problem was less, or a part of the solution or life without the problem was happening. By exceptions we mean those occasions when the problem is not so much a problem, when things are even a little better or there is a different interval between troubles. The question is 'what was different about those occasions and how did the service user manage to make that difference?' Of course, sometimes the difference will be brought about by chance or by another person. He kept out of trouble because he was in jail, or he kept sober because he had no money for drink. However, if there is always change, no problem is always the same. So what was different when it was different? As de Shazer points out, rather than proving the rule, these exceptions are exceptions *to* the rule and are the seeds of future solutions, the key to the lock and the clue to the mystery of how the person can be unstuck from where they are. It is partly a matter of amplifying small differences and building a picture of the future without the problem. Solutions are therefore built by the dialogue between service user and worker, talking in detail about the exceptions the person has noticed, about how they did that, about what difference it makes, about what others notice and say about it. The conversation builds up the positives, focusing on what the future without the problem will be like and focusing on the user's strengths and abilities, their confidence and their willingness to work hard at progressing.

In pathology assessment some normative model is used and people are judged against it; problems are seen as resulting from some failure in make-up that needs to be corrected (Walter and

Peller, 1992). The approach used in *constructive social work* seeks to avoid focusing on deficit; instead, it looks to potential and strengths. It looks to those times when the problem is less a problem, to when the user is doing something that is helpful to them, when they are being wise or strong or responsible. By building up this OK part, a person is able to fix the non-OK part. It is considered dangerous to focus on pathology or weakness since talking of problems makes them grow rather than diminish. But talking of strengths makes them stronger, and therefore identifying strengths and possibilities, affirming and complimenting them and talking about what the user is doing that is useful is a crucial part of *constructive practice*. The approach focuses on amplifying strengths rather than on correcting weaknesses.

Linked to strength is personal agency. Discussing how a person manages to do something difficult, how they create exceptions, how they choose what is good for them, not only builds up the sense of self-power but also the awareness of ability and strength. Not only does one not see pathology, one clearly and steadfastly sees personal agency and capacity. While the protective services need to address problems, they also need a balanced picture. To get that they need to spend time discussing the problem-free aspects of lives. We need to get off the problem because as Durrant has recently commented (SFT E-mail list, 1998) 'how the client wants things to be is not necessarily the opposite of, or the absence of, the problem'.

If workers are strengths-focused and ask useful questions, service users will reveal their capacities and then it is for workers to notice them, point them out and underline them. In suggesting tasks they will then be more likely to say 'If it ain't broke, don't fix it. If it works, do more of it.' This brings us to the principle of utilisation.

Utilisation

This principle was developed by Milton Erickson (see, for example, de Shazer, 1988, p. 139) and has been described in numerous examples by those who observed his work. It means observing closely what the service user brings in terms of strengths, abilities, unusual characteristics and special differences and talents, no matter how small, and *utilising* them in interventions. For example if they like to grow things, using that activity or metaphors relating to growing to build a helpful intervention. This involves mobilising the OK parts of a person's life to create possibilities to help the non-OK parts, and the belief that the former can fix the latter. Since everyone has OK bits, everyone has the potential to fix the non-OK bits. Underpinning this is a firm belief that, where personal change is required, the service user already *has* the solution and every crisis is a growth point.

In statutory work it can be difficult to maintain this belief and only too easy to distrust people and discount their strengths. Workers who work too much on their own are most prone to this pessimism and therefore we feel teamwork is essential especially in assessment work. Not only does it make for more productive assessments but it also makes space for more constructive work in which workers can switch from a risk focus to seek out evidence also for a more optimistic story – using *all* that the service user brings, not only the negatives.

Emotions, meanings and actions

As one listens to distress or stories of pain or loss one seeks to communicate empathy, to accept, to acknowledge and to validate and value how people are feeling. O'Hanlon (1995), however, adds to this important and familiar process by suggesting a 'twist'. He refers to it as 'Carl Rogers with a twist' because he adds the possibility of change. 'Being depressed is really difficult' – 'Yes, I've been really depressed' – 'So you've been depressed a lot *lately*'. The 'lately' opens the possibility of talking about when the depression was less. 'She doesn't care for me or our marriage' – 'So what she's done gives you *the sense* she doesn't care'. The word 'sense' opens the possibility that it is, at least in part, a matter of one person's perception.

O'Hanlon pays considerable attention to the distinction between emotions, thoughts and actions. While this distinction is never totally clear, it is useful, in validating people's feelings and in saying that people are not accountable for them, to add that they are however accountable for their thoughts (what they say to themselves), their words and their actions. Feelings may place a restraint on our ability to think, speak and act, but we are accountable in that we always have some control. Holding people accountable is not the same as blaming. Blaming refers to the past; considering yourself accountable is intended to refer to the present and the future; it refers to the self-agency we have over what we say and do, whereas feelings are seen as spontaneous. Critics, for example Dermer *et al.* (1998), say that some element of blame (of the oppressor) is required on behalf of victims, lest they blame themselves. She then distinguishes between unproductive blame and 'other-directed anger' (p. 242), adding that the former is not useful in creating change, while the latter identifies injustice in relationships and identifies an obstacle in the context of a solvable problem.

In an existentialist way, O'Hanlon places less reliance on the noun aspect of emotions and more emphasis on the verb. Having a depression or being in love, makes the emotions of depression and love into nouns. If they are treated as if they are verbs, then there is more possibility for self-agency and for empowerment. We can talk of how we 'do' depression, what method we specialise in for doing it. Likewise, when we think of love as a verb, as doing something, we can consider possible ways of vitalising it or changing it.

Emotions are to be respected and listened to but they are seen as part of something, of some situation, not as separate entities that can flood over us (Gale Miller, SFT E-mail list, 1998); they are in a sense language games, and so we move on as soon as possible to asking how people were able to deal with their difficult situation, so as to identify strengths and encourage change which will bring new emotions with it. As language games, they are *part* of something, not separate entities that cause certain effects. Emotions then need not in themselves be a matter for concern – social relations are replete with emotions, from grief, to joy, to boredom. If a service user expresses emotion, workers listen, but dramatic displays of emotion are not deliberately sought, such as crying by an individual or fighting by a group. Workers express respect and acceptance for emotions and then move on when the person feels listened to and acknowledged.

Perhaps confidence (or optimism) is an emotion; if so it is an important one. Is determination/motivation an emotion? If so, it too is very important. These notions/feelings are examples of moving the language game to where the distinction between emotion and thought or belief is less clear. Confidence and determination have more to do with being *constructive* and with considering the possibility of change, acceptance, or whatever the goal may be.

Later, when we discuss practice approaches, the use of scaled questions about confidence and about determination will be looked at closely. Measuring these is a useful way to encourage change.

Trust and confidentiality

The two issues that are often blamed for the decline of demand from service users for talking to social workers, are lack of *confidentiality* and lack of *trust*. To some extent neither of these becomes an issue in *constructive* work. Confidentiality becomes less an issue because there is less interest in past problems and the curiosity is searching for strengths rather than weaknesses. The worker is puzzling out how the user manages to have exceptions, rather than what has gone wrong. As the work progresses, a story of success and competence is built up which anyone would be proud of and would want people to know about. In any case, confidentiality usually surrounds bad news from the past, whereas this approach constructs good news for the future – much of the talk is about what will be happening when the problem is no longer a problem. Confidentiality is an important professional value but its limitations in social work ought to be fully explained. Needless to say, when faced with information about illegal or harmful behaviour, the professional and agency guidelines will still apply.

With regard to trust, the worker owes it to service users to deliver good service. But since the important agent of change is the person themselves, rather than the worker, and since the worker aims for minimal intervention and goes with the goals of the service user, so long as they are moral and legal, the issue for the service user becomes building trust in self rather than worrying about distrust in the worker.

The core value of this orientation is one of intense respect for individuals' views and efforts, as well as for their potential to help themselves. The approach seeks to balance this value with a professional stance that opposes injustice and oppression in all their forms and which requires workers to share their views, model appropriate behaviour and challenge abuses. Because social work works with the marginalised it cannot be neutral about the forces that marginalise people or deny rights, equality of opportunity and dignity. But we take the position that brief is best, that workers should aim to get out of people's lives as quickly as possible and above all that their work should be effective in helping people meet their needs. It believes therefore in the regular evaluation of outcomes.

Reflexivity

The reflexive involvement of service users in shaping and evaluating services and in developing a future in which workers' and users' efforts will be more coordinated and therefore more constructive, is key. But what are the attitudes and relationships that are associated with reflexivity?

We see it principally as reflection-in-action, rather than reflection after reflection has taken place. It is reflecting as action happens so that the action is thereby changed as it happens. This is self-reflexivity when it is limited to one's own mind; it can be relational reflexivity when it is shared with service users, when there is talk about what is happening or about ideas being considered.

I reflect + I change as I reflect = I am reflexive

Relational reflexivity leads to joining with people in creating the service they want, and worker and user having a joint say in how their relationship is going or needs to go. Clearly in transcultural work this is very important, but perhaps it is equally important in work with people who appear like us because we can then so easily assume too much shared meaning. In this, reflexivity helps us to remain curious about other people's meanings, even their meaning for common words like 'guilt'.

In statutory work, usually a certain degree of challenging and the introduction of different perspectives is necessary. However, people can be asked for their views on the differences and this seems to reduce the gap. Having listed some options, asking about what would be the easiest place to start addressing some difficult issue can be helpful. In challenging a service user's perspective, for example, on safety for a child, we can ask questions like 'Will this achieve the goal?' or 'Will there be a time when you will be able to look at what's difficult for you?' In a sense, questions about the business is a most useful part of doing the business. This is not to say that we only talk about talk – there can be what John Burnham (1997) calls 'reflexive spaghetti' (reflecting on reflections about reflections) which can interrupt and delay *doing*.

The fact that every service user is different makes us distrust positivistic approaches or a belief that there is one way that works best for all. User uniqueness calls for a careful, thoughtful approach and reflexivity slows us down so that we can go faster. A prime aspect of this is where it gives us time to reflect not only on a notion but also on its opposite and on its different types. For example, a loss may automatically lead us to assume sadness, but if we slow down and ask 'Are you sad or are you feeling something else?' we may discover that there is more of the 'something else' (relief perhaps). If someone is blaming themselves we might ask 'What would be the opposite of that for you?' In a discussion about time we may ask 'How long has the two weeks felt for you?', or in discussion of the future, 'Will that be next week or next year for you?' In report work we might ask what the service user would say about what was needed.

Questions about kinds of a particular emotion also help workers and service users to check out our meanings – 'What kind of guilt is it, productive guilt (realising you need to take responsibility) or non-productive guilt (giving up because you didn't take the right action last time)?' This is about asking the other person even if you think you know their answer; it is about remaining curious and checking every assumption. There can also be some questions about questions – asking what kind of question has been the most useful, or asking for feedback about a question that may have been insensitive. Better to co-construct the process with people by asking them about it! It is like researching the work with them as it happens so that they can benefit more from it as they become more part of it, and so that more possibilities than we might first assume can come to light.

Karl Tomm (1987) has developed a range of reflexive questions, some of which are based on supposing that the situation is different; for example, 'Suppose there was only one parent in the family, how would relations be different?' or 'Can you list what does not need to be changed?' or 'Which of my questions could have offended you the most?' Tomm argues that this sort of reflexivity 'focuses more heavily on the explicit recognition of the autonomy of the family in determining the outcome' (p. 182). We would add that it also avoids resistance, is a more transparent process and makes for more constructive work, based on joining the resources of service user with those of the worker. It is as if the user and worker are supervising their joint project as they go along, in tune with each other in an aesthetically pragmatic improvisation. This ensures that parallel monologues are replaced by ongoing dialogue.

Art or science?

The approach is sceptical of our ability to understand people. It suggests that the very nature of language leads to muddles, in that the best one can do is misunderstand a communication since we cannot know exactly what the other person meant by their words. Muddles don't seem very scientific. No one would use a muddled accountant. For that matter who would use an accountant who constructed figures or who changed their meanings? 'Creative accounting' does not have a good name; on the other hand creative football is considered special, as is creative music or writing. So, is *constructive social work* then more like art than science? We are creative wordsmiths, working with service users to sculpt new meaning, new possibilities, new strengths with people. Part of the art is the skill to find positives, to use questions that draw them out into view, to use the information people bring as raw material for creating something different with them even when they see their situation as a crisis. The Chinese characters for crisis suggest 'opportunity', or as McNamee (1992, p. 197) puts it 'a moment of freedom from set ideas'. Constructive work involves improvisation, not unlike jazz perhaps, and it also involves considerable discipline and practice. Great footballers and musicians base their artistic improvisation on discipline and skill. In *constructive social work* the discipline involves staying on the surface and not giving in to the temptation to fall for our own hypotheses; the discipline also to resist becoming too interested in problems rather than solutions.

Talking creates by amplifying; amplifying health, strength and resilience is much better than repairing weakness. Psychology and other sciences however have much invested in pathology and 'problem talk'. This current is very powerful. One needs to be a skilled and creative swimmer in it. This is particularly so in many areas of work such as child welfare, mental health and criminal justice – where notions of risk seem to dominate (Kemshal *et al.*, 1997). We will be referring later to the work of Turnell and Edwards in Australia in developing the 'signs of safety' approach. It takes discipline to resist the pathologising discourse of labels, such as Attention Deficit Disorder or Post Traumatic Stress Disorder. Great discipline too is required in holding to the principle that the service user has all the inner resources they need (agencies may provide external and material resources and information at times) and it is for workers to 'lead from behind' rather than see themselves as the providers of solutions.

This and the previous chapter have ranged over many of the important concepts and principles of *constructive social work*, in an attempt to present *useful* theory – *useful* in the sense that it helps to unpack why we do what we do. In this sense, there is nothing as practical as good theory and in the next two chapters we set out the two aspects of these ideas in practice – *creative narrative* and the *discipline* that keeps us within the philosophy. In the next chapter will look more closely at how narrative ideas and methods make for creativity.

5

The Art of Resistance

> Externalising conversations have a part to play in the decon-
> struction of modes of life and thought that are constitutive of
> people's lives. (White, 1993, p. 129)

This is the first of two chapters setting out ways in which
constructive social work can operate in practice. This chapter will
draw mainly on narrative ideas and will show how we use them to
help service users. Attention to language is key.

O'Hanlon (in Bertolino and O'Hanlon, 1999) tells the story of
Ernest Rossi observing Milton Erickson and trying to understand
what theory he was using with a client. As he tried to think out
what was happening, he stared at the ceiling. Erickson noticed this
and said something to the effect that 'there is no one on the ceiling
Dr Rossi, the client is over here'. We need to come down from
theory-land and be with service users, concentrating on their
words and detecting their 'language viruses' and especially attending to their various figures of speech, to what they include and do
not include. Such approaches use similes such as 'it's like being
in prison'. Various metaphors are common, such as 'travelling',
which includes making headway, on the move, being pulled back,
chugging along, on the wrong track, going up blind alleys; or 'fun-
fair', which includes being on a merry-go-round, taken for a ride,
on a roller-coaster. Such approaches use generalisations and exaggeration. Words like 'brick wall' appear. Knowing or understanding may be called seeing or feeling. The importance of attending to
language carefully is that we need to respond in similar figures of
speech if we are to engage. This is our best way into the other's
world; it helps us to see what we otherwise would miss; it affects
our level of consciousness, enabling us to share in some small way
with the other's experiences.

O'Hanlon maintains that we tend to underestimate the prevalence of metaphor. Take the world of banking, for example: they

float loans, have *liquid* assets and *slush* funds, *hard* cash, *frozen*
accounts and *rising liquidity;* the bank is the *bank* of a river!
Cooking is another major metaphor. We have *food* for thought, we
let ideas *percolate,* we let situations *simmer* and we put problems *on
the back burner.* It is always worthwhile listening to these and joining them, for in the joining we create for ourselves the possibility
of influencing the metaphor when it contains a virus for impossibility, and of putting in its place a virus of possibility or a frame of
new metaphors. This is like cognitive-behavioural work but with a
twist. The twist is that rather than correcting dysfunctional language, we ride with the language to get to the experience, so as to
be able to introduce possibility. Later in this chapter we set out
frames for various metaphors, particularly for the externalisation
process. O'Hanlon like most others writers stresses the need when
first listening to a problem, to pay particular attention to language,
to adjectives and metaphors. 'Observe and listen to people whom
you are working with and they will teach you everything you need
to know' (Bertolino and O'Hanlon, 1999, p. 21).

Validating

We want to emphasise the need to validate people's inner
experiences and feelings, but with a twist that opens the door to
possibility. *Possibility* is in some respects a 'small' or 'realistic'
word; it can mean 'a slim hope' but this smallness or slimness is
important especially where impossibility has taken over. O'Hanlon is quite cautious about stepping into the future too quickly,
where a person is unable to picture a future without the problem.
In these situations, he says, premature talk of solutions can leave
the person behind. He therefore looks for the tiniest possibility
in the story, perhaps a moment when the person delayed a little
before submitting to the problem, and he works on this 'chink
of light' to expand hope that some change might be possible.
He prefers to 'just *open the door* to possibility-land, and wait for
the person to walk through it first' (London Conference, 1995).
We will therefore make tiny challenges to generalisations, for
example by asking 'always?', but we prefer to follow, rather than
lead. All constructionist workers say that to make rapid progress
one has to go slowly, clearing the way, as one clears the ice in front
of the puck in curling.

Not seriously acknowledging feelings slows down the move towards solutions if the person feels 'you don't understand', therefore we need to make sure they know we understand how bad the problem is before we challenge anything or rush into solutions. Rather than seeking to convince people that they have exceptions, we invite them to convince us. 'I have been suicidal for two days', 'Did you feel suicidal before two days ago?', 'Yes', 'How did you beat it then?' Therefore we want to develop some possibilities *before* we begin to work on exceptions; we try to make some holes in the impossibility story, even if only to ponder 'Perhaps you will be less depressed *sometime* in the future?', '*So far* you have not been able to . . .', 'You can't feel safe *right now*', or '*just yet*'. '*When* you find a way to . . .' Here the seed of expectancy is sown – possibility is introduced into the problem. It is possible a time will come when . . . As validating frees up possibilities, possibilities free up exceptions and goals. But if the despondency is great, it may be better to suggest only small possibilities such as '*Perhaps* it will be a question of just learning to live with it'. If the person says 'You don't get it – it's too bad', go back, slow down and validate. Their response tells us if we have invalidated them or if we have opened the door to a possibility.

Many people are made to feel that no matter what they do they never get it right, and many others are made to feel they do not matter. Therefore we need to acknowledge and validate people's *inner experiences* before they can consider or be open to possibilities. They need to hear that they experience what they experience, that it's OK to experience it and that it's OK not to experience it *and* that they don't *have* to feel or not feel what they feel. But on its own this validation is not enough; the possibility of change needs to be introduced – possibilities need to be co-constructed with them. Whereas the conversations in traditional work included the expression of feelings, developing insight and being adversarial towards resistance, *possibility work* uses conversations of collaboration, of shared expertise, of partnership in goal development and of shared language, in building resistance to the problem

Externalising

White (1993) maintains that when the events of one's life, especially one's problems, are storied as external to one's self, the story can set out ways by which the problem influenced the self and affected relationships and self-image. The *externalisation* of the problem is a major shift in the problem-saturated story; the problem, for example, can be seen as the oppressor and the self the heroic resistance fighter. This separation and standing back from the problem, from one's problem story, helps to recover a sense of self-agency and develop an ability to intervene in one's life and in the 'life' of the problem. Furthermore, once an example of resistance is discovered its meaning can be discussed – what does it say about the person? For example, with questions such as 'You managed to resist drink then – what does that say about your ability to do so again?' people can be invited to re-describe themselves in a story that can include the courageous stand against the problem, and there can be talk of the implications for the future. 'How will this knowledge affect your relationships, when others hear about it?' can be asked concerning when the new inclusive story is performed before others. Also, people can themselves be the audience for the telling performance, as well as others, and the alternative stories 'become available to be performed' (White and Epston, 1990, p. 17).

The externalisation of problems helps people to separate from their own subjugation. It is empowering to ask what beliefs are maintaining the problem, beliefs such as a sense of failure at not reaching certain expectations or norms. What effects do these norms have on us and our relationships? What options have we for challenging them? Can we refuse to be oppressed by them? As we externalise problems and enable people to consider the effects of techniques of power on them, the new consciousness that is created leads to these techniques becoming challenged and people's survival strategies become identified and valued. The oppression is 'exposed'. Occasions when people could have participated in their subjugation and refused to do so become significant events. We can then ask 'How did your refusal undermine the problem?', 'What other opportunities might there be to do this again?'

In all *constructive practice*, the problem is seen as not in the person; nor is the person the problem; the problem is the problem. Worker and service user can work together against it.

Alternative stories are generated from this externalisation of problems and examination of significant events, and space is created for neglected knowledge and experience to become meaningful.

Protest at subjugation is encouraged. Experiences that do not fit with the powerful norm but show the person operating and relating satisfactorily will speak of ability and strength, as 'local' and neglected knowledge comes to awareness and performance. People come to value and appreciate their struggle to constitute their own lives.

White (1996) spells out a distinction of major importance; this is the distinction between *internalising conversations* and *externalising conversations*. *Internalising conversations*, whether with self or others, employ ways of speaking about life that omit/ignore context, that separate personal experience from the wider politics affecting matters and that avoid the wider issues associated with the production of the problem. Second, they objectify people by locating problems at central inner 'sites' such as character, personality and motivation. Then they pathologise people's lives and relationships with language like 'disorder', 'psychopathy', 'dynamics' and 'dysfunction' while claiming to speak of the true nature of the problem. Finally, these conversations are associated with the technologies of the government of people's lives, with normalising judgments and with cooperating with the 'ruse of hidden power' in inviting people to police their own lives. In general, they also support the Western cult of individuality.

Externalising conversations, on the other hand, whether with self or others, emphasise context and seek to re-politicise experience. They contribute to the deconstruction of narratives that objectify people and they challenge the dominant views through which 'disorders' and 'pathologies' are constructed. They develop an 'exposé' of the techniques of the government of lives. Externalising conversations also facilitate the 'naming' and 're-naming' of the dominant forces affecting people's lives and they invite people to identify the influences of oppressive 'truths' and the practices associated with them. In being assisted to evaluate these influences, people are encouraged to establish alternative stories or 'preferred identity claims and alternative preferred practices of self and relationship' (White, 1996). With these distinctions in mind and with the insights of narrative theory and of Foucault's analysis of power, we can set out the process of working with service users as follows – a *process* that may span one or more meetings. Frequently it would not flow in this order or stay together as one piece.

Following the usual introductions and brief social engagement, we ask the person to tell the story of the problem that is of concern to them or to others, during which we pay particular attention to the 'local' language used and to the meanings being employed by the person. We are thinking of the person as oppressed by the problem which in some way is pictured as outside the person as if it had a life of its own. This orientation leads to questions and responses that develop an *externalising conversation*. We believe that 'people's lives are shaped by the meanings that they ascribe to their experiences, by their situation in social structures and by the language practices and cultural practices of self and of relationships that they are recruited into' (White, 1993, p. 38) and therefore we move towards externalising problems as soon as possible and creating negative emotions alienation towards them by the following questions.

We ask about the negative effects the problem has had on life and relationships, on self-image and on the opinion of others, seeking detail of the harm done by it: what is it causing them to miss out on?, what is it doing to their reputation? In asking those questions we introduce a language that implies that the problem is external, that the person is OK, that it is *the problem*, not the person, that is the issue and that is having negative results. We use the language of oppression, domination, subjugation, enslavement and recruitment, finding the specifics of how the problem is dominating the person, as we ask questions like 'What attitudes have you been giving your life over to?'

We then get a contrast between this way of being and the person's preferred way, so that the person is invited to take up a position on the problem. 'Is this life with the problem your preferred way of living?' 'Is this havoc acceptable to you?' 'Do you want to go on cooperating with this problem and its influence in your life for the future?' 'Would you have invented this way of life for yourself?' 'So since it is not enriching for you , it is not ideally suited to you?' These and similar questions that suggest the problem is not the person construct a sense of alienation with the problem which, by this point, can often be given a nasty name, a name that draws on the person's own descriptive language, such as 'dark cloud', 'the monkey on your back', 'the smelly neglect' or 'the sneaky temptation'. It is best if the name of the problem is based on the service user's own metaphors. For example, a boy one of us worked with recently called his temper a 'Wild Wolf', and together we then developed strategies to 'tame' it. There can then be questions about how the person might have influenced the problem, perhaps by allowing it in or by accommodating it in some way.

This then is but the start of the externalisation and alienation processes, processes that begin to deconstruct the problem and challenge practices that support it. The next step is to examine how the person was 'recruited' or 'seduced' into cooperating with the problem . 'So how did you get recruited into these ways?' One can use Foucault's thinking about the hidden processes of power in the dominant stories of one's culture. 'What ideas around you invited you to go along with this practice?' This is where the problem is politicised and connected with the powerful influences operating against people in our society – ideas about style, size, gender roles, race and family relationships; pressures to live up to expectations and desires created by business conglomerates, managerialism, family expectations and so on. 'How were you invited to embrace this subjugation in the first place?' 'How come that the victim joins in the oppression and blames her himself?' 'What were the triggers that got you to submit to all this?' 'But am I right that you now want to make your life your own again?' 'And you want to have more say about your future?'

Externalisation opens up the problem to attack by the person; there is a major shift of focus, very different from the person feeling they are open to the attack. It makes it possible for service users to describe themselves and their relationships differently and to start authoring a story they can be proud to tell others. In this way it aims to empower the service user so that they can begin to take control of their situation. White believes the process reduces conflict between worker and person, and between person and family; it paves the way for cooperation in fighting against or escaping from the influence of the problem; it empowers people to create more possibilities, be more effective problem solvers and, most importantly, it undermines people's sense of failure. By this point the beginnings of an alternative narrative have been made – a villain (the problem) has been found out.

There is an important caveat, for where the problem is the person's violence or abuse of others, externalisation may not be appropriate. In these cases people must be held accountable for these behaviours and workers need to beware of the risk of minimising that accountability. However it is useful to externalise some of the beliefs and attitudes that help maintain the abuse – secrecy for example – so that other ways of dealing with problems can be explored.

O'Hanlon, on the other hand, separates the feeling from the viewing (the stories of impossibility) and the resultant behaviour. He agrees with White and Epston that it is empowering to *question the viewing and externalise the doing* 'to move the problem out there and develop a different relationship to it, so the person doesn't feel so dominated' (Bertolino and O'Hanlon, 1999, p. 198), but the inner experience is to be accepted, acknowledged and validated, with the possibility twist.

The *viewing* involves stories, ideas, beliefs, frames, interpretations, language habits concerning problems, solutions for life. Some of these will be OK but some will not, and will lead away from goals, block access to them and invalidate and close down possibilities. We need to challenge and poke holes in such stories and *create uncertainty* about them. This will include ideas we have about our feelings: for example 'I shouldn't feel sad'.

Therefore we challenge and cast doubt on four kinds of ideas, on four 'problematic stories'. These are:

- impossibility ideas – 'He can't change his spots'
- blaming ideas (attributing bad intentions or bad traits) – 'She's attention seeking'
- invalidation stories – 'You're silly and over sensitive' or 'I shouldn't be feeling like this'
- non-accountability-for-actions stories – 'I can't help it, it's my personality, it's how I was brought up'

These are problematic stories that need to be externalised and weakened with the possibility virus. Sometimes they may even be externalised as *the* problem. Concerning the question of blaming or not blaming, Lerner (1987) has distinguished two forms of blame: non-productive blame and other-directed anger. Dermer *et al.* (1998) say the former 'obscures each person's responsibility' (p. 242) and is not useful, but the latter is useful 'in identifying limitations placed on subordinate groups by dominant groups' (ibid). This anger recognises how powerful people and structures constrain people and how they impede belief in one's ability to change. It also identifies social injustices that require social change. Lerner claims, from a feminist perspective, that other-directed anger is important for personal reorganisation and esteem and it helps put the problem into a solvable context for the oppressed. O'Hanlon distinguishes blame from *accountability*. Accountability empowers and promotes self-agency; blaming alienates – it does not invite people to responsibility. Accountability attributes responsibility, whereas blame attributes bad intentions and bad personal characteristics such as selfishness – it does not invite cooperation, rather it tends to close down possibilities. We would add that both other-directed anger and accountability for self open the way to possibility stories, stories of validation and stories of accountability for change. Interestingly, this emphasis on acceptance, validation and also on accountability matches the tensions and ambiguities of 'liberty and discipline' that 'lie at the core of social work' and which we discussed in Chapter 2.

The process of externalisation is used to separate the person from the problem. This in itself is a powerful validation of the person. We like to find a name for the problem that will convey its subversive and oppressive nature. The language of the problem is like a virus: it seeps in, it invites one to fail, to be negative; it makes difficulties sound fixed and hopeless; in fact it makes it very difficult to talk about them without inflaming them; it is disrespectful of potential, it discourages and invalidates. We need to know its 'game': rather than play it we need to alienate ourselves from it; we need to see that the past may have led to our feelings but we can be responsible for our actions in the future. The exceptions, whereby we resisted the problem, are important and empower us to restore (and re-story) what worked in the past. This is about reconnecting with a sense of possibility and hope. It is about building a better identity story and then finding evidence from friends and family that supports the new valued story. We then invite speculation about the future that will come from the new story and how the future of the problem will be affected. Finally we seek to develop a social sense of the story, talking to others, talking of the person's membership of the anti-problem 'league' and how the person plans to no longer associate with the problem and how he or she plans to get it 'out of my club'.

Building on White's work, O'Hanlon (Bertolino and O'Hanlon, 1999) has developed seven steps for externalising problems:

1. Naming; or giving the problem a personality, as if it had tactics and intentions to dominate or undermine the service user.

2. Find what effect the problem has had: how the person felt, what the experience was like, its effects on relationships and so on.

3. Exception finding; times when things were a little better for the service user, when they made choices they are proud of, when the problem was not able to push them around or when they refused to believe its lies.

4. Explaining what these exceptions mean for one's qualities and identity; using good choices or successes to open the way to a better identity, how are they the sort of person who can do this?

5. Widening the evidence for the new story; past successes, evidence from the family and others that strengthen the valued story, finding evidence that might help explain the exceptions.

6. Consider what sort of future might result from all this; what will happen when they continue to resist the problem, and what will be different as they continue to stand up to it ?

7. Developing the social dimension; finding others to whom the story of resistance can be told, finding ways the service user can be consultant to others with such problems; how can they advise the worker?

Metaphors for externalisation

Metaphorical frames are commonly used in narrative work; they enhance externalisation, promote heroic resistance and courageous opposition to problems. O'Hanlon (1995) has developed a useful taxonomy from which workers can select fitting metaphors. In each set the first questions helps *deconstruct* the problem; the second helps develop the *hero/heroine story*:

- *Oppression.* How does the problem try to intimidate, silence, coerce, you? How do you resist, withstand, speak up to it?
- *Imprisonment.* How does the problem try to tie you up, lock you away, sentence you to death, hold you hostage, brainwash you?

How have you liberated yourself, served your time, got parole, escaped, got time off for good behaviour, won a reprieve?

- *Spying.* How does the problem try to infiltrate, recruit, give you disinformation, try to undermine you? How have you uncovered the truth, done counterespionage, trusted yourself?
- *Sports.* How did the problem try to get a grip of you, tackle you, pin you down, get you on the ropes, get you in a corner, get a choke hold on you, cheat you? How did you loosen its grip, play fair, get back up, get out of the corner, score against it?
- *War/violence.* How does the problem try to attack, try to bully, defeat, push you back, gain ground, try to ransack you? How did you counterattack, marshal your forces, hold your ground, outflank it?
- *Seduction.* How did the problem try to entice, sweet-talk, promise the moon, invite, whisper in your ear, coo you? How did you close your ears, stay faithful, keep your head, spurn, say no to it?
- *Supernatural.* How did this monster try to possess, haunt, try to suck your blood? How did you drive a stake through its heart, exorcise the ghost?
- *Crime.* How did the problem rob, steal, embezzle, highjack, try to 'con' you? How did you foil, catch, get justice, get restitution, appeal against it?

Note the use of the word 'try', which implies 'not always successful'. This is important so as not to give the problem too much power. 'Try' leaves an opening for more exceptions. However, when we come to the second question, concerning the person's resistance, 'try' is avoided because we want to build up the success.

In using metaphors one needs to be very attentive to the service user to see if the particular metaphor is working for them. If it appears not to fit for them, we should consider that perhaps the solution is not in that metaphor and one has to change to another metaphor.

One of us recently worked with a 'disaffected' schoolboy who was in trouble for fighting in class, and so on. He presented himself as uncooperative, 'disaffected' not only towards school but towards social workers. His only goal was to get out of school, join the army and become a boxer. This provided a ready-made opportunity for boxing metaphors. When the conversation was about getting his problems 'on the canvas', 'fighting clean' and 'getting back to his corner' he became fully engaged and was able to develop strategies to get the situation 'on the ropes' and 'avoid being disqualified'.

Inviting people into a hero heroine identity, in which there is personal agency, courage and self-value, is a major step towards change and empowerment. Actions that do not serve the person well, stories that blame or invalidate, or that close down possibilities, need to be externalised. This is not about getting rid of a part of self but changing the relationship with the problem. On the other hand, especially if one has been traumatised, one needs to internalise and embrace those experiences or aspects of self when one has devalued self, or has been devalued or doubted, be they feelings, memories, parts of the body, sensations or perceptions. To re-establish links with dissociated aspects of self, it is important to value experience, incorporate it into one's story, give it room. For example, O'Hanlon (1995) suggests that a person considers one thing they could do to approach and value an aspect of themselves and to imagine they are feeling/experiencing that aspect in the presence of someone who unconditionally loves them. At all times we invite conversations for accountability and action and decline invitations to blame or invalidate.

In this 'Re-storying' work O'Hanlon has coined the phrase 'wordsmithing' (London Conference notes, 1995). This skill refers to selecting words carefully, selecting possibility words, and permission and empowering words. It refers to making distinctions, between feeling and action, between what was done to one and what one did, between perception and fact. O'Hanlon likes outline or vague words, that are so bland that the person has to provide much of the specific meaning; for example 'you can draw upon experiences, wishes, dreams and abilities and *anything else you need*, to achieve your goals'. In summary, he uses stories to co-construct change, to open up options and to leave the person free to decide whether, and how, to act in new ways.

Particular attention is paid to those special occasions when the hero heroine stood up to the problem, made it wait or exercised some control or power over it. There can be detailed discussion of what these exceptions say about the person and the person can be invited to chose between being that sort of person or being the person who submits to the problem. 'Which way of being really suits you best?' When the person decides to continue to resist the problem, they are invited to tell others about that and to make the story of their resistance live by finding an audience for it.

Storytelling

Storytelling (helpful accounts by the worker) might have several purposes; it not only introduces new possibilities but it helps assess which possibility appeals best to the service user. It can evoke resources, memories of earlier resolutions; it helps transfer solutions from one context to another. It joins with people, normalises, guides discussion and addresses objections. Stories can be embroidered to hold attention and they can be animated with tone and gestures. They can include humour and metaphor, speaking about one thing but referring to another.

An important use of stories is in resurrecting alternative identities. To achieve this it is helpful to hear from other people who do not view the person as crazy or incompetent and to find out hidden or un-storied aspects of them that do not fit their disempowered view of themselves. Discover their best moments. It can be helpful to connect them with others who have had similar struggles and who have found various solutions. Talking about or with others helps to normalise their situation. This talking helps to invite the person to experiment with different possibilities that he or she had not previously considered. Stories enable people to stick with their experiences and to consider multiple meanings concerning them.

Here is an example of a fictional guru story:

A traveller in Tibet came upon a training school for gurus and was invited to observe a session. The old master/mistress started by saying to the students that this would be a crucial day for their development and it would be demanding. They would enter a large dark square hall, 'the hall of a thousand demons', and their task was to find their way to the exit at the far end, but on the way through the hall they had to face all their worst fears and most dreaded nightmares. But there were two pieces of advice to help them: (1) they should remember that most of their fears were of their own making; and (2) that at all times, no matter what, they should keep their feet moving.

The traveller was curious as to which advice was the most helpful, so waited at the exit to interview the students as they emerged from the hall. They all reported that in their terror they forgot the first advice and that the second piece of advice was the most useful.

We have used that story in various contexts, including supporting anxious students through a degree course. People get differing messages from it, and 'feet moving' can mean going through the daily routine of lectures, reading, note-taking or just 'keeping the pen moving'. Stories somehow by-pass the head; they seem to give access to another part of the self; they can influence the past, the present and the future. People can fill in the spaces and give them a personal meaning. Stories change the viewing and thus the doing. They may even be part of good nurturing. But most of all they enable people vicariously to experience possibly being different – they provide the experience of possibility.

Stories can also help people to decide what to do in difficult situations:

A teacher asked a social worker to talk with a child who was crying a lot at school. The girl seemed very distressed, especially approaching weekends. It transpired that her parents had recently separated and she was being forced to have 'contact' with her unloving and uncaring father with whom she never had a good relationship. Her main memory of him was of abusive shouting at her mother and coming home drunk. As she told her story of helplessness, it became clear that most people were afraid of her father; her mother wanted her to see him 'for peace sake' and the child felt she had to do this or everyone in the family would 'get it'. After exploring several options, the worker could find no one who could help the child; the court had ordered weekly contact. The child felt her father was seeing her only to get even with her mother. The visits were miserable for the child and her father was always cross with her. But there seemed to be no way out.

The worker was reminded of a common Western movie tale of a quiet little town being bullied by a tyrannical gang, of whom even the sheriff was in fear. It was only when one unarmed citizen decided to take a stand, because no one else would, that the tables began to be turned on the oppressors. He mentioned this story to the child and said 'Sometimes people just have to do it themselves – it looks like you might be the only one who can start to change things, but think carefully about your own safety.' After some time wondering together about what she could do, how she could trick him or undermine his power, she came up with the idea of sabotaging the visits by 'giving him a rotten visit'. Her eyes lit up as she pondered on subtle ways of making the time with her miserable for him. With very little encouragement she was able to plan pains and aches, coughing fits, spilling her drinks and so on. She laughed with glee at the thought of spewing out a well-chewed mixture of hot-dog and coke over his shoelaces. She loved the idea of secret power, so much so that she was almost looking forward to the next meeting. This empowerment, however, took a different turn. While she felt better about the next contact, she decided to hold back her 'big guns' and 'play along' with being given treats. Her father seemed more friendly and they talked better than ever before. During several more visits she never needed to use her weapons. All she had needed was someone who believed in her, who valued her and validated her story and who believed she had the imaginative resources to handle the problem. It was the Cowboy story that helped her to first experience the possibility of devising actions that could turn her story around.

We seek to empower, and give permissive affirmations, such as 'you can', 'it's OK, 'you may', 'you could', 'you don't have to'. We avoid blame, collusion, mind-reading, going over negative experiences and negative injunctions such as 'you shouldn't'. We seek to *challenge* injunctions people use, such as 'you must . . .' or 'you shouldn't . . .' and self-devaluation such as 'I am bad'. We often do this in a permission-giving way, to sum up positives from the conversation and go on to give permission to make choices. For example, 'Let yourself feel what you feel, think what you think, sense what you sense, and just be as you are.' If this leads to a contradiction it is all right – 'You can tell me about it, and you can *not* tell me about it, and you don't have to'. The *permission* is for feelings, not for actions unless they are not harmful, immoral or illegal. The person can focus inside and listen to some of the possibilities they have been talking about. The service user *can* be less angry, but they don't have to, *and* they can continue to be angry, and *they don't have to.* 'Its OK to . . . and you don't have to'. In doing this the worker closely watches the service user for responses or signs of fit, joining the person in the experience, being with them in it, not knowing what they will take from this personal 'verbal letter'. It is like a soul-to-soul chat, in which the worker tries to get to the point, not worrying that he or she may be off course much of the way because, if one is responsive to the person, their responses will guide one as if one was on auto-pilot. One has no choice but to trust the auto-pilot when flying in another person's inner world!

It is hoped that the ideas in this chapter will encourage the development of creative flair in *co-authoring* new stories of resistance, courage and accountability with people, as workers draw on their metaphors. Creativity, however, is at its best when the disciplines of the work are well established. The next chapter will outline these and suggest several ways of avoiding the indiscipline of not staying within the philosophy of *constructive social work*.

6

Discipline for Possibilities

The solution is not necessarily related to the problem.
(de Shazer, 1991, p. xiii)

Introduction

In this chapter we discuss a further set of ideas for how *constructive social work* could be made practical, and draw upon what has been termed the *solution-focused* approach which offers interesting ideas about operationalising the philosophy we have outlined in Chapters 3 and 4. This approach has received much interest in recent years, particularly in various forms of therapy and counselling, and particularly in North America. However, rarely has it been drawn on for developing mainstream social work practice in the UK. We use it here in an illustrative way to demonstrate that some of the ideas we have been discussing thus far have been informing different approaches to practice for some time. However, such practice is varied and the potential for development enormous. This chapter offers something of a case study to present, in some depth, one range of possibilities for practice which have been influential and which have stood the test of time. At the end of this chapter we will suggest that what it does *not* say may be as important as what it does say. Perhaps the major strength of such ideas is that they provide something of a discipline for the work – a discipline for possibilities.

The solution-focused brief therapy (SFBT) approach was developed mainly by de Shazer (1982, 1985, 1988, 1991, 1994), Berg (1992, 1994) and their colleagues at the Milwaukee Brief Family Therapy Centre. It is interesting to note that de Shazer's training and background is not in therapy or social work, but in research. For many years he studied the work of others, and was greatly influenced by people like Milton Erickson, and John Weakland and the work of the MRI (Mental Research Institute) in California. Basically, he sought to strip practice down to its essentials, searching for what worked, what it was that made the difference. From these essentials de Shazer has built the approach and tested it rigorously over many years. He argues that it is easier to train someone who comes from a non-counselling background and who is not biased by the knowledge of various psychological and social theories but who wants to listen to what it is people are actually saying. Having watched him at work, however, he is clearly a helpful and thoughtful practitioner and we have learned much from the simple (but not easy) discipline of his talking.

It's just talking, but not any old talking, as we shall see. The approach used is now practised widely in agencies of all kinds and many other writers have described their versions of it. For example Walter and Peller (1992) and Selekman (1991) and The Brief Therapy Centre, London, use this approach, as do individual social workers in agencies around the world. The central principle is that talk *constructs* the future and change. The talk leads to change arising 'from either a difference in how a person views his or her world or by a person doing something different, or both' (George, Iveson and Ratner, 1990, p. 3). The problems are already constructed; what matters is *constructing solutions*. Therefore the emphasis is on problem-free talk, discussing when the problem is less, is absent, is less a worry, in the knowledge that service users already know what they can do and are able to do it but that they do not yet necessarily know this. There is no search for the cause of the problem; there is considerable detailed discussion of exceptions to the problem, of how to have more exceptions and of how behaviour, talk and feelings will be different in the future.

This approach grew out of detailed observations of and experiments with practice, rather than any specific theory as such. In that sense it is atheoretical. However, de Shazer is greatly influenced by the philosophers Ludwig Wittgenstein and Jacques Derrida and ideas from Buddhism. Social constructionism says there are no incontrovertible social truths, only stories about the world that we tell ourselves and others (see, for example, Hoffman, 1993). Language builds up our meanings and even our identity. If we accept this, it will be clear that since *language is constantly changing* and varies from culture to culture, so too our identities are temporary and shifting, and since we strive for stability and control, there is a constant struggle with the dominant discourse that shapes lives and says what *is*. But essentially, *stability remains an illusion – change is inevitable*. Though this idea is developed here from the nature of language, it also fits with the ancient Buddhist philosophy that life is like a river, for it is constantly changing.

We find that the solution-focused approach provides an excellent discipline of thought which, when combined with the narrative ideas discussed in the previous chapter, produces many of the qualities of our *constructive practice*. The elements of that discipline will now be examined.

Exceptions

Exceptions are said to 'prove the rule', but not in this approach. When people describe being stuck with a problem and they are 'in a static situation in which the "same damn thing" keeps happening, then this can be called "the rule"; what is happening in their life when the problem is absent or lessened, can be called the "exception *to* the rule"' (Ratner, 1989, original emphasis).

At the start of work, using the SFBT approach, as people state their reasons for attending or ask for help or state their problem, their feelings are accepted and acknowledged and their words are listened to with great care so that discussion of the situation uses their language. But as soon as possible, the worker asks about exceptions to the problem – those occasions when the problem was less a problem, or those occasions when the person felt stronger or more confident, or those occasions when bits of the solution were happening. This leads to enquiry as to how the person managed to make that exception happen. The idea is to move to problem-free talk. Because talking constructs, talking problems creates more of a problem if one is not careful, whereas talking strengths constructs more strengths. However, one cannot move on if the person is not ready. One hastens very slowly at this point, waiting for the person to feel accepted and valued. There is something of a 'tightrope' to be walked – 'on the one hand we must acknowledge the experience of the (person) to whom we are talking and validate the experience of frustration, hopelessness, unfairness and so on; on the other hand, we do not want to focus on the problem to such a degree that we help it seem larger' (Durrant,

1993a, p. 53). Workers try to avoid solution-forced work, so they 'stay near' the person, but not so near as to be drawn into the problem story when they could be asking about exceptions or talking about other strengths. Talking of exceptions is central to this shift. *Exception-finding questions* focus the client's attention on their own problem-solving resources and are one of the central features of the solution-focused approach (Carr, 1990). Many have seen the approach as merely being strengths-focused; it is much more than that – it is a whole philosophy that believes that people have the seeds of solutions within them and that constructive talking can build new futures without examining problems.

Since there is nothing that happens always, there is an assumption that there is always an exception. Exceptions, however, are frequently discounted by service users as only proving the rule. But they contain the seeds of solutions and they need to be brought to life by talking about them as significant events that tell us more about solution than any analysis of the problem. Yet if they are not asked about they go unnoticed. In discussing 'change, difference and agency' in Chapter 3, we mentioned how knowing what it is that makes a difference is key to empowerment. Exception-talk looks for what is different when the problem is less or absent; it recognises and underlines this difference so that it 'makes a difference' (de Shazer, 1991, p. 156). Talking of exceptions puts difference to work for the service user and increases that essential sense of personal agency.

Weiner-Davis (1993) carried out research into the process with de Shazer in 1984 and an interesting finding was that many people reported some change for the better occurring between making the appointment and actually attending, but they did not report it unless asked. From this the 'pre-session-change' question was developed. Pre-session exceptions are especially useful because they are clearly attributable to the service user and not to the worker's efforts, and this opens up talk about how the person did that. This talk underlines and constructs the person's sense of self-agency. As each exception or piece of progress is discovered it is followed with some version of 'how did you do that?' This phrase, despite being a TV cliché in Britain, is powerful in developing self-agency. It contains two key words that can be emphasised in various ways – 'you' and 'do'. It was not anyone else that did it and it was not just talked about, but done. This practice is not 'just talk', it is also concerned with real results in terms of self-agency. It appears to help move the 'locus of control' in people's lives to inside themselves. This is a major shift for many service users who have given up because they feel their lives are controlled by forces outside of themselves, by teachers, parents, officials or by oppressions perhaps from peers, partners, police and social workers.

Exception-finding questions

De Shazer has reported (1997) that a clear picture of the 'day after the solution' is the best predictor of success and that he has had more success with the 'miracle question' version than any other. Having obtained a picture of the 'day after the miracle', the next question asks *if any small part of it is already happening* sometimes. This question generates 'after the miracle exceptions'; these exceptions can be more helpful and meaningful to people because they are directly related to goals, whereas other exceptions may be seen as more random. These small exceptions, days when things go better, are vital building blocks for solutions. People are encouraged to describe them in detail so as to amplify them and hopefully repeat them. Using the exceptions that service users report is a perfect example of Erickson's principle of 'utilisation' (de Shazer, 1988, p. 139) – using everything the person brings to the session: strengths, mental processes, anything they do that is useful.

Exceptions are those times when the problem is absent or lessened. They are not necessarily times when one is overcoming the problem, as in narrative work, because solutions in this approach have only a 'nominal relationship' (de Shazer, 1993a, p. 119) with the problem. Solutions are constructed by putting 'any differences that are noticed to work in such a way as that difference opens up the possibility of new meanings, behaviours etc., developing' (p. 116). If exceptions are within the person's control, once they are noticed and their importance talked about, they can be repeated. These are *deliberate* exceptions. Of course if they are not deliberate but due to something outside one's control, to chance or to others, they cannot be so easily repeated and they are known as *spontaneous* exceptions. But they are still important and if they can be *predicted* they may be more in one's control than first thought. We will look at 'prediction' tasks later.

Negotiating goals with various service users

Many service users may be vague about their goals, or may not be able to consider anything long-term; some simply have no idea of what they want, while others want nothing but to get away from the worker. Many know what they do not want but have difficulty in saying what they do want. Because this opening stage of the work seems to be so vital, going very slowly is probably wise, puzzling out with the person how they will know when to stop meeting. Drawing on a solution-focused approach, well-formed goals are:

- Specific and achievable.
- 'Small rather than large'.
- In process form; the doing of something.
- Here and now rather than in the distant future.
- Positive, rather than negative; that is – they consist of the presence of something rather than the absence of something, doing something new rather than stopping something old, beginning rather than ending.
- In the person's control.
- Expressed in the person's language; written as they say it, free of worker interpretation, 'Salient to the client' .
- Perceived by the person as needing hard work.

Effective goal-setting, especially when working with '*visitors*', those service users we visit or who visit us only because they have to (mainly statutory cases in unwilling contact), is never a matter of telling a person what to do. Telling is doomed to being ignored, whereas a question has a chance of engaging, so long as it is not a 'why don't you?' For example, a person asked for help to cope with the death of a partner so that she could get on with her life; the worker assumed that that meant help in 'letting go' of the partner, but later learned the person wanted help with 'holding on' to the partner in some way, so as to get on with life (a more spiritual goal perhaps). Berg and Miller (1992) recommend always finding out what the service user *wants,* then agreeing with their goal, so long as it is legal and ethical, and being sympathetic with their plight. Offer compliments and, if they are referred, enquire about their views on the demands of the person who referred them.

Complainants, those who want to change other people, are often victims in some way of those they complain about, or victims of some other circumstance or fate. They may have experienced their own attempted solutions as failing; in any case they usually see the future solution as in someone else's hands. Such people need to be empowered to 'recognise that there are changes they can make so their lives will be better' (Berg and Miller, 1992, p. 57) and to accept that they, and not just the persons they complain about, sometimes need help.

In developing goals with '*customers*', those who want help to make some personal change, Berg and Miller (1992) recommend five options possibilities:

- Asking questions about pre-session change (change made since making the appointment).
- Talking about other past and present successes.
- Asking future-focused questions, such as the 'miracle' question.
- Using scaling questions.
- Asking 'coping' questions.

The worker's stance in asking these various questions is one of curiosity and some respectful puzzlement at the person's unique way of making things better. The more successes are talked about, the more people are encouraged to repeat them, the more they will be likely to feel the solution is not only theirs but is right for them. Goals may often be routes to other goals but the assumption is that they are right for the person at this point. However, in all goal-setting, it is not a matter of going along with anything a person may want to do; the worker needs to feel the goal is legal and moral. As de Shazer has said, if one is to go to jail, let it be for what he or she has decided! 'Pre therapy goals are what the client brings in but the worker and the client figure out what is doable and what they both are willing to do' (de Shazer, SFT E-mail List, 1998). A last word on goals – 'when a sailor doesn't know what harbour he's aiming for, no wind is the right wind'. Of course, in their controlling/protecting role social workers often persuade people to move towards the agency's goal and they may be sometimes justified in being manipulative in doing so. But helping people to realise their own goals and to notice their own abilities can hardly be called manipulative.

The 'miracle question'

According to this approach an important technique in helping people formulate goals, to express what they want and to start looking to the future, is the 'miracle question' . It goes like this:

'Suppose that when you leave here, you go out and do what you are having to do, you get home, have something to eat and later go to bed; and while you are asleep something miraculous magical happens and the problems that brought you here vanish, in the click of a finger; but because you were asleep you don't know this has happened. When you wake up in the morning what will be the first thing you will notice that will tell you that this has happened?' (Based on various versions from de Shazer and Berg)

This is a very long question that has many important features. The most interesting is that the miracle is an ordinary miracle that happens following the ordinary things a person does. Secondly, it gently invites the person to step into the future when things are better and to picture the difference; it helps them to articulate the very first signs of that difference, to build a video-image of the goal s, as the worker goes on to ask for more and more detail of what will be happening, what will be said by various people, how various people will be affected and what difference that will make to themselves and others. In this way the solution is constructed without discussing the problem or *how* it can be overcome. People's affect can undergo a major change, as they describe and construct with the worker an alternative way of being. This is often the beginning of the hope that is necessary to get change started. The most important thing this question does is that it disconnects the problem from the solution and as other people's reactions are talked about it generates interactional descriptions; talking about other people's reactions and conversation reinforces the changes and their possibility.

There are some people who say they do not believe in miracles or magic and who cannot go along with this question. For them the question needs to be changed to something like 'When the problems that brought you here are solved, when this work has been a success, what will you or others notice that is different?' Others respond well to being invited to consider 'the kind of miracle that can really happen'. Most people can imagine or fantasise. One of us has been successfully using the 'Back to the Future' version (proposed by O'Hanlon and Weiner-Davis, 1989, p. 106 and modified by Milner, 2000). We say:

'You know the Michael J. Fox film *Back to the Future*, where the mad professor takes the youth into the future in a car that can time-travel? Let's get into the car and fly to your house as it is when your problems have all been dealt with. We park outside and creep up to the window – you are inside. What do we see you doing?' We get as much detail as possible and then ask 'Suppose you see us and you invite us inside and we ask you How did you start to achieve this?' Then, 'What else did you do?'

In this way the service user begins to talk to their competent self, as it were, and often locates ideas and solutions that otherwise would have gone unnoticed. Another variation is the '*crystal ball*', gazing into the future together, talking about what is there, how it was achieved. These techniques help people who find it hard to discuss the future to begin to 'just suppose' that change has happened. If it cannot be pictured and constructed in words it is unlikely to happen; if it can be talked about in detail it becomes more and more possible. Durrant (1993a, p. 21) has commented that 'problems are what get people stuck, and a focus on these may lead to more stuckness. Solutions are the changes people strive for, and a focus on these allows us to be more forward looking.' We would add that this focus not only looks to the future but makes it more achievable and helps construct it. Imagining *a better* future is an important first step to change; it is an important strength and tool.

Scaling questions

Another important technique in constructing change can be the use of 'scaling' questions. Any scale can be used but the most obvious one is the 0 to 10, with 0 being 'the pits' and 10 complete success. People can be asked to place themselves on the scale as they are now, for example 2, and again where they will be when work can finish. They often settle for less than 10. The next question is 'What will you notice that will tell you that you have moved up *one* point?' People seem to need to know the next small step.

Scaling questions are also asked in relation to the person's *confidence*, or optimism, and their *willingness*, or motivation. For example, 'If 0 stands for no confidence that you can make progress (or perform a task) and 10 is you are fully confident, where are you now?', or 'If 0 means you are very doubtful if you want to be doing this and 10 means you *will* do anything under the sun to solve it, where are you now on that scale?' 'What will you notice that will tell you that you have moved up one point from there?'

The use of such questions helps the person to get away from the idea that they are either in the problem or out of it; they begin to see that gradual change is within their power. (Nor is solving problems a once-and-for-all thing; it is much more grey than that). As de Shazer (1994, p. 104) points out, the scale is set up 'in such a way that all the numbers are on the solution side'. As the person attributes a number to himself or herself they are able to express something that may be too difficult to put into words, and frequently the number comes as a surprise to the worker who up to now has been listening to words. Having a number makes it more concrete when asking what they will be doing when they will be one number higher. No one need know exactly what the number stands for but they will know that 5 is better than 4. 'The numbers get their meaning from the scale to which they belong; they are content free ... but when we ask "how will life be different when you move from 5 to 6?", these future-orientated questions help the service user to begin constructing progressive change' (Milner and O'Byrne, 1998, p. 150).

In considering a problem such as depression, scaled questions get away from the idea that the person is either depressed or not depressed, as if there was an 'on–off' switch. So by asking 'If 1 is how depressed you were when you asked for help and 10 is when all depressing feelings have gone, where are you today?' Any reply by the service user that is above 1 would show that the depression is less of a problem and the person is moving towards their goal (de Shazer, 1994). Many service users say that the scale questions are the most encouraging part of the process; yet they feel odd and mechanical to workers when they start to use them. John Weakland once said to de Shazer (1994, p. 92) that 'by inventing one of these scales you take a whole damn amorphous thing and reduce it to a number; now its real and concrete. In a logical sense, that's an impossible task. But you do it, and now it's real.' De Shazer says that since you cannot be absolutely certain of what another person meant by his or her use of a word or concept, scaling questions allow both worker and service user to construct a bridge, a way of talking about things that are hard to describe – including progress towards the client's solution.

Scaling questions can be useful in assessing with people their self-esteem, any mood they may have, the quality of their relationships, progress of any kind – all aspects of life that are frequently difficult for many people to express.

Some other potentially useful questions

Coping questions, or *getting by questions*, can be useful when no exceptions are possible, as in cases of loss and other 'facts of life' that we all have to cope with some time or other. In these situations, people cope better at some times than at other times. How do they do that? What is different about those times? 'The situation sounds impossible – how *do* you get by?' 'How come things are not worse?' Then a scaled question about coping can be added.

In responding to replies to the miracle question, exception-finding questions and scaled questions, the worker always asks for more and more description. Probably the most used question in the approach is *'what else?'*, seeking out what else will be happening or what else will people be doing or saying. Every piece added to the talk of the future helps build future change. There is no rush – time is taken to construct well each piece of progress. While it is called brief, going slowly paradoxically helps it to be more brief in that goals are reached sooner. Similarly, the goal development stage is taken slowly.

Walter and Peller (1992) compare the process to movie-making, where the service users are the directors of their own lives and workers are assistants. Users are also the main actors. The work simulates the making of a video of them moving towards their goal, so that they can step into it and *experience* what they want in a positive way; for example they may describe 'I am sitting calmly, telling ... that we are going to the school together and ...'.

Goals are described in *active verbs* rather than a static state – for example 'loving' rather than feeling in love, or 'solving' rather than being helped. Questions and discussion therefore are of change *in process*.

For those who can only describe their goals as wanting something not to happen, usually something distressing such as a feeling, a habit or another person's behaviour, since this goal is the absence of something rather than the presence of something, they are asked 'What will you (or sometimes "they") be doing *instead*?' The emphasis is on the 'doing' and the 'instead'; something *different* that *will* be happening.

Sessions therefore are an interweaving of goal-talk and exceptions-talk. Should the person say they have no goal or no exceptions, the talk moves again to the future and to *supposing* the problems have gone – 'Just suppose that happens, what will you be doing differently?' and 'Does any small piece of that happen now sometimes?' Since the person has been taken into the miracle frame they often can recall exceptions they could not recall earlier. If the problem is feelings, they are switched into actions – 'What will you be *doing instead*?' The discipline avoids exploring feelings in the traditional manner.

While future-talk and *future certainty questions* are useful necessary for the creation of change, the far future is less useful than the near future. 'If I were a fly on the wall what *will* I notice you doing tomorrow *when* you begin to manage better?' 'What *will* your daughter notice?' 'What *will* she say *when* she sees that?' 'What difference *will* that make?' 'What *will* you say to her?' Notice the assumption behind the language – 'will' and 'when' are used because they assume the change will happen (it is only a matter of time); 'if' is avoided because it assumes it may not happen. 'Future certainty language conveys the suggestion that things *will* get better . It's like saying "I know you will be able to achieve this" without saying it' (Durrant, 1993, p. 58).

'*Suppose*' or '*let's pretend*' is used rather than 'if', and of course since pretending to do something is the same as doing it, doing can be experienced in the pretence. Therefore if someone still maintains they have had no exceptions and they could never do things differently, the task of pretending the change has happened is often used. It is easier to do something if you have already experienced the result. For many this is not easy territory and they will often answer 'I don't know'. It is important not to read this as resistance; it takes time, and more talking, to shift the mind-set into new possibilities. Odd as it may seem, it sometimes helps to ask 'So if you did know, what might you say?' A person may smile at the illogicallity of that but go on to reply.

The break: planning an intervention/feedback

Many of those who use this approach take a break after doing this work for 45 minutes or so. This helps the worker to think differently, as they will have been doing some thinking like the service user in the meeting. During the break they study the words used by the service user (having taken notes in the session) and consider whether the exceptions are 'deliberate', in the person's control, or 'spontaneous', not in their control or in the control of someone else.

Based on this analysis they 'make an intervention', that is they will give the person a message and also sometimes a task. It is a question of deciding what to do that will be useful, and part of this process is figuring out what not to do. Thinking about what not to do helps us to consider evidence differently and knowing what not to do can be more important than knowing what to do, even if it means we sometimes do nothing more than compliment service users or invite them to simply notice what else it is they do that is helpful.

The Milwaukee group suggest that *the feedback after the break* can have three elements in it:

- Compliments – using the person's own words to give feedback on what the person is doing that is useful, the strengths shown, the family qualities, the honesty and so on.
- A linking statement to the task: for example, 'Because you know what helps you to handle the temptation to drink too much . . .'
- The task, which may be, for example, 'Do more of the same', or 'Take notice of what is happening that moves you up to 4', or 'three days next week pretend that the problem is solved and see if the others can tell which days you are pretending, and next time we can talk about which days were really better'.

The feedback could begin with some expression of empathy for the problem the person has and a comment that it will take hard work to solve it; then compliments and admiration for the good things they are doing. The link could be 'So because of all this we have this idea that might be useful to you', followed by a task.

With unwilling service users, such as those required by law to meet with the worker ('visitors', in de Shazer's language) giving positive feedback, *compliments*, on what the person is doing that is useful, encourages them to feel that they are cooperative and able to work hard doing what is good for them. The worker may have a struggle sometimes to find some small things to compliment but by cooperating with these small things one can win cooperation back. Successes are made more significant by talking about them and underlining them, even cheering them. Cheering success varies from worker to worker. Some can do it excitedly and be effective; others need to do it quietly and subtly. And cheerleading is not to be confused with running ahead of people with lots of worker's ideas and getting excited about the worker's solutions. It is the service user's efforts, honesty and so on, that are to be cheered when that is appropriate, not if there is nothing to cheer. If unwilling people are required by law or others to continue in contact, one can go on later to explore what else they can do to get what they want, even if it is only to convince the referrer. By treating people in this way, as far as possible, they seem more likely to willingly participate in some respect.

'Complainants' too respond well to compliments about putting up with the other person, for their ideas as to what needs to change and so on. However they need to be encouraged to see that only they can take action if the worker has no mandate to see the other person, but this cannot be rushed. Since 'complainants' goals are about other people they are more likely to be good at *observing* the other, so they may be asked to notice change in someone else or to list when they are less problematic, and then asked in the next session if they themselves were doing anything different when the other person was different. *Observation tasks* are frequently used for parents and teachers and can be given an added element of self-observation. For example, 'Continue to monitor John and observe too, so as to notice and report back, how he manages to behave better sometimes and also observe what you are doing that is different around these times.'

Observation tasks, when applied to the service user's self can also be most useful in finding more exceptions. For example, 'Observe what it is you are doing when you overcome the temptation to drink', or simply, 'Observe those times when you are less depressed, so as to tell me what was different', or 'Count those times when your son was behaving better, so we can talk about what you both are doing when that happens'. Durrant (1993a) gives these examples – 'Observe what happens when you keep your temper under control; keep a look out for any things that you do which are in the direction you want things to go; see if you can catch the teacher out when she's not on your back, and note down what you are doing different at those times' (p. 88) Another good example of an observation task is inviting a schoolchild to 'Observe what the teacher is doing that shows he cares about you and is trying to help'. A teacher can be invited to look for anything the child is doing that is positive; talking about these things later can 'make' a better story for all concerned.

The F.1 task (F.1 is shorthand for 'standard first session task') asks the person to *notice* and list all that is happening in their life that they want to continue happening. This is useful for clarifying what change is wanted by listing all those aspects of life that do not need to be changed; this can sort out what does need to be changed. Incidentally, reluctant service users are often impressed or at least curious with a worker who is so interested in *not* changing things.

Pretend tasks play a large part in this work and are a creative way of introducing change without losing face. 'Pretend to do . . .' sounds as if they will not be really doing it. Pretending is only pretending, but it is also 'change without changing' (de Shazer, 1991, p. 115). As we mentioned above, pretending to do something is virtually the same as doing it. De Shazer argues that it is not the same as 'acting as if' – acting is a very deliberate thing, whereas pretending is more spontaneous. It is experiencing new behaviour without trying too hard. If others are asked to notice when one is pretending and when one is doing the same thing but not pretending, they usually cannot tell the difference. They frequently report that the person was not pretending when they said they were – so the question becomes 'Could they have been doing it for real?'; for example, being free of depression. Given a straight task, some people will say they cannot do it because they 'are not like that', but when asked to just pretend on random days to see if others can spot the pretence, it suddenly becomes possible. Pretending can be the rapid road to change. 'For the sake of solution development, it is much easier to act your way to a feeling than to feel your way to a new action' (Walter and Peller, 1992, p. 78). Pretending will include some talking, both to oneself and to others – *making* meaning with action and words.

Sometimes people have to start acting recovered in order to start experiencing recovering. Pretending 'serves to disconnect the solution construction and development process from the problem and to bypass the client's historical, structural perspective and any disagreements about what the problem really is. Once the solution develops ... it no longer matters what the problem might have been' (de Shazer, 1991, p. 114). In working with a family group, one can ask each member secretly to pick two days in the week ('secretly' means they are to lie about it if asked!). On those two days they are to pretend the miracle has happened and notice how the others react to them differently. The others are to try to spot it but to keep that a secret too, until the next session. This task appears to work well even if no one does it; if they think the others are doing something different, or doing something more, they will respond differently. This at least leads to a different internal dialogue and possible different external conversations. But when the changes are experienced and talked about they will be amplified.

A prediction task is given to invite the person to predict when some spontaneous exception will happen again. Predicting exceptions increases them; predicting lack of exceptions increases the lack of them. This is another interesting example of the power of words – it is important, for example, to say 'Predict when you will overcome the urge', rather than 'Predict when you will give in to it'.

It has been found that people can get better at getting predictions right by practising, and of course if they can predict something its spontaneity is questioned – they can sense some self-agency in the matter. This task creates a self-fulfilling prophesy; predicting the exception leads to behaviours that increase the likelihood of the exception. 'It is as if the client knew all along what the elements of the exception pattern were, but was simply unable to describe them' (de Shazer, 1991, p. 88). It is as if people sometimes do not know what they know, until their knowledge is activated in some way that makes a difference and their self-agency is empowered.

The suggestion to '*do something different*' may seem vague, but specific suggestions can seem as though the worker knows best. When it is left to the service user to decide what to do there is a message that it is assumed that *they* will know what is best, but in any case it appears that it may not matter much what they decide to do so long as it is different since it may be that it was the repetition of the failed 'attempted solution' that needs to change. Where people feel hopeless or stuck one can say, 'When what you are doing is not working it is important to do something different. It almost does not matter what it is, so long as it is different.' Any difference will interrupt the pattern, and this can be especially useful in relationship difficulties or parenting conflicts.

An alternative to 'Do more of what works' is 'Now that you know what works, do more of it' (de Shazer, 1988, p. xiii), or 'practice doing that more often'. These seem to be very simple ideas which perhaps our traditional training causes us to undervalue. Being constructive probably works best when it is kept simple!

The thinking process of a first meeting with a person might be summed up as: having explored the 'Day after the Miracle', consider 'what does the person want to change?' If the conclusion is 'nothing', simply use compliments; if the conclusion is that he or she wants 'others' to change in some way, use compliments and/or observation tasks. If the person wants to make some personal change, consider what is he or she able to do? If you conclude that the answer is 'very little', you could suggest an observation task or a pretend task. If what they can do is unclear you could consider a pretend task or an F.1 task. Finally, if they can do a lot, ask if what they are doing is helpful; if it is, suggest they do more of it; if not, suggest that they need to do something different.

This summary is not intended to be prescriptive; nor is it suggested that workers need to keep it in their heads. It is offered to create possible tentative maps of typical ways of thinking through the process. It certainly is not the only way to be constructive; an alternative version can be seen in Milner and O'Byrne (1998, p. 151). In helping those who are new to the approach, the suggested questions may be useful in keeping workers to the central philosophy that service users are the best experts in building solutions to their problems. The questions may also help to keep workers within people's discourses, be they children, women or men, and to ensure that conversations reflect people's own world views.

Second and subsequent meetings

In subsequent sessions the first question is 'What is better?' The assumption is that things cannot stay the same and asking for news of 'better' promotes the expectation of progress as well as making it more likely to be talked about and the difference noticed. There will be times when the person will maintain that nothing is better and that must be responded to appropriately.

The 'EARS' process is central to the ongoing process and it consists of:

- *Eliciting* from the service user what exactly the changes are. When something is better, the question is about how did they make it better. If they attribute the progress to someone else they can be asked how are they going to maintain the improvement. They can also be asked how confident they are about maintaining the improvement.
- *Amplifying* these changes by asking the service user what difference the changes made, who noticed the changes, what they saw that was different, what they said about it and so on.
- *Reinforcing* the change by complimenting the service user.
- *Starting* over again ('What else is better?'), discussing any further changes that are reported by the service user and how he or she can 'do more of the same' (Milner and O'Byrne, 1998, p. 151).

Here the process might be:

What is better? If something is better, go through the EARS process above. But if nothing is better, ask if there are any changes. If there are none suggest the person needs to do something different.

If there are some changes, ask if they are goal related; if they are not, suggest they need to do something different; if they are goal related, ask if it is enough; if it is not, ask what else needs to happen; if it is enough, terminate. The comments about the summary of a first meeting also apply to this summary. (See Milner and O'Byrne, 1998, p. 153, for another version.)

A scaled question about progress can be an option for starting subsequent meetings. It can be followed by 'So what else makes you at 5?' Scales used early in the session seem to influence the whole session to be 'progressive'.

A useful question to help maintain change is 'What do you have to do to stay on track?' (Berg and Miller, 1992, p. 135). This can lead to discussion of how to spot back-sliding just before it begins and how to identify strategies for use in high-risk situations. The focus, however, must not be on preventing something from happening (that is not about the presence of something – not a well-formed goal); building on and talking more about what they *are* doing that *is* working is more useful than trying to stop something from going wrong. As Berg and Miller (ibid) suggest, focusing on 'high success' situations and promoting when the person is likely to be successful is better than focusing on 'high-risk' situations. Setbacks can be seen as signs of success – one cannot slip back if one has not moved forward. Maintaining gains is more important than preventing relapse.

When a person reports that there is no change, the assumption is that the change was not as large as they were expecting. Nothing can stay the same. Frequently, people say nothing is better if they have had a bad spell shortly before the session – this causes them to feel the whole period was bad. Therefore one can ask 'How was the first day after our last session ... and the next ...?' and so on, looking for the change. In the rare cases where no change can be identified, the conversation moves on to those things that do not need to change, and the next task will be about doing something different. If setbacks are reported they need to be acknowledged. The conversation can address how it was different from other setbacks, how they managed to limit the damage this time, what difference did others notice, what was better? It may help to ask what they learned about themselves from the experience and what they *will do* differently in future.

Questions – too few or too many?

By 'too few' is meant that the same few questions are asked of everyone, over and over again. While the questions seem set and the words are often repeated, in practice the same question can be said to be never asked twice, for as de Shazer (SFT E-Mail List, 1998) has said, it is the answer that indicates what the question was and since we never get the exact same answer there is always difference. We agree that ritualistic use of others' questions is improper because it is not connected to process (Gale Miller, SFT E-Mail List, 1998) but these oft-repeated questions are questions whose usefulness has been well established, and that is the measure of a good question. That is not to suggest that the questions we present have to be used or that workers are not capable of developing more useful ones.

In solution-focused practice questions are connected to people's 'folk method' and ways of talking. Technique is useful for learners, be they social workers or jazz players, but in the long run it gets in the way of performance. Others argue that it helps to keep work impersonal and more efficient and brief. A way of talking is a language tool and skilled talking finds ways of achieving the purpose with the least effort. In this regard, the search for the most useful questions has been valuable.

Are there too many questions in the process? It is not a matter of question after question like gun-fire; there is much listening, pauses, reflection and a lot of self-restraint. These questions are part of moving slowly at the beginning, checking well and improving (mis)understandings, listening and clarifying, taking turns in question and answer in a collaborative conversation. The urge to rush to 'do' is powerful in social workers; we are arguing for more talk before the action so that taking action will be more economical and brief, and workers can 'get clear out of people's lives', as a recent service user was heard to say. The urge to do can be acceptable but it needs to be accompanied by the skill not to do. Minimalism is good efficiency but it is also empowering and respectful, and difficult. This approach seems simple when it is described, but it is difficult to maintain in practice, partly due to prior training and practice based on other assumptions. Sometimes it is felt to be confusing; perhaps that is because it is simple – simple but not easy. It is one approach to constructive talking and stresses that constructive talking needs to watch what it talks about and ensure that the conversation is 'progressive' not 'digressive'.

The main discipline is in the questions and, on the face of it, it can look rather formulaic. But it is much more than a set of tools.

The questions are embedded in the orientations set out in Chapters 3 and 4. These show the attitudes and assumptions that accompany the apparently set questions. However, in our experience of working with students, those who try the questions without grasping the philosophy make little progress. They tend to give up on the process as soon as the service user replies 'I don't know'; this, we believe, is due to a lack of conviction about the basic principles, such as the view that service users possess all the potential that is needed to reach their goals, allowing for the fact of life that some people with special needs need special external resources. We believe that service users *do know* the answer to 'How did you do that?' if only we wait for them to find it, as we ponder with 'I wonder . . . how did you manage that?' and wait for them to discover what they know. We see such questions as providing something of the discipline for *constructive practice.* They compel and help us to avoid questions and practices associated with work based on diagnostic thinking or hypothesising, and they keep us focused on searching for the service users' abilities and unique ways of cooperating. In this sense what they do *not* suggest is of key importance. But discipline alone does not make good jazz; the creativity an improvisation of the ideas outlined in the previous chapter is also needed. This brings us back to the question of art again.

If workers are to develop their creativity, they need 'never do anything always' and remain flexible about their engagement with each person. They could safely work less hard at doing, more hard at thinking about the quality of their talking. They will know they are successful at this when service users are working harder and talking more, especially talking more about strengths, exceptions and the future; when the discipline of constructive questions is combined with the flowing narratives of re-authored living. This is not very different from the ease with which an artisan does work that would require great effort from others.

Frank Thomas (Internet, 1998) likens the approach to a traditional flute maker explaining his carving methods; 'the branch will tell you how to carve it . . . each piece of wood has its own qualities, which you must respect. In each one lies a flute – my job is to find it.' So too the social worker's job is to point to, and help underline, resources as the service user reveals them. This is a form of art.

Does brief mean fast?

We cannot emphasise enough, however, that to adopt this type of approach one needs to work very slowly at the beginning. The first push away from problem-talk is the hardest. It reminds us of the data that a rocket uses 40 per cent of its fuel to lift the first inch off the ground! The lift-off seems very slow but it must not be rushed. To do fast work with people requires one to go very slowly at the start and to gently move from problem to solution talk. Service users may first consider a solution that reflects a dominant culture story and it may be useful to explore 'what else' might be useful. The problem is very attractive to both user and worker – it tempts us to look for the 'cause'. Stepping into interest in exceptions is the first inch towards bringing the solution into the present. 'When are you now doing some of what you want to be doing?' 'How do you do that?' or 'How did you decide to do that?' – these questions can put the service user in the driving seat from the start. The worker remains curious and always takes seriously and respectfully what the service user says. Provided all this happens, the approach has been shown to frequently produce results faster than other approaches. It is called 'brief' not because is has to be brief, but because it frequently happens to be more brief (see Chapter 8).

The ways of working described in this and the previous chapter fit with the orientations outlined in Chapter 3, and the interventions go further in that, while respecting people's definitions, they help service users to *redefine themselves and their situations* in a unique way that makes it possible for them to *attain their goals* in life with the minimum of intrusion by workers. 'Change talk' is a constructive process of meaningful communication, and a mutual achievement of the service user and the worker. It produces a body of something (commitment, hope, understanding, empathy, trust, pride) to which both can appeal in a crisis, or if things take a turn for the worse. It can be a 'cultural resource' for the service user, for coping or for improvement change. It constructs a 'changed reality', and represents a new set of aspirations and commitments for the future, experienced as both strengthening and in some sense binding. Despite its prescriptive appearance, we would suggest it helps workers to remain focused on strengths and possibilities.

7

Constructive Social Work: Two Examples of Practice

> Of all the paintings I've ever seen
> and all the artists I've ever known,
> I've never seen any more imaginative
> than those artists of conversation,
> who choose their words like colours from a pallet
> to co-create a picture of hope
> within the souls of their fellow citizens.
>
> (de Stefano, SFT E-mail List, 1998)

The stories in this chapter are based on work we personally know but the original accounts have been changed; the situations, agencies, workers and service users are all disguised in various ways to protect confidentiality.

The purpose of this chapter is to demonstrate, in a very concrete way, how the use of the approaches we have been outlining can look or feel like in practice. In our view it is difficult to think of any service user with whom the approaches outlined in the previous chapters cannot be used. In this chapter we will be considering practice with difficult and demanding work, and we also want to suggest that in many ways the workers seem to be working less hard, in a way that could avoid stress for them. This is mainly due to the basic premise of *constructive social work* that: *it is not our brand of 'jazz' that creates change – the service users bring all the possibilities for change with them.* In this approach, it is for us to get out of their way, and listen to them rather than listening to our theories.

Needless to say, we do not suggest that the way the workers in these stories use constructivist ideas is the only or best way. A mix of solution-focused and narrative ideas are used as and when they fit. In the first story the worker has been asked to help a family in which the adoptive parents feel they can cope no longer. It may be felt that such situations require fairly rapid progress when people are desperate for relief from an intolerable situation. This is family work. At times the social worker is talking to an individual and at other times to the group or a sub-group. Our experience has been that hearing about the problem, without making matters worse, can be the most difficult part of such work. One may have to act as a strong 'chair' of the meeting, ensuring turn-taking and so on. But the most important, and quite difficult aspect, is respectful listening and yet stopping family members from going into a long detailed account of the problem or the problem behaviour. It is often necessary to say 'OK, we'll come back to that, but first I have an unusual question for you'. But let's see what happens in this, the first of two examples:

'And then the dog died'

Paul and Lucy contacted Social Services saying that their two adopted children, Susan aged 15 and John who was nearly 14, were so 'impossible' and 'out of control' that they thought that they could no longer cope with them. They felt terrible at having failed and at having to ask for the children to be accommodated. Lucy was now quite ill with her nerves; Paul was having to detach himself to survive the endless rows.

The children had been adopted as babies and had presented no major problems until the last few years. Gradually there had been ever-increasing aggravation in the family. Lucy had suffered from depression for long periods and Paul had given up trying, having tried everything. They had tried to get support from friends, one of whom is a counsellor, but things continued to deteriorate. They felt the children had cost them a terrible price and were about to destroy them and their relationship. So they had decided to act. With great regrets, they were asking to have the children removed.

The work was allocated to a woman we will call SW and a visit would be arranged shortly to meet the whole family. On visiting, SW said she had seen the referral notes and knew a little about the situation and how upsetting the arguments and rows must be. Having carefully and slowly validated their feelings she mentioned that this huge upset must feel like a monster invading their lives and she was here to see firstly if there were any ways of ousting this fellow. She said it might help if they could figure out how he got into their home, how was he being invited in or welcomed and who or what were 'the friends of Upset'.

This startled the family members a little and they took some time to follow the idea, but then they participated at least for part of the conversation. Lucy said that money shortage was a friend of Upset – she was not able to give the children much pocket money and their friends seemed to get a lot. Paul and Lucy worked long hours on low pay and had to watch their spending but the children did not understand this. Could misunderstanding or lack of clarity be a friend of Upset? It could be. Were there any others? Lucy mentioned Susan's social life. Also the anger that was between her and Susan when she was often out very late. Susan said that mother did not like her friends and nagging was a cause of Upset. Then there was a brief discussion of the effect Upset had had on them and their relationships. The parents found it easier to answer than did John and Susan and between them all they expressed several negative effects. As they participated the word 'Aggro' was used – Aggro was killing the fun they used to have; it was wasting their lives and causing illness and it looked like breaking up the family. Did they want it out of the family? They all said Yes.

SW then asked each member in turn what would they notice happening that 'will tell them' that Aggro has left their lives. Slowly and patiently she invited various descriptions of 'what they will notice' themselves doing differently and what kind of things will they be saying to each other, and how that will feel? What difference will it make to them? They made various replies describing changes and better interaction. On occasions they slipped into blaming each other but the worker continued as if Aggro was to blame rather than any one person, and they could all work together to drive it out if they wanted that.

She then asked if it might be possible to notice when Aggro was coming towards the house or sliding under the door. Lucy said she could smell it a mile away and the others said they could notice it starting in various ways. SW wondered if there were any ways it could at least be made to wait outside or be pushed off before it got a grip on them. Paul commented that Susan had 'good antennae' and could warn people so they could divert it before confrontations started. Lucy introduced two other friends of Upset and Aggro: her own long hours at work and the untidiness of the rooms and the bathroom – wet towels left on the floor, and so on. No one paid much attention to her, and the children called her 'nag'.

Next SW asked them a series of 'scaling' questions. 'On a scale of 0 to 10, with 0 being the pits, where would you put the situation now?' They gave replies from 1 to 3. She asked them also to scale how determined they were to get Upset out. The parents said 10 (they would do 'whatever it takes') – Susan said 5 and John 6. Finally she asked them to scale how confident they were about being able to succeed – this question brought replies between 2 and 4. SW said that as it seemed that what they were doing was not working, could they do something different? Could Lucy experiment with being slack and not bother with such things as wet towels or washing people's clothes? Paul interjected that he could easily get slack about being the children's taxi-man. This was ignored but the idea of Lucy getting slack caused some amusement – it was too unlike her. Then John mentioned that Dad always backing up Mum was a friend of Upset. Lucy talked of how terribly upset she got with worry – she often cried for hours. SW suggested that perhaps Lucy worried and cried for everyone and if the others shared it a little she might nag less. This amused Lucy, who smiled, saying 'I really do'.

At this point John offered to make tea if Susan would help. She agreed and they went to the kitchen. Lucy and Paul repeated how terrible things had been and how this meeting did not reflect the level of trouble they were in, yet they said they had to admit that the children had surprised them this afternoon. SW moved off the problems by asking them about what they would like to be doing when the monster is out of their lives. They seemed at a loss to answer; they mentioned going to the park when the children were small but they seemed very uncertain about any vision of the future, as if they were going to be at a loss without the children.

Tea arrived with Susan and John exchanging minor insults. They all agreed to notice what small improvements they could make to stand up to Aggro over the next two weeks, by which time SW would like to see them again. The parents agreed to allow Susan half an hour's leeway on her coming in time. Susan commented 'if only mother could chill out'.

SW added that 'chilling out' might become the family slogan; perhaps they could notice what they are doing to chill out a bit, so that they could talk about it. SW suggested that next time she would like some more time alone with Lucy and Paul.

Two weeks later SW visited Lucy and Paul and asked what was better? Lucy did not reply but was concerned because Susan was distressed at the thought that her parents could not cope with her and had asked for outside help. This was discussed and it was agreed that Lucy would say she would rather have her (Susan's) help than outside help. Again SW asked what improvements there had been and Lucy replied that the first week had been quite good. SW showed she was pleased at this and asked how they had managed to do this but they found it difficult to answer. They did not know. SW waited and pondered 'I wonder how did you do that?' Then Lucy was filled with gloom as she told of how John had stormed out of the house this week, though he returned after an hour and a half. Then Paul mentioned how John had surprised them by joining in prayers for children killed in a school shooting that had been shown on television, even though he normally showed no sign of being religious.

SW steered the discussion towards their need to work as a team over the children's behaviour. Together they pondered on ways of doing that, on the children's growing independence and on the importance of their own life together. They talked of how tired they were of one problem after another. SW commented that family life is usually 'one damn thing after another'; it was only when it became 'the same damn thing over and over' that they needed to take urgent action.

There was then some discussion about how they decide things. Paul felt he was in between Lucy and the children. They wondered if that was a bad place to be and he added that he was never sure what Lucy expected of him. He felt she kept moving the goalposts. SW suggested they have a go at deciding what to do about Susan's late hours here and now. They tried but it was difficult. Lucy said she complains and Susan flounces out of the house; they worry that she is in danger and even though she always returns safely they attack her over it and she explodes in rage. SW brought them back to deciding on sanctions that were enforceable. Paul tried to get Lucy to say what was fair but she became upset, saying she could not cope with Susan's friends staying overnight; she was too tired and the house was too small. Paul agreed with her comments and Lucy then moved to asking him what about when John came to her at work asking if he could stay out overnight. It was agreed that it might be better if Lucy stalled on such occasions, listened gravely to the request and said she would have to talk to Paul about it. They thought there were some requests they could talk about in advance so that she could say 'We have thought about that and have decided that ...'

SW returned to the issue of Susan having friends in. Lucy changed her position saying that on the nights when Susan was going to the club she would prefer if she would not stay at a friend's house but bring a friend home instead. 'Moving the goal posts again,' commented Paul. Lucy seemed to vacillate between wanting to be firm and wanting to indulge. Paul complained about how she backs down on decisions and Lucy added that it was because she was harassed and worn down by the children.

SW asked what they could do about keeping calm and avoiding being stressed out. They said they could give all requests a hearing but, like a broken record, when taken by surprise always say that they needed to talk to the other.

Lucy asked 'Are any other families like us?' SW repeated that for most people life was 'one damn thing after another' and she asked if they had any ideas on how to be slack over rooms and wet towels. 'What would happen if you sabotaged them back?' Would that be better than emotional haranguing? Lucy thought they might get the idea eventually 'by the quiet process of having no clean clothes' but she frowned that she might never get that slack.

SW raised the question of Lucy and Paul having time together, if only for a walk or to sit in a pub. Lucy talked of how they are going to a wedding and she felt sad that the children were not invited. SW asked if it could be good to have time without them as they were quickly becoming more adult and might require less supervision. Perhaps they could practise having some private time together and not tell the children what they did. Some such secrets could be helpful; even if they did nothing, they could pretend they had!

Some other ideas were shared (these are referred to in the following letters).

Susan and John then asked if they could come in and they were thanked for their patience. SW said she would like to write to them all to sum up the many good ideas they had and she would visit again when they wanted it and in any case would ring in about six weeks.

Letter to the parents:

Dear Lucy and Paul,

It was good to meet you both last Tuesday and I was impressed by the start you have made in your own minds to change things, so as to get Aggro out of your home.

I know you are realistic enough to accept that all families have the normal difficulties of living and of raising children and this means 'one damn thing after another'. However, it is very wearing, especially if you are unwell. In this regard, you recall how the possibility of Lucy seeing her G.P. for some temporary medical support was discussed. Even though life can be wearing and is hard at the moment, it need not be a cause of disappointment since most families are in similar situations of one sort or another.

I was also impressed at the start you had made at getting a tighter system for managing the children's behaviour and a united front over rules, for agreeing consequences of broken rules and for agreeing expenditure on the children.

You recall how we thought that it might be useful not to threaten anything unless you are sure you will do it. Also you decided that you need to carry out what you promise or threaten, but after a warning has been given. All this will take some time; there is a lot of talking to be done in private without the children present and you will need to help each other to get things really clear.

Even if you do have problems to sort out, you recall our conversation about having some time each week when you are alone and keep secret what you do and what you talk about. This could make some space between you and the children, so they will be more likely to get closer to each other. In all this, do not try too hard; chill out a little, as Susan said, and begin to plan ahead for when the children have left home. Many couples seem to find it scary to contemplate life as a couple again but I feel you will be well prepared and will enjoy it.

Finally, you recall our discussion about blame and about how we can only be responsible for our own words and actions. As parents, if you have erred at all it could be that you tried too hard. You may now need to make the sacrifice of beginning to be more slack, letting the children do more for themselves, so they can move on to adulthood.

I have written to Susan and John but I have not mentioned the ideas we have shared but I have asked them to look out for some small but important changes you might be making and to see how they can help you make them a success. I have however asked then to not 'let on' to you when they spot the changes, so you need to watch out for some surprises perhaps! My good wishes are with you.

Yours sincerely,

Letter to Susan and John:

Dear Susan John,

I am sorry I did not have much time last Tuesday to talk to you much after seeing Mum and Dad. I was impressed however at learning that you have been able to make some subtle changes so as to reduce the hold that Aggro has on your lovely family.

I have worked out some more suggestions with your parents about small but important changes they may wish to make and it will be interesting to see if you can spot the difference. When you do, do not 'let on' to them but talk among yourselves about the best ways of making them a success. If you can't spot the changes it means your parents are being really cool about not letting on to you what their new ideas are.

Have fun, not Aggro, and help Mum and Dad to be as cool as you are. One thing that may help them to worry less is to do occasional little things to surprise them about how adult you are. Watch their faces; when they notice they will not need to try so hard to parent you. That is what I mean by 'peace being a two-way street!'
Best wishes.

Yours sincerely,

Six weeks later, SW telephoned to enquire how they were. Generally things were much better and it was not clear that a visit was needed, so SW suggested they list what was better and notice how they were making this happen.

Ten months later; phone call from Lucy who was very tearful and upset about John. She felt his recent back-sliding was due to his birth mother, with whom he has had occasional contact for some time, rejecting him. John was saying he now wanted to go into a children's home. Lucy was very 'down' over John. He wanted to be out of the house all the time and when they tried to exercise any control he would scream and shout at them very abusively, saying his friends were allowed to be out late and so on. It wasn't that he was allowed out but he was never in and they never knew where he is. He lied about where he went and he associated with lads who have been in trouble over drugs and crime. Paul arrived home from work and came to the phone briefly.

SW reminded them of the talking about working together. A united front was still missing; Paul felt John didn't seem to hate him, only Lucy. They returned briefly to the conversations about united decision-making, so that neither one of them was blamed alone. Susan was doing fine and was in contact with her birth mother whom she sometimes visited. SW arranged a visit for the next day.

Next day SW visited; only the parents were in. She was surprised to be informed that their dog Scottie had been taken to the vet and had died the previous evening. They were all saddened by this but John was very upset, they said. He had turned to Lucy for comfort and they both comforted each other. The wall of hostility and anger was breached and they were feeling much more positive about each other. SW commented that before this loss they probably did not know they could be so loving. 'We often think we don't know how to do what we have to do, but we sometimes surprise ourselves.'

They talked about life being tough at times and SW told them how she had been talking to a fourteen-year-old who had been fostered since she was two and who was now in a children's home. She was full of complaints about the place, saying there was too much noise, fighting, lack of peace and privacy and there was a lot of bullying. Her freedom had been narrowed down and she had to be in bed by 9.15 on week days. If she visited anyone she was taken there and collected by 8.15. She had to do her ironing and she had to share a room. Lucy thought she could share this, in a low-key way, with John if he mentioned a children's home again. They then reflected on their ups and downs and on their fear that John, who was very bright, would waste his education. SW told the story of when she was at college she was amazed at the second and third chances people had. Many of the students had made serious mistakes in life but they had matured through them; it was amazing how the education system provided all sorts of ways of getting higher education without doing well at the GCSE or 'A' level stage. Maybe some people need to make mistakes despite good advice, in order to mature; there were always chances to get back on one's feet and do well. She knew a friend whose son seemed to waste time at school and only wanted to get a job and have more spending money. But after a few years he said he wanted to go to college and they supported him in doing that. Now he has gained his Higher National Diploma and works for a TV studio. So children end up doing things in their own time and it seemed that parents are there to support and not to despair when the timing is not the timing they feel is right. 'Young people have amazing potential but they don't always know it at first.'

Susan was fine now, working in a departmental store in town. She thought she might leave full-time education after her 'A' levels and find permanent employment.

As Lucy and Paul talked, it seemed their desperation had dissolved following the events of the previous evening and John's friendlier behaviour. They felt nothing more needed to happen at present. John was back at school. SW said she would ring in a couple of weeks.

Phone call to the family two weeks later. Lucy said John was still fine and going to school. He was more friendly and communicative. They had been to an animal rescue centre and John had chosen a puppy, Sam, whom they were busy training. Lucy wanted to see how things went and did not want to give John the impression that she always had to run to Social Services for help when things went wrong. So it was agreed that no regular contact was needed. Lucy would decide if it was to be needed again in the future. Also she and Paul had had pay increases and felt more secure financially. She was taking more time out to be with Paul and they took the new dog for walks and were beginning to be less totally involved with the children. As Lucy sounded less emotionally fragile, SW asked her some scaling questions. The situation was now at 8. And confidence? That too was at 8. SW complimented her; Scottie's death and Sam's arrival may have helped, but it was mainly the family members' strengths that had helped them work things out. 'You could say your OK parts have been able to fix the not OK parts.' More compliments and good-byes.

Some specific comments on this piece of work. Firstly, the worker validates the feelings of the parents though the comment is addressed to the whole family. She avoids exploring the problem (the family will bring her back to that often enough) and very early in the meeting begins to externalise the problem, giving it a name based on their language. This helps to avoid a blaming story and as she explores who are the friends of upset, she gets a non-blaming analysis of what is happening – *their* analysis. Questions about the influence of the problem help to create an alienated relationship with it, which brings the motivation to get rid of it. Then rather than worrying about how to do that she invites constructions of the future that they would see as satisfactory interactions. This creates the sense of goal.

Next, as she moves on towards tackling the problem, rather than sorting out any problem person, she asks about 'spotting' the problem coming and how they might work together to keep it at bay or overthrow it. Scaling introduces the sense of gradual steps from what is already some progress (no one scores anything as at 0). Then various options for 'doing something different' are introduced, some almost paradoxical, some playful, some based on established family therapy ideas. There is no worry about being purist – if it fits, try it; if it works, do it more.

As family members slip back into a problem story from time to time, she avoids '*making* too much of it', but keeping a balance between showing that one hears what is said and also avoiding amplifying the problem is always difficult.

Notice the subtle insertion of tasks that invite people to *notice* what they are doing that is helpful and also to *talk about it* so as to *build* it up. When they say they do not know the answer to important presuppositional questions, she waits or asks again with different words, for the assumption is that they do know – if they can have a go at saying it, they can realise that. The assumption in some of the questions, of course, is that they have control over what they do and to do it they must know how to do it; if they know that, they do not need solutions from the worker.

There is a good deal of normalisation going on – a form of reassurance familiar to most people – as well as some behavioural insights such as not threatening what one cannot or will not carry out. There is also some side-stepping of the problem; rather than tackling the storm head-on, she asks about how will they create some calm, and their replies show that they have many excellent ideas themselves.

The use of letters may be familiar to some readers. Writing them can be hard and time-consuming work, but our experience is that they save time as they amplify the impact of meetings and most service users read them carefully. Change is constructed by language and written language can provide an additional 'cementing' of the spoken word.

Readers will also probably have noticed the use of stories to communicate ideas. They are less like professional knowledge as they draw on 'local' knowledge, but more importantly, they provide people with the indirect *experience* of successful action or outcome.

Perhaps the key issue is how the discipline of the process keeps the worker from showing interest in dysfunction or its cause and how it keeps her uncertain about solutions and curious about the family members' ideas for co-constructing the changed future.

This second example shows the approaches being used in quite a different situation:

Letting go of a baby

Trudy, aged 17, was raised in a succession of children's homes and foster families. As a child she was sexually abused. She now lives in a small flat; her child Tess, aged 18 months, is being fostered subject to an Interim Care Order. Trudy visits her boyfriend, Jim, daily; he lives nearby and has been known to have been violent in the past. Trudy has a bruised eye due to Jim hitting her a few days ago. A court case is pending to decide on the release of her baby for adoption and a Guardian Ad Litem is involved. If the application to court fails, Social Services will seek a Full Care Order. Trudy, visiting her social worker, had walked three miles from her boyfriend's house on the sea front.

Trudy started with the news that she has fallen out with her boyfriend – she hit him. Nothing is going well for her except for getting a kitten which is just old enough to leave its mother. SW comments that she is good with very new animals. She then asks how is Tess? 'She's OK, her chest is not fully better but she's off the nebuliser now – just inhalers, she's got a lot of eczema.' She last saw her on Monday but they both were very tired and fell asleep.

SW asked 'Suppose when you are leaving this meeting you feel that it was really worthwhile coming, what would have happened to make you think that? It has taken a lot of effort to get here, so what needs to happen to make it worthwhile?' 'I need counselling since Tess was taken from me. I miss my appointments and I missed the court. I'm trying to get Tess back but it all goes on my record. I have a good relationship with Jim but today is a bad day. I said I'm going to hit you – he said go ahead and I did.' SW asked what was her main issue. It was Tess. 'Tell me about it.'

Trudy said people were acting as if she had a mental disorder -'But I haven't'. 'Like my Dad's drinking and violence – I know I have a temper but it's my temper, not my Dad's.' 'What's your temper like?' 'I lose my temper and then I have to swallow my pride and say sorry.' SW asked if she felt out of control. 'It feels like I'm trapped. Not going anywhere, but it's not me holding back, it's Social Services saying I can't get a house with Jim. They say concentrate on Tess, but Jim supports me and that gives me some energy. My self-esteem and motivation have gone up since they took Tess away because I'm fighting. It's taken me seven months to realise I want her back.' 'How do you get on with the Guardian?' 'He's OK, he knows I love Tess.'

SW took up the issue of the bruised eye. Trudy said Jim only hit her once. 'Once too often', remarked SW. 'Has he hit other people?' 'His ex-girlfriend says so but she is trying to get back at him.' SW said that she could understand that Trudy needs a relationship and she can't always put her child first without any consideration of her own needs, but it did not sound like the best situation in which to get Tess back, so could they talk about Tess's safety.

'How would I know if Tess was safe with Trudy?' 'She'd be happy.' 'How would I know she was happy?' 'She'd be talking, playing, smiling and nosy as usual.' 'What would you be doing that would make her do those things?' 'I'd love her.' SW looked at her questioningly and she added 'feed her, clothe her, care for her'. 'When they took her away she had had that fall and had bruised her face; what happened?' 'I asked my foster father to take her to the doctor. Next thing I knew there was a letter under my door saying I'm not having her back.' 'How come she fell?' 'I was sitting on the settee and she was up on my shoulder so she could see out. She fell. Then while I was in the bathroom she fell off the bed. There was a red mark on her face so I sent her to the doctor's. He said it was a grabbing bruise.'

SW said 'It does not sound like the Trudy I know – you always fuss over her. What was going on to make you behave like that? Had you been having a smoke or something?' 'Well Paul and Sally were around and we were puffing on a spliff.' 'But that can make you very relaxed – all those loose muscles and you holding her up!' This led to a discussion of responsibility. While Trudy did not accept full responsibility, she did not blame anyone else for the fact that Tess did come to harm. SW talked of how her mothering was OK before that and she seemed comforted by that.

'So what will be best for Tess if your mothering isn't quite what it was?' asked SW. 'She'd be best adopted, but honestly I don't think I can do it. I'd feel like I had thrown her away.' 'Do you need to fight all the way to prove to her later that you did your best?' 'But I've not been fighting all that hard – I missed appointments. They don't get on with it – I'm fighting for myself 'cos she'll think I gave her up.' Tears. Though it was very emotional, the meeting went easily from there on. Trudy was able to put herself in Tess's place. She had worries about how good a job the adopters would do and what her friends would say, but 'they' could have Tess. The only thing now stopping her signing is that she still really wants Tess and will feel ashamed.

SW asked about how will she save her face. She thought she would accept the guardian's report – let him decide – he is responsible and leaving it to him is the responsible thing to do. She liked him and felt he was fair, and she can still fight but only a bit.

SW asked what she will be doing for herself and talked of the need for self-care. She will go out with Jim and treat herself to a trip to a theme park. She will also ask for counselling.

SW congratulated her on her bravery and on finding her own solution. She replied 'I thought I needed a second chance but Tess needs a chance more than me.' That was it! More tears, as she and SW had a good sniffle together!

This is a much abbreviated account of one meeting with a service user who could probably be said to be mainly a 'complainant' rather than a willing 'customer'. The situation contains conflict between the rights and needs of a mother and those of her child. The child's right to safety is paramount. Managers in Social Services had decided, on strong evidence, that removal and adoption of the child was necessary, and legal steps to do that are in hand. Yet the dignity of the mother is important and her well-being will be affected by how she comes to terms with her enormous loss. Given the statutory role of the social workers in such a situation, it would not be surprising if engagement was quite difficult.

When Trudy arrives there is a social stage of asking how she is and how the child is and some details about her health are offered by Trudy. Then, quite early, the worker asks a future-orientated question, namely the 'worthwhile' question, which asks the service user to consider what will be a good outcome for this meeting, or what would she like to achieve in it. With the use of a supplementary question the answer is, not surprisingly, to get the decision about Tess sorted out. The answer may be self-evident but the worker presumes nothing.

As frequently happens, the service user develops a story of life being controlled by others and the worker stays briefly with this but picks up on a positive – Trudy is not fighting the guardian.

Trudy's bruised eye cannot be ignored and her acceptance of violence from her boyfriend almost includes a defence of him. This is not condemned and she is not blamed, although the social worker makes her own values explicit, and the provision of safety for the child is kept central. Questions about building safety lead to disclosures that are admissions of neglect. They then move on to a conversation about responsibility, facing consequences, that is harm to Tess, while avoiding blaming. Trudy is not harangued but is asked for her view on what is best for Tess. Trudy knew the answer.

The gentle but firm talking together, including compliments where that was appropriate, seemed to bring out the humanity of Trudy. She still had a most difficult question to face (how to let go without losing face), yet the worker avoids offering her ideas and trusts Trudy to know how to do it. Then she moves onto how Trudy will care for herself. Again Trudy knows, and ends with a moving statement putting her baby before herself.

There is a sense of the worker getting close despite their very different backgrounds and parts in the story. It almost looks easy as they cry as two women together, yet there is no hint of unprofessionalism. It seems that the more difficult the piece of work, in terms of avoiding deficit or a problem-focus, the more discipline is needed to stay constructive. The social worker in question said afterwards that it is the solution-focused approach that does this for her most clearly, and she drew on this here.

A number of descriptions of narrative and solution-focused work have been published, covering situations, problems and work settings too numerous for us to discuss. However, we provide an annotated summary of the best-known publications in Further Reading at the end, so that the way such approaches can be used, refined and developed can be explored in more depth.

8

Constructive Assessment

> Problems are seen to maintain themselves because they maintain themselves and because clients depict the problem as always happening. (de Shazer, 1991, p. 58)

It is perhaps 'assessment', more than any other aspect of the work, that distinguishes social work from counselling or therapy. Counsellors and therapists may form assessments of people or of their problems but these private thoughts are not usually for the use of courts, managers or review panels.

Social work assessments, on the other hand, especially in statutory agencies, are usually written formally and are for the use of others in authority. This assessment work is essentially the work of *making judgments, so that decision-making can be better informed*. In this chapter we will attempt to address this important part of the social work role. But the issues involved are numerous – assessment is a most complex, controversial and demanding activity (see, for example, Meyer, 1993, and Milner and O'Byrne, 1998).

The traditional notion of assessment implies comparison with some sort of measure or norm and is therefore based on rationalist assumptions. It relies on positivist notions of being able to clearly know reality, and it has therefore invited social workers to attempt to present not only data but judgments *as if they were certain*. Courts search for certainty even in the impossible area of predicting child abuse as if the social sciences ought to be able to provide clear answers, and yet the law itself is far from clear and is open to interpretation and change. Teubner (1989) has remarked that professionals who act as expert witnesses will, in court, often give unequivocal replies to questions about motivation and causation which, back in their own scientific domains, they would regard as unanswerable. The way child psychology is offered in court is quite different from that used in treatment contexts. Judges seem surprised if non-legal experts differ while legal experts differ with relish. In court, non-legal experts are under pressure to come to a consensus. There is a tendency for theories of child care to be given a certainty they never had originally. Parton (1998b) has begun to explore *the value of uncertainty* in social work, arguing that uncertainty needs to be rediscovered; it is a fact of life, for while social workers may make mistakes and some of the tragic deaths may have been preventable, *many are not*. Workers can identify the potentially dangerous cases very well but it is much more difficult to identify the acutely dangerous. Such judgments are riddled with moral and civic issues like 'responsibility taking' which are ill-defined. As Jan Fook (2000) has demonstrated, experienced social workers have developed a construct of professional social work expertise which allows for uncertainty and conflict, and also for a sense of ultimate direction.

We would argue, however, that to pretend that there is certainty where there is little, is not good practice; we need to be open about the practical-moral nature of assessment work and not offer false certainty. There may be several conflicting plausible explanations and yet no established cause. Fook believes that social workers know that they are dealing with uncertainty; they are faced with multiple realities and so they make moral judgments about the adequacy of a given account, using notions of motive and intentionality. Knowledge based on formal empirical research does not help much with this form of accounting for decisions about what are unique situations. But recognising reflexively the 'undecidability and indeterminacy' of situations may be at least part of the way out of the current trap. Such a move by social workers could not, however, be possible without wider support. But better to have honest accounts of struggles with judgment and understanding than to search for false certainty. Such a change, we maintain, would improve the quality of assessments.

Even though the notion of assessment sits uncomfortably in the constructionist frame, we believe the constructionist approach has much to offer the process. Therefore, having briefly stated what assessments are expected to do, we will consider some of the theoretic issues flowing from constructionism, then examine what implications these have for the various parts of the contents of assessment reports. We will then consider their implications for the assessment process, before suggesting what a *constructive assessment* report might look like.

Assessment reports are expected to set out factual data concerning the service user in an accurate and truthful way, stating how the information was obtained, what were the sources, and 'identifying steps taken to verify information' (Home Office, 1995, p. 8). This data is intended to be objective or at least free of subjective reframes or of 'the terminology of aggravation or mitigation' (ibid, p. 9). Next, they are required to provide an analysis of the person and the problems they have or present, providing some explanation of, or deconstructing, a particular strange state of affairs, as it were, and attempting to summarise the person's needs, resources and risks. Lastly, they are expected to recommend what should best be done about the situation, what intervention might be tried and what the prognosis is for the future. In brief they collect data, make judgments and offer recommendations for decision-making.

Smale *et al.* (1993) suggest that there are three types of assessment processes:

1. *The questioning model.* This process of data collection is not unlike detective work, finding 'facts' and collecting statements from various witnesses; then, like Sherlock Holmes, making deductions and producing a diagnostic opinion or at least a *professional judgment* about the matter in hand, and especially about the risks involved. To arrive at the conclusions, the worker will have asked many questions, perhaps following a set format, and he or she will then have processed the answers, or shaped the data, in accordance with some theory, or agency or professional agenda. The social worker is the expert, though he or she may be called in court to back up judgments or to be cross-examined about how they were reached.
2. *The procedural model.* Here the process is dominated by agency check-lists and risk matrices. The task is usually to judge whether a person fits the criteria for certain services; little judgment is required and the so-called assessment is mere information gathering – the rules or policies decide what should happen.

3. *The exchange model.* Here people are viewed more as experts on their difficulties 'with an emphasis on exchanging information' (Milner and O'Byrne, 1998, p. 29). What people say is not interpreted, but is taken as a basis for helping them locate inner resources and potential, and for deciding how best to work collaboratively with people to get to goals defined by them, assuming these goals are not harmful, immoral or illegal. These assessments aim to be empowering and needs-led.

We will be suggesting that *constructive assessment* is most closely related to the exchange model, but also that *constructive* ideas can contribute to the questioning model and be helpful in improving the quality of these types of assessment as they are often employed in risk situations.

Theoretic issues

Firstly, there is the question of whether the medical model of 'assessment before treatment' is appropriate in social work. In the medical world it is seen as important that the correct disease is treated, as in the mechanical world it is important to diagnose a problem before fixing it. But problems of relationships and behavioural problems are different – 'cause' is much more difficult to find. In dealing with psycho-social problems, Reid (1978) suggests that assessment *in* or *through* treatment is more realistic (the root of the word 'diagnosis' is the Greek *dia* (through) and *gnosis* (know). Even in some areas of medicine the trial-and-error principle applies; it is only *through* trying certain medicines that doctors know if they are the right treatment. In the social field this certainly applies; it is only through working with a person that one can know what will be useful in helping them; if something has never been tried how can it be ruled out? The matter is more problematic when we move into the *constructive frame*, where it is not necessary to understand a problem in order to build a solution. Furthermore, constructionist approaches maintain that *explanations* of human problems are, in themselves, highly dubious. De Shazer argues that explanatory theories stop us needing to listen, or at least they interfere with our listening. While it is not possible to not theorise, how well we listen depends on whether our theories are 'grand' or 'local' theories. Grand theories produce labels rather than reliable explanations, so they render people less human. Diagnosis stops dialogue and therefore diagnostic theories stop the constructive process.

A *constructive assessment* would question the whole notion of cause in behavioural matters. Cause may be clear in mechanical or biological problems, but while a person has any shred of personal agency, how can one say with any measure of confidence what 'causes' a person to do something? We suggest the term 'invitation' is more useful. People and situations, and events and emotions, *invite* certain behaviours and a person decides whether or not to respond. Their response may depend on the strength of the invitation or not; people may decide to go along with an invitation or to recoil and do the opposite or do nothing. Searching for an explanation of how a particular invitation influenced or failed to influence a person may be futile; in any case, it will hardly lead to a certain answer. If we impose our pre-determined theories of cause, rather than listen to unique personal experiences, we may inflict on people the same damaging process that is part of their problems to begin with. If we must provide explanations we must therefore always remain open to alternative explanations.

Secondly, an understanding of the human 'person' is at the centre of any assessment. As McLeod (1997) sees it: in psycho-social thinking the self is a combination of mechanism (energies) and organism (id); in humanist psychology the person is an organism; and in early cognitive psychology an information processor. These images lead to images of change; 'a mechanism is "fixed", an organism is "healed", a computer is "re-programmed", a person "grows"' (p. 90). For a constructionist, these images fail to convey the experience of being a person at the beginning of the twenty-first century; they omit people's capacity to reflect on their situations, to challenge the given, to construct changes in living as *social* beings. Traditional practice relies on notions of a 'bounded autonomous self' (p. 91) at the core of people. Winnicott's idea was of a 'true self' with many layers of false self , like an onion. Constructionists would say the (false) self we present is our only true self; Lacan (1981) would say there is no core, only a 'lack', and self is an illusion made up of (sometimes conflicting) bits of stories, and is based on the creation of a pretence that there is no 'lack' at our centre. In the traditional Western view, self is seen as mature when it gains independence; Lacan would say independence is an Anglo-American construction based on the assumption of a nurturing benevolent society. Narratively, maturity is acknowledging a lack and a need of others – meaning and identity are negotiated with others. For Winnicott a positive identity meant a high esteem of oneself; for Lacan and some more recent French writers, identity is storied, reviewed and re-storied over time as we take bits from various experiences and relationships. Cushman (1995) argues that 'self' is central to Western conditions such as isolation, mobility, privacy and consumerism; it sustains capitalism and our political system even. But in constructionism a 'person' is an active and relational being. McLeod quotes MacMurray (1961) as maintaining that an isolated agent makes no sense, as agency assumes relationship and words like 'self' and 'anger' refer more to things we *do* than to any state. A *constructive assessment* would ask how, for example, anger is constructed and used, what stories there are to tell of it, what relationship the person has with it.

The same with problems; a constructive worker externalises the problem and asks 'relative influence' questions: 'What influence has the problem had on your life? and 'What influence have you had on the problem's life?' At first sight this seems as if the problem, rather than the person, gets the blame for the trouble. But there is no let-off; the service user is held accountable for his or her actions. Though responsible behaviour may have been 'restrained' by influences, the person is still responsible for doing something to put matters to right and for 'standing up to' the problem. This shift to looking at problems as outside people means that the person's relationship with the problem is more important than the cause or nature of the problem itself; that nature is largely constructed by language. This theoretic shift is not an easy one and communicating it to people in authority is certainly not easy – their damaged property, for example, is all too real.

Thirdly, in *constructive social work* change comes about by talking about life without the problem or by creating a better story or by challenging old narratives so as to co-construct better ones that lead to changes in meanings and then in behaviours. In assessment, talking about life without the problem seems to be missing the point, but it is there that hope of change lies. Externalising makes space for a better story to emerge; how well a person is able to do that cannot be guessed at unless there is time to actually try it. Assessment *before* intervention therefore seems not to fit in this way of working.

There is also a sense in constructionism, with its emphasis on 'local knowledge' and on subverting taken-for-granted oppressive 'truths', of 'rendering strange the familiar' (White, 1993, p. 34) rather than explaining the strange (Sherlock Holmes). There is a sense of 'staying on the surface' rather than digging for explanation. The worker is not the only expert; users are often more expert than us in the problem – we may be more expert in thinking about solution-development but we can only build solutions *with* people since they have the raw materials.

Lastly, knowledge is always incomplete but that does not mean that we know nothing. Yet, 'because what we know about problem causation is so very limited and because clients know more about the particularities of their lives than [we] do, [we] are right to limit the use of predetermined theories of problem causation and to emphasise instead each client's own personal theory . . . [and] be willing to take their stories seriously as providing some extralinguistic reality about their lives' (Held, 1995, p. 254).

The content of assessments

There are a number of elements that can be seen to make up an assessment : data collection; analysis; the assessment process; and a number of assumptions.

Traditionally with *data collection* there has been an emphasis on reporting the 'deficits' in people's lives and, as Gergen (1990, p. 353) put it, 'common actions are translated into a professionalized language of mental deficit, and as this language is disseminated, the culture comes to construct itself in these terms'. Competence reports on incompetence, in a search for historical truth.

Constructive assessment, on the other hand, searches for a balance of data and includes problem-free data. It seeks to offer a balance of *strengths* and *deficits* and it searches for the 'narrative truth' about how people experience and deconstruct the facts and what they mean to them. Spence (1982) defines narrative truth as 'the criterion we use to decide when a certain experience has been captured to our satisfaction'. We would suggest it is dangerous to think that it is possible to discover if a person's story fits with actual events and practice is more about creating stories that people can live with (McLeod, 1997, p. 86). We 'facilitate the emergence' of a better story.

Bruner, J. (1986a) in discussing narrative approaches points to an important principle that the dominant story always has important 'lived experiences' missing. A sense of 'persons engaged in action' may be missing and exceptional behaviours that contradict the dominant story are unnoticed if we listen only to the dominant story. Without a belief in exceptions and a search for exceptions, data will be misleading. For this search to be successful, a human engagement is required where the worker comes from 'not knowing' and is able to listen, having engaged in 'problem-free talk' and asked exception-finding questions. Only then will a story of personal agency be found that challenges the dominant one. Scaled questions provide a description from the service user's perspective probably more easily than most questions. We have found that Scale Sheets (see appendices, particularly Appendix 3) help further. They can contain numerous questions that fit the situation; they can be worded in positive language, yet the columns allow for 'not at all' answers, but also for various answers between 'no' and 'yes'. These kind of helpful instruments empower people to tell a story that may otherwise be difficult to tell because it has several shades of grey. The Scale Sheets in the appendices are first drafts and we recommend that workers devise their own versions to fit better the situations they are assessing.

There are two aspects to a *constructive* approach to *analysis*. One is de Shazer's view that problems just happen; it is impossible to say for sure what is their cause or what is the cause of the cause, so let's forget it – in any case this knowledge is not needed for generating solutions. Causal explanations are suspect, usually pathologising, and come from the worker's head rather than from the data.

Then there is the narrative view of White and others that when working with the person, problems can be deconstructed, so as to expose the oppressive narratives that enslave people or at least restrain them from responsibility. White and Epston (1990) hold that by exploring how the problem 'recruited' the person and then continued to oppress them, an alienation is created in the person's relationship with the problem, so that they can make a choice to fight it. Here, persons are seen as storied beings – storied by powerful narratives, for example a history of failure, but capable of re-authoring themselves. In both these approaches blame is avoided but responsibility/accountability is mobilised. This, however, is rather difficult to do in one meeting, particularly if one has to deal with the current risk culture that tends to dominate how assessments are devised. Discussing completed Scale Sheets helps to develop a reflective story that frequently throws up surprises for the worker that allow for further exception-finding and a 'thicker plot' for the story.

De Shazer is interested in assessing whether the potential service user is motivated to change and has confidence that change is possible. He wants to know if the person has exceptions they can talk about and whether these are spontaneous or deliberate, and whether the person can answer clearly 'the miracle question'. But he says that none of this is a sure indicator of whether intervention will be successful. If there is any indicator of success it is probably that well-formed goals based on acute listening to people's use of language is key. White, on the other hand, searches for the hero/heroine story among the problem-saturated story and for a decision to stand up to the problem's influence, for a change in the relationship with the problem.

In the *process* of constructive assessment there is close *engagement* with the person; an attempt is made to 'bridge the difference gap' (Milner and O'Byrne, 1998, p. 68) between the person and the worker. Considerable effort goes into *negotiating* perceptions, exploring the mutual subjectivity and assumptions of the worker about the person's life as well as the assumptions by the service user about the agency and its staff. This also involves *acknowledging differences* in background and experiences which makes possible the emergence of a shared critical dialogue in which misunderstandings can be addressed with cooperation. Jordan (1990) maintains that where such a *dialogue* is not achieved and service users are perceived as uncooperative, the conclusions reached are greatly affected. An openness about culture and values and about lack of knowledge of the other person's beliefs is required, and this will lead to inviting the service user to help the worker to see life as they see it. Without such a humble 'not knowing' position, a black female service user, for example, will rightly see a white male worker as coming from another world (Milner and O'Byrne,

1998). White workers have been criticised for failing to acknowledge the strengths in black people; respectfully asking about
people's struggles and survival in the face of structural inequity,
not just discussing the 'wounds' but also the capacity for nurtur-
ance in their communities, is necessary. In our view, at least some
lack of sameness has to be addressed if there is to be a moral
dialogue and human contact that is accepting, respectful and
mutually empowering.

Like anthropologists, social workers carrying out assessments
have values that interact with the very essence of the work, that is
in constructing accounts of people's lives and making judgments
about them. There is a need, therefore, to move from trying to
'reproduce' lives on paper to writing more collaborative accounts
that draw on the meanings of service users. Since many of the
service users' lives include experiences of being devalued,
oppressed and powerless, and of having impossible expectations
imposed on them, Milner and O'Byrne (1998) suggest using some
of the following questions:

- What expectations do you feel you are not meeting?
- How do you think you are coping?
- Do you expect too much of yourself?
- Are your burdens such that no one should be expected to do
  better than you?
- How good do you feel about who you are?
- How appreciated are you by others?
- Could your difficulties be due more to a lack of resources than a
  lack of ability?
- What traditional supports are lacking for you these days?
- What particular strengths have helped you to keep going?
- Where could we start building a network of support?

Use of Scale Sheets, followed by discussion of the answers, can
lead to the co-construction of a detailed story that has the balance
of needs and strengths that we discussed earlier, and the strengths
focus encourages a closer, more trusting story-telling, since it has
a sense of cooperation and excitement at the discovery of facets
that the service user may not have been aware of until he or she
answered the question.

In our view, service users need to tell their stories and workers
need to listen to these stories of personal experiences, not only

stories of the problem but stories of life in a wider sense. White and Epston (1990, p. 41) put it as listening to the 'previously neglected but vital aspects of lived experience' and to their 'unique outcomes' that often fall outside the dominant story. White wants to know if a person can talk of such outcomes, for it is in talking of them to an audience that the possibility of personal agency grows. Can service users have a voice with which to re-author themselves, for there is implicit power in having such a voice?

Perhaps the main difference between traditional assessment and *constructive assessment* is the different attitude of the social worker towards 'truths', stories, as well as towards their role. There is always some element of detective work but there is a world of difference between Sherlock Holmes and Columbo! If we can ignore the shabby raincoat, Columbo brings an attitude closer to what we are attempting to describe. Rather than appearing as superior authority figures, social workers could have the confidence to be diffident, to be informal, to engage in a conversation that helps to give the service user a voice. That conversation may be driven by various theories but workers need to realise what these theories are and question whether they are the most useful. Furman and Ahola (1992) maintain that one can even use a fictitious theory to develop collaborative understanding of a situation. Milner and O'Byrne set out how this can be done if the service user, for example someone abusing drugs, can pretend that his or her problems are caused by a gremlin who lives solely for that purpose. The person can be invited to list the behaviours that the gremlin likes to see and also those behaviours that it dislikes. In this way service users' understandings are examined in a non-threatening way. If they wish to defeat the problem they can see what behaviours to change, avoiding those that the gremlin likes and increasing those that worry it.

Bill O'Hanlon offers a summary through his Web-site of what he sees as key *assumptions* that should inform the assessment process. This is followed by a series of *considerations* which we find very suggestive. We have changed some of his language for brevity.

Assumptions:
- Assessment and interviews are interventions; workers and service users co-create problem definitions.

- Whatever is focused on in the conversation, has its 'prevalence' increased.
- Service users have the resources to make the necessary personal changes.
- Rapid resolution may be possible more often than we think.
- It is not always necessary (nor possible) to know the 'true cause', history or function of a problem.
- People are accountable for their actions and can change regardless of background, mental status or emotional state.
- People are resistant and/or uncooperative when we haven't listened to them, have blamed them or have not been helpful to them.

Considerations:
- Assessment is always an on-going process, changing as we learn about the person. We don't have to get the 'right diagnosis' before making interventions.
- Who thinks there is a problem, and what have they complained about. That becomes the focus.
- What are the goals? How will we know when to stop?
- Be specific about what the problem-free future will be like.
- What is the smallest noticeable change? [Hint: it may already have happened.]
- What is the person motivated for? What does he or she want?
- What can they do well? (look in their life experiences).
- Explore exceptions/previous solutions, times when the situation was better.
- What were the best coping moments?
- Past strengths, problem related and not problem related.
- Present strengths, during the assessment process.
- Future strengths via 'the miracle question'; get 'video-type' descriptions.
- What are the patterns of the problem? How is it performed?
- Search for regularities of action, interaction, time, place and so on. Get a specific 'video' account.
- Scan the potentially harmful actions of the person or of others in their life (for example, violence, substance abuse, self-harm) that may not be obvious or may be minimised initially.
- Acknowledge and validate each person and her/his point of view without closing down the possibility for change.

Murphy and Pardeck (1998, pp. 16–17) have some strong words to add to this discussion and argue that:

> reality is situational and community based. What it means to be poor, homeless, an old person, or a person with a disability is largely defined by persons experiencing each of these personal situations . . . and by other social systems such as family, group or organisation. Practitioners must be sensitive to these definitions in order to conduct appropriate assessments.

Risk

For some years now, risk has moved centre-stage, certainly in social work in statutory agencies, as the focus of attention (Kemshall *et al.*, 1997). It is a notion that strikes a certain fear into the hearts of workers and managers alike, as society, especially the media, has developed an insurance mentality and is quick to lay blame when things go wrong. This situation has changed the relationship between workers and service users (potential and actual) and often seems to result in workers seeing those they are assessing as 'the enemy'. This makes partnership virtually impossible. So how can risk assessment be addressed in a more positive way?

We have discussed the need for balance in information gathering, collecting positives and exceptions to the problem, as well as information on need, problems, deficit and danger. (See the Signs of Safety Scale in Appendix 2.) But this alone is not sufficient for decision-making about risk.

Prospect Theory provides some interesting insights. Kahnemann and Tversky (1979) have shown how workers making decisions about risk tend towards the direction of risk or caution depending on whether or not the initial choice is framed in terms of losses or gains – that is, in terms of options that involve losses or that involve gains.

Firstly, if options are framed in terms of *gains*, workers will be more likely to be *more risk averse*: that is, they will tend to opt for a *certain*, though perhaps *smaller*, *gain* as opposed to a larger gain that is less certain. They will therefore be less likely to gamble on losing a certain gain.

Secondly, if the options are framed in terms of *losses*, workers will tend to be *more risk seeking* and therefore will tend to favour a larger loss that is uncertain and avoid a smaller loss that is certain. That is, while avoiding small and certain losses, they will tend to gamble on *larger losses* when they are uncertain.

Framing situations in terms of gains can result in more caution, and framing situations in terms of losses can result in more risk-taking. This may seem to be a curious paradox. Most social work situations can be framed in terms of gains or losses. Many social workers seem to feel that a focus on losses is more distrusting and therefore safer. But all it does is lead to the service user being seen as the enemy and greater risks being taken eventually. Unfortunately some social work legislation encourages this. For example the Children Act 1989 does not convincingly define the welfare of a child in terms of gains; the criterion for a court order is possible losses to welfare in comparison with a similar child. But 'cautious behaviour (by workers), that is opting for certain gains, is more likely to lead not only to re-evaluation and contingency plan-making, but also to creative and effective social work' (Milner and O'Byrne, 1998, p. 176).

We suggest that framing situations in terms of *certain versus uncertain GAINS* would avoid 'risky shift'. It will not avoid difficult decisions but it will lead to safer judgments. *Constructive* approaches, we would suggest, will facilitate thinking in terms of gains. Milner and O'Byrne (1998, p. 161) state that 'the way in which service users' situations are framed to emphasise gains, reduces risk in practice and increases creativity'.

Turnell and Edwards (1997) argue that risk assessment in child protection assessments is only half the equation; the other half is 'the discovery and development of *safety* for the child in the present and the future' (p. 181, original emphasis). They quote research by Farmer and Owen (1995) that shows that the preoccupation with risk means there is too little time in child-protection case conferences to consider the needs of the family and what should be done. To balance the equation we need to elicit the family's views on competencies, goals and existing safety so that cooperation can be enhanced. The goals of the agency need to be clear in terms of what needs to be happening for safety to be satis-factory. Families often do not know this. So we ask how will both the agency and the family know when to stop meeting? What will people see happening? But Turnell and Edwards also show that it is not for the agency on its own to decide what should be happening. That leads to workers hounding reluctant families who feel others' values are being imposed on them; rather it is vital to ask the different family members 'for their understanding of what the statutory agency needs to see' (Turnell and Edwards, 1997, p. 183) so as to be satisfied. When this is respectfully asked of them they often feel empowered to 'spell out ideas that would satisfy the agency' (ibid). It is also important to find out what the family want more generally – they may lack some essential piece of domestic equipment, for example.

So-called unmotivated people may say they want the agency 'off our backs'. This may be a very appropriate goal, for 'these sorts of indirect motives are often powerful mechanisms for harnessing the energies of parents under investigation of child abuse' (ibid, p. 184). Turnell and Edwards's signs-of-safety approach explicitly outlines signs of risk alongside signs of safety. They also claim that, due to the power of language, sufficient safety is often not only found *but also created* by the process. They suggest an assessment therefore should:

- Clearly state agency goals in terms of 'what constitutes enough safety for the case to be closed'.
- Incorporate the family's strengths and resources.
- Encourage what the family is already doing to create safety and draw on identified exceptions to neglect or danger.
- Include the family's own safety ideas as far as possible.
- If the family's general goals are likely to increase safety, draw on them too.
- Use those people who are willing and able to take action.
- Where possible, agency plans should be presented in the light of the family's aspirations, and their position on the problem.
- Include compliments where people are already moving towards their own or the agency's goals.
- Be specific: for example, not 'father would like to be a better parent' but 'he would like to learn better ways of disciplining the children' and add his ideas for how he would learn that and what difference he would expect to see.

Scales, such as those in the appendices, can help collaborative assessment, even in the most difficult situations. Eve Lipchik (personal communication) has drafted one for assessing whether to work with situations of domestic violence. This is controversial in some quarters, but if both parties want a non-violent relationship, given sufficient motivation and safety precautions, she has found ways of successfully helping such couples. She asks scaled questions about feeling cared for, feeling respected, trust, feeling comfortable alone with each other, ability to be honest without fear, not humiliating each other in front of others, respecting the need for sex or the wish not to participate at times, resolving differences without serious argument, trying to win in debates, able to call time-out to cool down if they fight, control of drink and drugs. People can give one of four or five scaled answers to each of these, providing a rich source for a comprehensive story and assessment.

De Jong and Miller (1995) say that pre-prepared categories 'may not reflect the categories the client uses to organise his or her experiences' (p. 730), and they suggest using the standard solution-focused questions about exceptions, about the day after the miracle, and coping questions. They also maintain that some people may be alienated and lack a sense of belonging and so are out of touch with their strengths and possibilities. Therefore we get nowhere unless we work collaboratively, affirming their perceptions and experiences, validating their efforts and successes. The 'miracle question' greatly facilitates the opening of possibilities. There is always more progress if people's own ways of working are incorporated into the plan and used in a 'synergic relationship' (ibid, p. 734) which expands both internal and external resources.

This is a far cry from the detached reporter, developing his or her own theoretic analysis and drawing up a plan for intervention back at the office. Kathy Weingarten (1998), writing about postmodern practice and the need to look for exceptions, quotes White and Epston concerning how there are always alternative stories to the ones that dominate lives. She adds 'I find that simply *believing* that the current version we tell about our lives is just that, a version, can promote the search for alternatives to a story that diminishes us in its performance' (p. 10). In practice she strives 'to bring my own voice in to the dialogue mix in a way that does not keep my thinking private, preferred, and privileged' (ibid, p. 7). Such a 'dialogue mix' is an apt description of a collaborative assessment process where ideas are constructed in partnership. The more difficult the situation, the more urgent it is to build such a partnership.

In conclusion, the shift in approach to assessment that we are suggesting very much follows that summarised by Bill O'Hanlon (Web-site handout, 1998) in the following way, where he compares the 'traditional' and the 'new'.

The traditional

- Conversations for true explanations.
- Searching for the function of the problem.
- Searching for 'cause', supporting ideas about determinism.
- A focus on history.
- Conversations for diagnosis, categorisation and characterisation.
- Encouraging conversations for identifying pathology.
- Conversations for inability.
- Conversations for insight and understanding.
- Conversations for blame.
- Attributions of bad intentions/personality.
- Adversarial conversations.
- Worker believes service user has hidden agenda that prevents co-operation.
- The worker is the expert; the person is a non-expert.

The new

- Collaborative conversations.
- Accepting/validating people's experiences.
- Worker and service user are partners in the process, though unequal.
- Conversations for change and difference.
- Presuming change.
- Searching for descriptions of difference and exceptions.
- Introducing new distinctions and using clients' distinctions.
- Conversations for competence/presuming ability.
- Searching for competence in other contexts.
- Eliciting descriptions of times when the person dealt with the problem in a way they liked.
- Conversations for goals and results. How will they know they have reached their goals?
- Conversations for accountability and personal agency.

- Holding people accountable for words and actions.
- Presuming actions derive from intentions, selves.
- Conversations for action (video descriptions).
- Focusing on what the person can do to make a difference to the problem.
- Introducing new possibilities for viewing and doing into the situation.

9

Does It Work?

Our mistake is to look for an explanation where we ought to look at what happens. (Wittgenstein, 1968)

It may be assumed that because of our critical perspectives in relation to science, rationalism and the increasing obsessions with monitoring and accountability, we would also be critical about any attempts to address outcomes. This is not our position. Our position on outcomes is that we owe it to service users to offer the best possible service. *Constructive social work* has many attractive characteristics such as respectfulness, engagement and dialogue, but a crucial test of ethical practice is a commitment to effectiveness in helping service users. *Constructive social work* seeks, therefore, to establish whether it is as effective as other approaches or not. Can it be shown that it produces comparable outcomes? In a professional culture increasingly dominated by obsessions with effectiveness, outcomes and being evidenced-based, it is clear that the approaches we are outlining here have to be prepared to address questions which in other respects could be seen to go against its central assumptions and principles. In this respect the development of *constructive social work* needs to be prepared to address questions which may not be of its making, but will be key for establishing its credibility to a wider and sceptical audience.

Very little evaluation of this approach has been done in social work settings as such, but there has been a considerable amount of research into the effectiveness of solution-focused and narrative interventions in a wide range of related settings, family work, work with adolescents, people with drink problems, offenders, people with mental health problems and those with school problems. Some of this work has been done by specialist teams and some by therapists of various sorts and some by qualified social workers themselves.

152

Evaluating SFBT (solution-focused brief therapy)

Over the years de Shazer's team and others have studied the effectiveness of brief interventions in various ways and, in general, these studies suggest that this way of working is at least as effective as others even though it tends to have shorter involvements in people's lives. Furthermore – and this is important for those who are concerned that such brief work may be shallow with short-lived benefits – most studies suggest that not only is the effect maintained over time but it actually tends to increase in its impact rather than wash out. We will take a closer look at these results and discuss some of their implications for social work.

Ever since de Shazer and his colleagues started practising SFBT his main research interest has been what service users and workers do together that is useful. Rather than comparing the model with other models, he has mainly asked service users if their goals have been reached and after how many meetings. This has been asked on several occasions, with similar results. A study in 1990 in Milwaukee (de Shazer, 1991) showed that 80.4 per cent of replies reported goals fully (65.6 per cent) or substantially (14.7 per cent) reached, and the average number of meetings was 4.6. When they were followed up 18 months later the success rate rose to 86 per cent. When the cohort was divided into those who attended for fewer than 4 sessions and those who attended for more, those attending for more than 4 sessions reported 91.14 per cent success and those attending fewer than 4, a 67.41 per cent success rate. In addition, 77 per cent reported no new problems and 67 per cent reported improvements in other areas since work finished. It must be borne in mind, however, that these were not 'scientific' studies in the usual sense of fully-tested measures, control groups and so on, and in any case the Milwaukee centre was able to contact only about 50 per cent of its clients. These findings suggest that the model deserves more rigorous evaluation.

At a conference in Glasgow in 1993, de Shazer reported that the latest Milwaukee study at that time obtained the following results (N = 225): follow-up at 6 months – 80 per cent success; at 12 months – 81 per cent; at 18 months – 86 per cent. Less than 20 per cent were self-referred, and the majority were from Social Services and Probation, and were poor and black. Ninety-seven per cent had fewer than 10 sessions; 4.2 was average; 55 per cent had 3 sessions. Intervals between sessions varied from 1 to 8 weeks. Termination and intervals were decided by the service users but these decisions were not predictive of success, nor were problem category nor any other factor. Attempts to predict who would be a success or who would fail widely missed the mark. Taking what people say at face value and good goal-setting seemed to offer the best prognosis. This study also showed that the average service user was at 7 on the ten-point scale in the last session and at 7.8 eight months later. People who were at 5 in the first session usually turned out to be single-session cases and at 8 months these were mostly at 10.

By way of a brief comparison, a study of the Mental Research Institute's (MRI) problem-solving approach showed 72 per cent 'success'; 40 per cent complete relief and 32 per cent considerable relief (Weakland *et al.*, 1974). Note that the study in Milwaukee in 1990 (reported above) *used the same research questions* as those used in this MRI study. In comparison, the Milwaukee study shows greater attainment of goals.

For a number of years, de Shazer, working with Luc Iseabeart (in press), has been consultant to a series of three-week programmes in Bruges for alcohol abusers, and has given the following verbal, and therefore incomplete, account of a study of the service (de Shazer, 1997). In week one, service users get education on the effects of abuse – the rest is solution-focused work. People can opt to work towards abstinence or controlled drinking, and have individual work, group work or family work. Twenty-five per cent get some detox if symptoms show up; 75 per cent get no medication apart from vitamin B. One-third are involuntary attenders. Out of a group of 500, at six months, 80 per cent still reported that they met their goals or that the problem was no longer a problem; at 12 months it was 78 per cent and at 18 months it was 86 per cent. Seventy-six per cent said they had no new problems needing help; 68 per cent reported additional positive changes not discussed on the programme.

A five-year follow-up study has recently been completed in Bruges (N = 250): 49.1 per cent were abstinent; 25 per cent were controlled – that is, taking no more than three units a day with one day off; 11 per cent claimed to be controlled but were not counted as they took more than the definition allowed; 58.6 per cent had no problems, 88.8 per cent felt good; 79.2 per cent had no more treatment, 75 per cent had no relapses (uncommon for alcohol follow-ups). A four-year study has also been completed (N = 150): 50 per cent were abstinent; 23.5 per cent were controlled; 57 per cent had no problems; 75 per cent had no more treatment; and again 75 per cent had no relapses. (These studies will be submitted for full publication.)

De Shazer and Berg (1997) summed up their evaluation studies in a report in the *Journal of Family Therapy* (UK) (vol. 19, no. 2) which set out their approach to 'what works?' and which stressed the need not to lose sight of the service users' goals or of their evaluations of our work.

Constructive evaluations

Various attempts have been made at more thorough studies of *constructive* methods of working, but as with all attempts to study methods of working, there are always difficulties. The main problem is to control what exactly is being studied. Is the model being correctly used? Is what is done really solution-focused work? In an attempt to preserve some 'programme integrity' some say that for work to be called solution-focused it must at least include future-talk and scaled questions; others say it should also include 'the miracle question' and a consultation break. Nevertheless, despite such difficulties some useful evaluation work has been done. We will first present some studies with some explanation, then some reports of *particular elements* of *constructive social work* being studied.

Peter Sundman (1997) reported on a study of a social work team in Helsinki, using solution-focused work in a community-based social welfare office where service users had problems such as addictions, mental disorders, physical illnesses and/or crises of various kinds. They were predominantly poor, known to the service for several years, and many were 'second-generation clients'. The team was not using the full SFBT model, just emphasising goals exceptions and positive feedback and incorporating 'a few simple solution-focused questions, remarks and suggestions' into the work. While there was no significant difference with a comparison group in terms of goal achievement, the service users were more satisfied, more goal-focused and more engaged with the workers in joint problem-solving; that is, the work was more collaborative. This may not be a striking result but, as Sundman says, since welfare problems do not disappear in six months, 'in the midst of the worst recession since the 30s', it was a good example of 'empowering practice'. Furthermore, the experimental group had more single men in it than the control group and it was felt that changes in their lives were more difficult to achieve than with people living in families. And there was a qualitative difference in that the experimental group thought that 'their own accomplished intentional actions' meant a positive change for them. The workers with the experimental group also had very scant training but, despite that fact, these workers 'began with a broader and more positive view of their clients' and the relationships became more personal, focusing on only a few goals that were based on a shared view, and the workers were seen as doing less work. So the conclusion was that even though goal achievement was not significantly different, the solution-focused way of achieving a goal 'meant a more positive change for the clients'.

Eakes, Walsh, Markowski, Cain and Swanson (1997) reported on the results of five sessions of solution-focused work combined with some narrative work, over ten weeks, with families with a member diagnosed as chronic schizophrenic, and compared them with a control group who received traditional medical therapy. The work included some externalisation of problems, a future focus, scaling questions and an emphasis on exceptions and competence, highlighting previous successes. The experimental group showed significant differences in expressiveness, active-recreational orientation, moral-religious emphasis and (less) family incongruence, as measured by various tested instruments. The scores indicated a healthy change towards more expressiveness and participation in social and recreational activities. There was more emphasis on value issues within the families and the group increased significantly their agreement on the social climate dimensions tested by the scales. Externalising the schizophrenia allowed the families to view the illness as one of many contributing factors over which they could exercise some control. 'Once problems are defined in those terms, they no longer appeared to create distance between clients and family members' (p. 152). Though acknowledging the real limitations imposed by the illness,

they appreciated each other's strengths more and their commitment towards overcoming the usual effects of the illness. Those in
the control group, on the other hand, had more emphasis on
medication as the healing agent and they transferred power and
responsibility on to medical staff.

Alisdair Macdonald (1994, 1997) has written about the results
obtained by his adult mental health team, using the SFBT
approach over six years. At the end of the first three years they
reported 'a good outcome' for 70 per cent of referrals. The
36 replies (out of 39) were cross-checked with the general practitioners. Sessions were monthly and ranged from 1 to 12 (mean
3.28). A 'good outcome' meant a report from the attender or
the GP that the problem was better – 23 (64 per cent) were better,
3 were worse and 10 unchanged. Combining the results over
the six years, 68 per cent reported a good outcome for an average
of 3.5 sessions. The level of new problems reported was low and, as
Macdonald (1997) says, 'contradicts the widely held belief that
symptom substitution or relapse will occur unless the "real"
problem is uncovered. The concept of flight into health is also
challenged' (p. 218). There was an equal outcome for social classes
but longstanding problems did less well.

Besa (1994) evaluated narrative-based family work with six
families. In five of the families the approach was found to have
produced reductions in parent/child conflict. The improvement
scores varied from 88 per cent to 98 per cent. The report states
that the approach was 'based on the notion that healthy exceptions
can be found within a problem-saturated story', that between-
sessions tasks initiate unique outcomes, that families can be
helped to re-author a new narrative about a child. In the sixth case
it was felt that the mother's change of shifts at work had made the
major contribution.

To mention very briefly some other outcome studies:

- Beyeback, M., Morejon, A. R., Palenzuela, D. L. and Rodriguez-
  Aries, J.L. (1996); 80 per cent of outpatients at a mental health
  centre achieved their goals.
- Burr, W. (1993); 77 per cent improved.
- Jong, P. and Hopwood, L. E. (1996); of 275 cases with a range
  of problems, 45 per cent of goals achieved and 32 per cent made
  some progress.

- Lindfoss, L. and Magnusson, D. (1997); solution-focused work in a prison in Sweden. Randomised study; 60 per cent reoffended in experimental group – 86 per cent in the control group. Also a pilot study – at 20 months 66 per cent of the experimental group and 90 per cent of the controls had reoffended. It was estimated that the reduction in reoffending saved 2.7 million Swedish Crowns.
- Lee, M. Y. (1997); a study of solution-focused family work; 64.9 per cent improved (goal achieved 54.4 per cent, part goal 10.5 per cent); average number of sessions 5.5.
- Vaughan, K., Young, B. C., Webster, D. C. and Thomas, M. R. (1996); Continuum-of-Care model for inpatient psychiatric treatment; 688 cases before SFBT model – average stay 20.2 days; 675 cases after SFBT – average stay 6.6 days.
- Wheeler, J. (1995); work in a child mental health setting; 44 per cent of 'routine' referrals, versus 69 per cent of SFBT referrals were 'satisfied'; other clinic resources used for 31 per cent of routine, versus 12 per cent of SFBT referrals.

Many of those developing SFBT and narrative approaches are more interested in studying how to improve it rather than showing that it works. An example of a study to examine potential improvements is de Shazer (1988), who reported on a study that showed that 'information talk' dominated session one; 'change talk' was common in second and subsequent sessions but rare in session one; 'change talk' was over four times more likely to occur after the worker attempted to elicit it and was more likely to continue when the worker responded to it in a positive way. Rigorous searching for exceptions promoted more 'change talk' even in the first session. This led to more second-session work moving into the first session and the average number of sessions dropped from 6 to 5. De Shazer is currently studying the question 'What pieces of the miracle have you seen recently?' If this is asked before going into the miracle question only 70 per cent report anything, but when asked after *exploring* the miracle question, 100 per cent reported 'something'. Fisher, Himle and Hanna (1998) have studied the externalisation of problems in work with compulsive adolescents. They sought to make the problem 'the enemy' as a major part of the work. Eleven of fifteen participants provided follow-up data and showed significant improvement after a 7-week programme.

Comparative studies

It is interesting to compare these results with parallel studies of other methods. We will next sum up some studies of other methods for comparison. We do not suggest that there can be any exact comparison and we realise that the rigour of the studies and their general methodology varies considerably.

The most noted study of non-solution-focused treatments for people with drink problems has been that carried out by the Rand research corporation in 1980. This looked at 3,000 cases from a 30-day in-patient programme, with Alcoholics Anonymous referral and other follow-up support, in the USA. Four years after finishing, 7 per cent were abstinent. Among the 93 per cent who were still considered to be abusing, 25 per cent said of their lives that they were 'doing normal things', which seems a contra-diction. This is not just bad luck, it is possibly a case of iatrogenic harm, since a large Canadian study showed that 50 per cent of those who stop abusing do so with no treatment at all.

Perhaps studies of the 'task-centred' approach in social work will provide a closer comparison for discussion purposes, accepting that there cannot be any exact comparison. We have selected the 'task-centred' approach for comparison as it is probably the most researched, and probably the most commonly used approach to problems. One of Reid's studies of the effectiveness of task-centred casework with children in their final year at school produced the following result. There were 87 cases of whom 77 were traced in a two-month follow up. Independent judges found that 21 per cent showed improvement, 70 per cent showed no change and 9 per cent were worse. (The judges studied case notes and agreed with each other in 75 per cent of the cases.) However, when clients were asked if their overall problem situation had changed for the better, 80 per cent thought it had and 20 per cent reported that it had not. One child said it was worse. In the opinion of 'collaterals', who tended to be less optimistic, 60 per cent showed positive change and 40 per cent did not (Reid, 1978). In a further result published in the same book, work with family problems produced these figures: 33 cases, 25 responded, 18 (72 per cent) said the main problem was at least a little better, 14 (56 per cent) said the problem was either a lot better or no longer present, and 45 per cent *felt* a lot better.

Reid and Epstein (1977) published the results of a series of studies. Task-centred casework with people with mental health problems resulted in 30 per cent considering it to be slightly helpful, 24 per cent moderately helpful, 37 per cent very helpful and 9 per cent not helpful. There were 196 families involved. A study of task-centred work with psychiatric outpatients gave these figures (N = 22): 17 traced after 12 months, 16 said their overall problem situation was better. A further study of mainly young psychiatric outpatients (80 per cent under 40 years old) who had 'favourable outcomes': 17 were found after 2 months and again 73 per cent of these reported favourable outcomes. A study of the task-centred approach in Britain (Newton and Marsh, 1993) suggests that learning to *apply* the approach, as distinct from learning *about* it, is far from easy and the results are disappointing.

These various results serve only to suggest a flavour of studies of other approaches and provide some context in which to view the above studies of SFBT and constructive approaches. Much more research is needed but there are huge ethical and methodological difficulties. Because the approach involves a certain personal 'artistic' flair and collaboration with service users in various ways, finding any 'pure' use of a specific set of techniques is difficult and inappropriate. We are not advocating that set techniques should be developed; rather we are advocating a new philosophy on which to base *constructive social work*, as well as some discipline for keeping to it because it works well.

How does it work?

We can only theorise about how *constructive* approaches contribute to change. At present we have studies that show effectiveness and studies that show the importance of certain elements within the approach. It will take a great deal more study to establish which elements are essential and why. But even then there is little chance of establishing how (or why) the approach as a whole, or any element in it, works. Narrative writers suggest that narrative creates lives and new narratives have the power to make changed lives – but how?

We suggest that all talking, in turn-taking conversations especially, *constructs an inner experience* that constructs the 'real' possibility of outer change, and this possibility *invites* the actual change or *empowers* people to opt for change because they have experienced it as a possibility. The approach also builds alliances with service users, listens to their feelings, their stories, their language, and incorporates this language in co-constructing a different future that entails personal agency on their part. All this adds up to a strong invitation and makes opting for change easier. We doubt if we will ever know, for example, how people manage to answer the miracle question (de Shazer jokingly says 'it's a miracle!'). That when people are asked constructive questions, and talk about their exceptions and how things can be better in the future, they do opt for change is sufficient for us at this point. We believe that the approach promotes personal agency; therefore the notion of 'invitation' makes more sense than 'cause'. It is about helping people to do what they want to change or to just get by; it prompts, it paves the way, it leads, it builds motivation and confidence; it does not *make* people change. There are many different types of invitation, some more influential than others and all depending on altering a person's state of consciousness in some way. Hypnotism is probably the most obvious example of powerful suggestions. Talk of change that has been experienced in conversation, in stories, in pretending, is probably quite influential. It can more easily lead to a 'suspension of disbelief' because the counter-belief is considerably strengthened.

Held (1995) discusses the possibility of research to establish the essential components of narrative work and also perhaps which components work best with service users' various narratives. She refers to the work of Omer (1993 and 1994), who finds that there are four elements that are particularly valuable, though not of universal effectiveness. They are: use of clients' narratives, validating the seriousness of problems, externalising the problem to make the client a hero/heroine and developing options for a new character. It is as if the service user provides the bricks in the form of his or her unique local narratives, the worker also provides bricks in the form of other stories or suggestions, and the known principles, assumptions and disciplines provide the mortar that holds the bricks in the wall. No two walls/solutions will ever be the same and we cannot tell what any particular solution will look like until it is built, though they may be built in a similar manner. After all, a basic assumption is that the service users have the resources that are needed and also know how to get what they want, but it is only by talking it do they get to know what they know. How exactly that process of 'linguistic production' (Held, 1995, p. 194) works will be very difficult to study since it is in part the work of service users and it makes every outcome unique. We feel, however, that the studies presented above show that positive outcomes can be demonstrated. A recent case we have been involved with in a supervisory capacity helps to show this. There was a boy of 10 years who had a serious problem with soiling. He was on medication and had various sorts of interventions that had not worked. Our colleague externalised the problem and the boy chose the name Poo Pants (à la Michael White). During a discussion about the problem's tactics and about various ways of defeating it, it was mentioned by the boy that Poo Pants was afraid of the dark and that while it liked white toilet paper it was afraid of green paper. His parents agreed to buy green paper and to become generally more playful about the problem even though they had begun to think that their son and the worker were both a little mad! Next week the boy reported that the green paper had worked and he had not soiled since the previous session. How did that work? The narrative was mostly fictitious! We suggest that this linguistic production had some extralinguistic reality embedded in it, that it helped to develop an experience of competence and power for dealing with the problem and that that experience, which involved some personal agency, paved the way for the boy to opt for taking control and for a behavioural change to happen. This is a theoretic explanation and there may be others just as reasonable. Some of the materials in the 'wall' were fictional but the solution was real enough. That they were fictional does not matter; so long as they made change seem possible they opened the door to 'change-land'.

When Bill O'Hanlon is asked if his *possibility* approach works he replies 'That's a tough one, partly because measuring the effectiveness is like nailing jelly to a tree. It's a slippery business' (O'Hanlon's web-site, 1998). He goes on to explain that there is also disagreement as to what is a good outcome or what is a reliable measure. He only has his experiences to present; clients usually end contact reporting satisfaction, so his impression is that it works. That too is the experience of Judith Milner (personal communication) who uses the constructive approach, working in Yorkshire with people of all ages who have been abused.

Does it address emotions?

Some critics ask 'Does it sufficiently address emotions?' and 'Are workers not responsible for being sympathetic to people's feelings?' Gale Miller, in a recent Internet paper 'Mind your Language', suggests that the best answers to these questions draw our attention to taken-for-granted assumptions involving the use of language. One assumption is that emotions exist independent of social context and our use of language. We assume that love, grief and anger are labels for realities (feelings) that exist separately from how we use these words. This helps us make sense of occasions when we feel 'overcome' by emotions that 'swell up inside us' or 'spill over' in tears, so that they are experienced as beyond our control. While such experiences are authentic, they do not explain themselves – that requires placing them in their social context. In our culture we define some events, such as a funeral, as 'emotional', and others, such as shopping, as non-emotional. We sometimes describe service users as 'showing appropriate affect' or not. Likewise, some workers look for emotions more than others. Miller believes therefore that we need to regard emotions as an ever-present aspect of our relationships with service users. Some will show tears in their dealings with us and some will not. These are simply different ways of being involved with the service, and with the activities of various meetings, and the different ways language is used by both parties. Emotions therefore are regarded as belonging to the context, rather than being 'internal' to some people. In any case how do we know other people's emotions, if not by our interpretation of behaviours, rather than by directly entering their heads?

Regarding emotions as ever-present in this way means that they are never disregarded but they are seen as context produced and based on interpretations rather than internal things that we 'get to', and it is enough for us to be competent observers of human behaviour and culturally competent at interpretation. Taking this approach, we than ask 'Are the emotions I am "seeing" useful in solving problems?' and 'Must all emotions be responded to in this way?', or 'What other options are there for responding?' Some believe that talking about a feeling makes it more stable, so perhaps we need to carefully elect which ones to talk about. Emotions that are shown physically need to be acknowledged since they are non-verbal communications; all emotions are to be validated but constructive approaches move on as soon as possible from emotion-talk to action-talk, as the more helpful progressive way of getting to a goal.

Is constructive practice gender-sensitive?

In setting out and developing our ideas about *constructive social work* we have been very conscious of whether and how our own 'storied' lives influence what we say, particularly our maleness and the impact of gender on the work. Many of the approaches we have drawn on *appear* to be gender neutral. In this regard Freeman *et al.* (1997) argue that it is important to examine how narratives are shaped by sociocultural biases and stereotypes. 'We need to examine our own biases, agendas and values and make them available for comment by our clients, colleagues and ourselves. Our collaborative aim is to explore the dilemmas that silence and separate us ... instead of lecturing about right and wrong, we can externalise the effects and operation of "isms" so the personal misery and social alienation they promote can be seen more clearly' (pp. 56–7). This leads them to develop useful ways for reducing women's and children's sense of helplessness. They propose, for example, a moratorium on mother-blaming by selecting facts that contradict self-accusation, or encouraging children to adjust their roles by consulting them as authorities in their own lives. When children discover their own solutions to problems, they are asked for their permission for this new knowledge to be used in helping others.

We would expect that women workers would be more likely to use the narrative approach with female service users as it offers a clear potential to include gender, sexual orientation, ethnicity and class. Yet this is not always the case. Milner (2000) found that narrative approaches, especially the externalisation of problems, fitted well with young males' perceptions. With young women who had internalised their problems, she found that the seemingly neutral solution-focused approach yielded better results in promoting self-growth and confidence. This may seem a paradox.

Clearly Milner is able to 'stay near' to the women with whom she works but it is not so easy to identify exactly what is different about this. The first step in understanding her style is to examine how she 'gets up close'. Firstly she makes her values explicit – for example a comment to a young woman who wanted to understand her partner's problems so that he would not beat her, that she does not consider it her job, as a woman who cares about women, to help her become a better-adjusted battered wife. She is also explicit about her view that giving evidence in court is a largely dangerous and demeaning strategy (see Lees, 1997) yet she supports young women who wish to take that action. Of great interest are the explicit comments showing how she actualises empathy in a particularly female way. According to Madge (1997), sympathetically receiving disclosures helps to recover resilience and so women workers may interject comments about the abuser during the telling of the abuse story. They are not neutral and service users respond with some initial surprise and then delight. There may be strong conversations about what they would like to do to abusers and this seems to be helpful in expressing anger about what was done to them. Milner has a predilection for a kind of humour that uses creative craziness. Abuse, she says, is too serious to be always taken solemnly and women enjoy having a laugh with her about terribly serious events. Women laughing about men is, in her view, a particularly womanly thing which a male worker would find rather difficult.

Dermer *et al.* (1998) suggest that feminist-informed practice supports women by encouraging them to connect with each other through groups, but this is to assume that they will 'naturally' find a consensus. But many women's preferred solutions are much more complex than this. The example is given of a young woman who sought help in coming to terms with sexual abuse by her father when she was a young child. Initially the work addressed her feelings of self-blame and various conflicting emotions about her father who appeared to be a good parent in other ways, but then it was discovered that he had abused all her sisters as well. When they linked together to share experiences, they each expressed different views, particularly about future action. One wanted him to be prosecuted, another merely wanted the police informed in order to protect other children, a third felt sorry for him and hoped to get treatment for him, and the fourth had difficulty in even acknowledging what he had done. Workers therefore need to address all these competing senses of personal responsibility, rights and wishes. Each one's story has validity and personal meaning and cannot be subsumed under any one agenda/umbrella, other than safety and personal control of one's own life. 'The personal may well be political but it is extremely complicated' (Milner, 2000).

Alice Walker (1983) developed the idea of 'womanist'. 'Womanly' could also be used to describe work with women who perhaps may need to reclaim their girlhoods in various small ways; for example, 'giving permission' for a woman to have girly nights with friends or spend one day a week being a teenager again can be a way of learning to like other women as adults, and thence herself.

The literature on solution-focused and narrative work does raise questions about practice that suggest that women's ways of dealing with solutions are different. In writing about alcohol-abuse work, Berg and Reuss (1998) challenge the male professional domination of this area and they add that 'many clinical indicators show that women are not comfortable with the conventional treatment approaches and prefer approaches that appeal to women's ways of problem solving' (p. 151). Berg claims that women tend to hide their misuse of substances, internalise their problems, are devastated by the destruction of relationships and self-esteem, have a sense of lack of control over their lives, a tendency towards self-blame, often take unrealistic responsibility for problems and feel vulnerable when making decisions. So she seeks to be conciliatory rather than confrontational, paying attention to personal issues and their personal meaning to women, as she builds consensus and negotiates goals. She uses a more tentative language so that women can more easily challenge her. For example, 'Some women tell me that they feel like . . . Is that how it is for you, or is it different?', 'I wonder . . .', 'Perhaps . . .' This reinforces the idea that the woman is unique and that her individual feelings are valid.

Lethem (1994) writes that the accomplishments of women may seem modest unless account is taken of the adverse circumstances in which they have occurred, and therefore it is particularly important to acknowledge this and to clarify what is and what is not within an individual's control. A helpful way to acknowledge achievements is to use the recovery charts in the appendices of this book. These reflect the components of resilience, thinking positively, having supports, underlining successes and becoming stronger women. Women can be helped, using this set of ideas, to re-story their lives in ways that enable them to respond differently to the oppressions they face. But because these oppressions undermine women and destroy their creativity, Milner (2000) maintains that they often need a 'kick start' in one or more of the following five ways.

Safety and control. Where one suspects that a woman is at risk, one can unilaterally 'put safety at the top of the agenda' (George *et al.*, 1990). Berg (1994) places the safety of children at the top of her agenda in her work on family preservation, by asking 'What could you truthfully tell social services which would convince them that safety is present in your home?' Assessing the capacity for safety, rather than predicting risk, has proved a useful way of incorporating child protection issues into work that remains woman-centred yet does not ignore the reality that children are more vulnerable than mothers in some situations. Violence shatters a person's illusion of safety; many women's lives are not very safe, and therefore exploring what control is reasonable can be a sound starting point, perhaps beginning by helping the person to gain control of his or her own thoughts and feelings.

Women reclaiming their bodies. Women who have been sexually abused often seem to dissociate from their bodies in various ways. Their seemingly reckless promiscuity and self-harm is most puzzling for their families. Dolan (1991) maintains that such women need to be helped to regain a sense of control over their bodies, but adds that this is 'a delicate step' for the worker and that 'it is imperative that the client feel not intruded on, lest the invasive aspects of the original trauma be symbolically re-enacted' (p. 165). She suggests that we follow the woman's easiest path, usually asking her about the times when she *does* experience feelings in her body.

Self-blame. A common theme in the lives of girls and women is that they take an unreasonable amount of responsibility for what has happened to them. They seem to internalise the violence as a relationship failure, even when the trauma happened in childhood. This not only relates to how women are socialised to take responsibility for relationships but also to the discourse about mothers, who are expected to love and nurture even in extreme adversity. They are often exercised by the question 'why me?', and we would suggest that a useful response is 'Which would be the more useful for you – to find out why or to get better?' Most opt for getting better, though it is possible to explore, in an externalising way, how they were 'recruited' into their problem. We can discuss the dominant discourse about mother love and how we have no choice about the family we are born into – in this story the parents we are given is a matter of good or bad luck and the plot is thickened by the way in which children are not allowed to dislike their lot. Where only one child in a family has been abused they are more likely to think there must have been something wrong with them or that they must have done something bad. Other questions may be 'Why did my mother not protect me?' or 'Why did she prefer my father to me?'

Challenging psychiatry. Women of all ages frequently complain of depression. As *constructive social workers* we have a problem with this as we feel it is a story imposed on people by a discourse based on pathology being the explanation of problems and expertise being required to diagnose and treat them. Even if such treatment works the person is left in a dependent role, still unable to have control of their own life. Addiction to Prozac is only another kind of misery; urges may be muffled but one can still be out of touch with one's body. As Furman and Ahola (1992) say, these diagnoses can become self-verifying and 'watchful wording' is needed to develop an alternative story of self-control. For example they use the words 'searching for a life direction' rather than 'borderline personality disorder'. Smith *et al.* (1998) say that diagnostic labels invalidate the means which people have found to communicate extremely painful issues which cannot be spoken of openly. Therefore psychiatric expertise needs to be challenged. Berg and Reuss (1998) suggest questions like 'What are you doing to make the medication work for you?' or 'What per cent (of progress) is the medication working for you; what percent is you helping yourself?'

Valuing oneself. Most of the referrers of the young women suggest that poor self-esteem is the problem. Self-esteem can be said to be a complex notion that includes self-concept, self-image and self-achievement. 'Selflessness' may be a more useful way of looking at this as it includes the wider effects of socialisation and of self-blaming. To help women get in touch with their authentic selves, Dolan (1998) has a range of useful exercises which can be adapted to the individual preferences of each woman. These involve tasks that require the woman to spend time on herself. It usually takes time for oppressed women to get used to this. As one woman said, 'I didn't take it all that seriously at first; I thought you were just being nice. But it built up and it made me realise that I am worth a treat.' Treats and pampering tasks, 'bed-room therapy', and 'comfort contingencies' for panic attacks can be an important part of 'womanly' work with women.

These ways of working are developed by *constructive* women workers; perhaps the underlying philosophy of the *constructive* approach to practice can help men to be more gender-sensitive, though high-quality womanly work will probably remain difficult for them especially where the person has been oppressed by men.

Conclusion

While we have demonstrated that various *constructive* approaches are effective, it is not our aim to argue for the development of these approaches on the bases of traditional evaluation criteria alone. Rather, we invite the reader to consider the new possibilities offered by *constructive practice* and to do their own comparisons with other approaches. Similarly while the emphasis is on narra-tive, talk and solutions, this does not mean that emotions are not taken into account.

We have attempted to address the question of gender and there is a number of other issues which we have touched on in this chapter, to which we will return in Chapter 10.

10

Conclusions: Some Central Issues for Constructive Social Work

> Whether it is pursuing a strengths perspective or other like developments in social work, we will see that our work is part of a larger intellectual landscape where head and heart form a new relationship. In moving beyond modernism, we may indeed discover the wise and deeply moral seedbed that has been with social work all along. (Weick and Saleeby, 1998, p. 38)

In outlining our *constructive* approach to practice we have argued that perspectives which draw upon constructionist, solution-focused and narrative approaches are particularly relevant at the current time and provide the basis for theories *for* practice which are relevant and useful. In doing so, however, we are very aware that some of what we have argued is contentious and that there are a number of overarching issues which we need to address. It is to these we turn in this final chapter. In doing so we aim to bring together some of the central themes which we feel characterise *constructive social work*.

Objectivity, realism and relativism

While there are numerous interpretations of what is meant by 'postmodern' perspectives we have suggested that a central assumption is that social and cultural realities are seen as linguistic constructions. Not only are individuals and the wider society seen as a series of texts, but scientific texts themselves are seen as

170

rhetorical enactments, with no ultimate logical or empirical warrant. In such a view, the distinctions between fact and fiction become blurred, as both are seen as products of and resources for communicative action.

As we argued in Chapter 1, social theory has been littered with terms such as late-modern, post-industrial, and post-traditional to point to a range of social, political and cultural shifts which are seen to have diverse but important implications for the way we understand the nature of contemporary society, knowledge, and identity. Perhaps more than any other it is the term 'postmodern' which is seen to capture the nature of these shifts and which has been subject to a range of heated and critical debates. The encroachment of anything associated with 'postmodernism' into social work is seen by many to be potentially dangerous. In particular, critics see in 'postmodernity' the triumph of relativism and nihilism, the collapse of standards and ideals, the loss of a vision of human progress and hence a failure to engage with serious debates about what to *do* in any practical sense. Quite understandably these are issues which have troubled those in social work (Gray, 1995; Campbell and Pinkerton, 1997; Pugh, 1997; Peile and MacCourt, 1997; Smith and White, 1997; Munro, 1998). Thus while some commentators may accept that some of the techniques we have outlined may have some attraction they may be unhappy at the overall philosophy and its implications.

Some of these concerns have been clearly articulated by Michael Sheppard (1998) who argues that the introduction of social constructionism and 'postmodernism' into theories *for* practice leads to an 'unrestrained moral relativism' (p. 775) and fails to take into account the practical roles and responsibilities that go with being a social worker. In particular, Sheppard argues that such approaches fail to recognise '*the definition of the phenomena* with which social work is concerned. Here there is a *core of objectivism*. Certain key areas of practice are deemed to have an objective reality, in particular that areas like child abuse and mental illness have a real existence, independent of our perceptions of them' (p. 771, original emphasis). These are clearly major issues for practitioners. How is it possible to develop a form of practice which draws heavily on constructionist and narrative approaches which does not fall into a relativism which does not recognise any reality beyond whatever we (subjectively) define it as?

The first point to note is that issues such as child abuse are not as objectively given, as Sheppard argues, for numerous researchers have now demonstrated that cases of child abuse have to be interpreted, defined and categorised every time they are potentially made available (Dingwall, Eekelaar and Murray, 1983; Parton, Thorpe and Wattam, 1997). But does this mean that cases of child abuse are neither real nor objective? Does this mean there is no reality outside language and does it mean we have to abandon any attempts at objectivity? Similarly, how is it possible to argue that values are central to what we do when it seems inappropriate to set down any categorical set of standards? These are clearly important issues. How we understand them has important implications for practice, and important if *constructive social work* is to be taken seriously.

At the outset it is worth defining some key terms. We take *objectivism* to mean that family of philosophical positions that assume the existence of some ahistorical framework to which we can appeal in deciding on what is objectively rational, true, good and so on. More particularly, objectivism assumes there are truths that exist independently of human wishes and beliefs, and that there are justifiable ways of establishing these foundational truths (Smith, 1997). Such a position is thoroughly consistent with the modern, technical-rational approach we discussed in Chapter 2. In contrast, *subjectivism* asserts that it is subjective experience that is the sole foundation of factual knowledge; while *relativism* is usually taken to mean any position that denies the possibility of any foundationalist framework, and asserts that we cannot get beyond conceptual frameworks, language games, theoretical assumptions and so on. In this respect relativism is often seen as a key assumption of not only 'postmodernism' but also constructionism and that as a result constructionism is also anti-real. As we will argue, however, this is not necessarily so and is not consistent with our position. While we are critical of a *naïve realism* and would want to encourage an approach which *problematises* reality, this is not the same as being anti-real and thus cannot be accused of nihilism and moral relativism. The point we want to demonstrate is that while we construct the world we are not arguing that *any* construction is as good as any other, and the reason for this is that there is a world 'out there' which influences and constrains. In this respect there are aspects of reality which are independent of our experiences, ideas, wishes and language. Such a position can be understood as a *minimal* or *subtle realism* as opposed to a *naïve realism* (Hammersley, 1992). This does not imply any particular theory of truth nor does it depart from the view that facts are theory laden. But it does move us into a much better way of understanding the way constructions and reality and the subjective and objective are related.

As we have seen, while the approaches associated with constructionism cover a diverse field, they do have a number of apparently quite common epistemological and ontological commitments. Constructionism generally endorses an anti-objectivist, anti-foundationalist view of knowledge. That is, knowledge of reality is not seen to be simply a matter of 'taking a look' at the 'facts' of the world in order to identify the degree of correspondence of those facts with our thoughts or beliefs – whether this be by direct perception or via representation. It is this naïve realism which constructionism reacts against. Such an approach is quite inadequate for not only does it fail to recognise that all perception and observation is assumption-laden but that we actively construct the world in the process of looking and articulating. It is in this respect that 'there is nothing outside the text' or language.

Constructionist approaches to knowledge therefore see it as proactive and anticipatory in that it is radically undetermined by the sensory stimulation we receive from the world. As such it is much more concerned with *meaning* than objective propositions about reality. Constructionism posits a proactive view of the person who struggles for and creates meaning via action in the world. Reality is assumed to have an 'error tolerance' (Noaparast, 1995) which allows for a variety of competing hypotheses and constructions. However, where this 'error tolerance' is exceeded, where the world says 'no' to our constructions, we appear to experience our most direct contact with the world. It seems we are not so much told what to think, as what not to think. It is in this respect that reality – whether it be biological, physical, material or social – can be seen to be constraining. In this sense, then, we cannot assume that any construction is as good as any other. While there are many possibilities, some may not be useful and some are likely to be more helpful than others. The way these are established is not just by reconstructing and re-storying but by using new constructions and stories to change and reconfigure the world. The way reality is constructed and reconstructed is an active process and reality is itself actively involved.

What is important is not just what language *means* but what language *does* – what it enables human beings to imagine and to do, both to themselves and to others. It is important to recognise that language, while key, is connected to and integrated with other technologies that make human beings capable of being and doing particular things.

As Held (1995) has demonstrated, the behavioural enactments that result from the new meanings/narratives/constructions developed by the service user refer to some extralinguistic or real events including those behavioural enactments themselves and their effects – they are not *merely* narrative reconstructions. In this respect it is important to recognise that a minimal or subtle realism is at play in any constructionism which aims to make itself practical.

If reality were exclusively structured and given form by our (re)constructions, then why should we ever be invalidated, shocked or surprised? The answer must be that there are discernible properties in the world and in our bodies independent of our constructions and which therefore impact on us – but not in any direct or uni-causal way. We are not so much shaped by events as shaped by the meaning we ascribe to outside 'noise'. This is not to say we can ignore what is going on but it is to recognise we can (re)construe it in a wide range of ways.

It is in this sense that reality, metaphorically speaking, has a 'voice' in the dialectic conversation we experience as living. We cannot experience whatever we like – and in this respect possibilities are not limitless. For example, if we choose to conceive of a wall as permeable and then attempt to walk through it, we can anticipate that the wall will resist. The world places limits on our constructions and its 'voice' is always evident if only in the background. This does not mean, however, we have to fall back on a dualistic separation of the world and the person, the objective and the subjective, or the real and the constructed. Each is embedded in the other. It also demonstrates that it is workers' and service users' social constructions of the real which should be the focus of our attention.

These issues are nicely illustrated in Gibson's (1979) discussion of affordances. *Affordances* refer to the possible uses of what is picked up in the environment. Surfaces are perceived as exhibiting certain possibilities for action such as picking up, for grasping, for walking on and so on. Such a notion not only accounts for the fundamental intentionality of our perceiving, but also accounts for the inherent meaningfulness in our relations with the environment. Thus meaningfulness is simultaneously co-specified by person and world. However, Gibson firmly locates these affordances in the (external) world. While this helps us understand why we do not attempt to walk through walls it does not help us to account for how we relate to social and cultural objects. Noble's (1991) discussion of the affordances of a mailbox is important here in developing the idea further for, as he argues, it is one thing to point out that a mailbox manifests affordances such as containership (in the purely physical sense) but quite another thing to explain the social usage of a mailbox. For example, the American mailbox, to the British eye, looks remarkably like a litter bin. As he argues, we are no longer dealing with the world of directly accessible affordances because we are dealing with objects, like mailboxes, that are socially sustained:

> We have now to lay down prerequisites for the perceiving of affordances and these prerequisites have to do with the cooperative linguistic community that symbolically invests and sustains objects and their affordances ... In the human community there just is a vast proportion of perceptual experience that is sustained by cultural rule – given prerequisites ... the relationship between persons and objects is now complexly mediated by a normative structure that is not connected with the visible affordances of objects per se. (Noble, 1991, p. 208)

What this quote underlines is, firstly, that affordances do not simply inhere in some object 'out there', but rather inhere in the relation of the person and the environment. Secondly it demonstrates that the nature of an object is not intrinsic to itself but depends on it being socially constructed that way. As Noble argues, ' "objects" are *realised*, they do not pre-exist' (Noble, 1991 p. 215, original emphasis). In this way we cannot separate the world from how it is constructed, nor can we assume that our constructions are not influenced by a world 'out there'. It is thus not possible to separate the person from her his world. This recognition of encompassing, unavoidable and intimate constraints of the world not only allows us to recognise the importance of realities which are endemic to social work such as poverty, deprivation and exploitation but also ensure we are not swallowed up by an anarchic relativism. Put simply, we are forced to recognise that any construction is not as good as any other.

Bill Warren (1994; 1998) has provided a very helpful way of understanding why constructionism and a minimal or subtle realism are not irreconcilable and why the concepts of *subjecting* and *objecting* are far superior to subjectivity and objectivity, and thus why we do not have to slip into mindless relativism. Following Deutscher (1983), he argues that it is important to replace the verbs *objecting* and *subjecting* for the nouns 'objectivity' and 'subjectivity' in order to capture the *process* and *activity* of what is involved. For *subjecting* and *objecting* are things we *do* and not states we achieve. In this context objectivity, or at least striving for objectivity, appears as much a focus of our actions in and on the world, as does subjectivity appear to characterise those same actions. Objectivity is thus better understood as 'disinterested interest' (1983, p. 54) – an interest in finding out how things work by reference to those things themselves, rather than with reference to how we would like them to work. It is consistent with the concept of objectivity suggested by Barbu (1956) in his discussion of the democratic mentality. By objectivity Barbu was referring to the capacity we have to be aware that we are governed by a variety of internal and external forces, and that it is this ability to balance the often contradictory elements of this complexity that displays the 'objective frame of mind'. Barbu characterises objectivity in terms of the individual's ability to look at the world through 'the categories of otherness, multiplicity, and formal relationship' (1956, p. 77). The most important of these is the capacity to understand another person, the non-self, or perhaps more significantly for us, the non-identical as having its own reasons for its existence within itself.

As Warren (1998) argues, we do not 'just dialogue', we dialogue about something as the object of our attention or interests. Such dialogue, with others, presumes a rich background of shared experiences. As individuals we seek to understand and make sense of our individual and social situations. In this striving we are always 'interested' in that our striving is always for a purpose and is thus always *subjective*. By definition we as individuals are never 'disinterested' and cannot escape our involvement in life and our attempts to understand and make it meaningful. It is in this sense that we construct the world. In doing so, however, we seek a degree of understanding that transcends ourselves – that transcends our *mere* subjectivity. When we attempt to convert objectivity into objectivism, in effect we *claim* a once-and-for-all 'complete' understanding: that is, we attempt or assume closure on the issue. In doing so, however, we have subverted our own subjectivity and our quest for understanding. What we have to recognise is that our attempt to pursue objectivity *arises from* our fundamental subjectivity and is not the antithesis of it.

We are arguing then that while we all start with an epistemological and ethical subjectivity we strive for and, in part, achieve objectivity in the sense of being able to recognise 'otherness'. However, it is important to stress that this is a *process* and not a *state* and hence is potentially forever changing and developing. In striving for objectivity we are striving beyond our *mere* subjectivity. In many respects it is this which is key to understanding 'what it means to be human'.

Constructionism can be understood, therefore, as an approach that tries to advance us in our 'objecting'. It aims to demonstrate how we, and others, subjectively construct more and more meaningful ways of objectively understanding who, what and where we are and how this might be otherwise. In this sense, constructionism is far from being anti-real and lost in *mere* subjectivism and unending relativism. Certainly the way we understand and use constructions does accept and assert there is a 'world out there' but that we have more freedom to interpret, construct and re-construct it than we may recognise. As we have tried to demonstrate, while there is room for manoeuvre the possibilities are not endless. Some constructions and stories simply will not 'work' if they are capricious. Constructions are tested out and validated 'in the world', which includes relationships with others, and it is as naïve to assume that one construction is as good as any other as it is to assume there is a reality which is readily discoverable and that there are foundational truths which can or should inform our actions. Our relationship with the world is more complex.

We also recognise that there is a danger of assuming that everyone is equally capable of redefining and reconstructing their own lives. Most of the people who come the way of social workers simply do not have the opportunity to free themselves from the implications of being located in certain key structures and oppressions related to class, age, gender, ethnicity, and disability. Material resources and structures of power do not disappear.

Thus, what we are suggesting is not that we should take up a position which is anti-real but one which continually problematises and questions what is taken for granted and hence tries to open up creative ways of thinking and acting. The focus is the human being's continual attempt to make sense of and change the world and the central role played in this by talk and language. The active agency of the individual in their social/relational contexts is prioritised. That there is a world to be made sense of is not in doubt – but how, ultimately, we make sense of the world is intimately related to the way the world turns out to be, but, not only is this complex but it remains, and is likely to remain, an open question.

Moral responsibility, truth and social work

It may still be argued, however, that such an approach is far from helpful in providing clear standards or goals by which social workers can make decisions and that it denies that values and morals play a part in practice. While we have tried to demonstrate that particular notions of objectivity and the real world are key to the approach, the way these are understood, it may be argued, does not help the practitioner rediscover their civic role. As we will demonstrate, however, this is not the case. Far from denying the ethical and moral dimensions of the work, it makes them central.

A key part of our argument from the outset has been that social work is a moral activity and that constructionist approaches to practice make this even more explicit and pervasive. However, it is a particular notion of morality and one which we see as very relevant to the uncertain times in which we live and the inherent ambiguity which we see as lying at the core of social work.

Zygmunt Bauman (1993; 1995; 1997) is the social theorist who has become most closely associated with the analysis of 'postmodernity' and the articulation of the place of values and ethics in contemporary times. His work challenges not only the assertion of many critics that perspectives which draw on 'postmodernism' abdicate morality, responsibility and values, but also the broader concerns that ordinary people are increasingly in a moral vacuum which needs to be filled with clear and simple moral rules and certainties.

In a paper in 1998 he outlines two stories from the Bible which he feels capture the two main alternatives that have been offered throughout history to account for the nature and explanation of morality (Bauman, 1998). The subject of the first story is the expulsion from the Garden of Eden. Before their expulsion Adam and Eve were not given any instructions or advice on how to live or what to choose, nor did they know that acts could be good or evil, as the words 'good' and 'not good' only appeared in the mind of God. Once they ate from the Tree of Knowledge this was to change, but unlike God they lacked divine omnipotence and omniscience and could thus make mistakes, take wrong decisions, and mistake good for evil. According to Bauman this is 'how they become *moral* persons – persons to whom things appear as either good or bad and who can pick either of them' (p. 12, original emphasis).

Bauman's second story is that of the law-giving act on Mount Sinai. 'When all the people saw how it thundered and the lightning flashed, when they heard the trumpet sound and saw the mountain smoking, they trembled and stood at a distance.' When Moses told the people they should follow the Law that the Lord announced, they answered that 'whatever the Lord said we will do' and the Lord spelt out in considerable detail what they should do and what they should refrain from doing. Having spelled out everything that would become the Law from then on the Lord commanded the people to follow his commandments and statutes as they were written but if they did not listen or bowed down to other gods, they would perish. If they did what God told them they would be good and if they did not they would be evil. For obedience they would be rewarded and for disobedience punished.

According to Bauman these two stories tell us what morality is about and what it means to be moral. The first story suggests that to be moral is to face a choice between good and evil, and to know that there is such a choice and to make choices with that knowledge. In contrast, the second story implies that to be moral is to follow strictly the command – to obey unconditionally and never to deviate either in deed or thought. The first story presents morality as a cruel predicament, eternal uncertainty and perpetual agony, while the second story presents morality as obedience to the Law and conformity. According to Bauman the social transformations associated with 'postmodernity' have laid bare the incurable uncertainty and ambivalence of the human condition, which are so central to the first story. For Bauman the loss of certainties means we can become fully moral, not amoral – the moment of 'post-modernity' is not an amoral moment but the opportunity to become fully moral. No longer can we hide behind rules and assume that our obedience makes us good. However, in refusing to hide behind the rules we are fully exposed to the anguish of responsibility and the consequences of our choices.

Following Bauman, this kind of uncertainty and ambivalence marks the key difference between *moral responsibility* and *contractual obligation*. The latter strives to be well defined and is convinced that the task of being precisely defined is feasible, while the state of being so defined is an ideal state to be in.

Further, Bauman argues that 'moral responsibility tends to grow in such situations in which contractual obligation tends to shrink, and vice versa' (1998, p. 19). It is the weakness of the Other which makes me responsible. It is the strength of the Other that makes me obliged. One is obliged towards the strong. One is responsible for the weak. We would argue that this captures the essential morality which lies at the heart of social work such that moves over recent years to proceduralise, contractualise and legalise not only fail to recognise its nature and core strength, but are in danger of undermining it altogether. This is perhaps even clearer in the following quote from Bauman:

> To put it yet another way: moral responsibility soars up in the face of an Other, who due to her powerlessness is incapable of supporting her welfare by soliciting on her own the obligatory and unforceable duties from other people; and reaches yet greater heights if the Other is too weak to render her needs visible and demands audible. *The weakness of the Other makes me powerful*: everything depends then on *my* taking up the responsibility and giving voice to the unspoken demand. I am literally responsible for the life and death of such Other; the difference between my assuming the responsibility and rejecting it is that between life and death. (Bauman, 1998, p. 19, original emphasis)

Bauman argues that the greatest paradox is that the greater the moral responsibility, the dimmer is the hope of its normative regulation and the more we need to act, the less we know what we ought to be doing. While it may be easy to spell out the guidelines and norms for insignificant responsibilities this is not so with larger responsibilities. For the larger the responsibility to be taken, the less sure we are of what taking up that responsibility would need to consist of.

He concludes with a statement which not only captures what we see as the core of social work but which is central to this book:

> Ambivalence is the only soil in which morality can grow and the only territory in which the moral self can act on its responsibility or hear the voice of the unspoken demand. In its unstoppable search for the meaning of unspoken demand and unconditional responsibility, the moral self will never reach the certainty it aims at; yet only while seeking such certainty can the self become and stay moral. (Bauman, 1995, p. 22)

There are clear parallels here in the way morality is understood and the way we have previously discussed objectivity and reality, subjectivity and relativism. In particular, those who get accused of being relativists do so because it is assumed they are arguing that every belief on a topic is as good as any other – however, Rorty suggests no one holds this view. 'The philosophers who get *called* relativists are those who say that the grounds for choosing between opinions are less algorithmic than had been thought' (Rorty, 1980, p. 728, original emphasis). As Sue White (1998) points out, it is usually inappropriate to rely on 'algorithmic' means to justify knowledge claims which are generated by some procedure which purports to be sure and certain and thereby is assumed to guarantee validity. All we do is shut down discussion and debate and thus increase the likelihood of inappropriate choices. The problem thus becomes not one of relativism but of trying to ensure we embrace and value dialogue, argument and discussion and thereby analyse in detail what might be competing or contradictory points of view.

These issues are further illustrated by Bhaskar (1979) who distinguishes between *epistemic relativism* and *judgmental relativism*. *Epistemic relativism* asserts that all knowledge emerges from and is shaped by its particular historical and social circumstances and that there is therefore no 'pure data' which is describable 'extra-linguistically' (Barnes and Law, 1976; Collins, 1983). However, *judgmental relativism* goes further and asserts that because all forms of knowledge are epistemically relative all are equally valid or invalid. Because they are all embedded in local historical, social and linguistic practices we cannot compare different forms of knowledge and discriminate between them. However, as Bhaskar argues, the assertions of judgmental relativism do not necessarily follow from the position of epistemological relativism. Indeed, in some respects the two are in opposition. First, judgmental relativism assumes that standards must be absolute or universal to be valid, whereas epistemological relativism identifies alternative forms of valid knowledge. Second, epistemological relativism is a stance one may assume when *talking about* forms of knowledge. But this is different from, and quite inappropriate, when *actually using* them. Thus the fact that an explanatory category or form of knowledge can be analysed *theoretically*, does not count, by itself, as a criticism of the *usability* of that category or knowledge (Collins, 1983, p. 101). The epistemological relativism implied in the former does not necessarily justify a judgmental relativism about the latter. What such discussions demonstrate is that not only are ethics central to making judgments but that the complexities involved cannot be avoided in any formulaic or straightforward way.

Logic, reason and ethics are brought down from their absolute, pre-existent heights into the creative, contextual web of day-to-day action and decision making. It suggests we shift from a conception of truth as *discovery* to a conception of truth as *process*, or put another way, we should focus on the *how* rather than the *what* of truth and virtue. In this sense any practice that attempts to claim a constructionist approach will be inherently *reflexive* – for the *what* of any system of knowledge and value is entangled in the *how* of its writing and speaking.

The issue becomes less *whether* there is truth, reality or virtue independent of accounts of it, but *how* such accounts are made adequate for their respective purposes and practices. Not only does it acknowledge the tension between the reflection of reality *in* language and the constitution of reality *by* language but also that morality and responsibility are implied on each and every occasion we think and act. It is a concern with the question of the moral responsibility for the Other which is at the heart of the 'postmodern' ethics outlined by Bauman and which we would argue has from the beginning been at the heart of social work (Horne, 1987; Jordan, 1990).

Allen (1993) has argued strongly that adopting a constructionist approach ensures that an awareness of values and ethics becomes central. Following Keeney (1985), she argues that it is important to move from a position of objectivism to one of responsibility where the worker acknowledges the active role they play in creating a view of the world and interpreting it. The hallmark of ethical practice is that we are reflexive and embark on a process which is mindful, respectful and aims to empower. The ethic of responsibility positions the worker as a non-expert who tries to open up a space for conversation whereby the user can actively redefine themselves, their problems and their preferred solutions. Dialogue and collaboration are key. The social work values of respect, self-determination and working from where the client is, are very consistent with such an approach. But rather than see individuals as isolated and atomistic it emphasises connectedness and relatedness.

Constructive social work: the key characteristics

What we have tried to demonstrate in this book is that constructive and narrative approaches to practice very much build on the long traditions of understanding the substance of *process* in social work, and we have tried to demonstrate that real outcomes are constructed in the process of talk and narrative. *Social work can be conceptualised as a narrative process with real outcomes.*

Traditionally, social workers have been, in practical terms, experts on process. However, this is in great danger of being lost to very deleterious effect. Yet social workers: know how to establish relationships with a wide variety of people needing services; can survey the environment for material resources and bring those resources together on behalf of clients; work with considerable skill in negotiating human systems, whether individual, family, workplace, neighbourhoods or communities, and mobilise the energies of these entities in constructive action; and are able to enter other worlds of meaning in order to offer help. These are all areas of expertise which have previously been commonplace among social workers but, we would suggest, the theory which informs such an approach has not been well articulated and, crucially, developed and refined in ways which address the challenges of our changing times. We feel that the major strength of explicitly drawing on constructionist and narrative perspectives for practice is that they provide a vocabulary for understanding and using the substance of process.

As we have argued, the constructionist approach does not privilege professional, disciplinary or expert knowledge over clients' knowledge. On the contrary, a person's knowledge of his or her experience (local knowledge) is viewed as an essential element of the work. In order to understand a human situation we must go to the actors themselves and the act of telling their stories not only becomes the focus of the work but a central way in which their situation can be improved. Such stories should not be diminished by the imposition of categories imported from an external, perhaps professional or organisational, world. Diagnostic labels, for example, as a primary form of categorisation, are seen as a means of reinterpreting clients' reality and taking control of their story and which are likely to reduce their sense of competence and confidence. In the constructive approach professionals bring their own knowledge to the helping situation but that knowledge is not accorded more authority than the person's own knowledge. Rather the social worker's investment in process is to assist people in identifying resources and opportunities which may have been hidden from them or framed in ways which were not helpful. In this view, a social work relationship is a partnership, with each party bringing something of value to the conversations. *A constructive approach emphasises process, plurality of both knowledge and voice, possibility and the relational quality of knowledge.*

Such an approach assumes that people, no matter what their circumstances, have significant resources within and around them but the way these are 'storied' is key to opening up new and more positive possibilities. Because social workers are experts in process, they can help people focus these resources to assist them best in accomplishing their goals and re-storying their situations. The social worker does not presume to know what is best and what to do. An ability to work with ambiguity and uncertainty both in terms of process and outcomes is key. The principle of indeterminacy suggests the fluid, recursive and non-determined way that social situations unfold. The general thrust is that social life is replete with possibilities and that the linguistic social bond proposed in our constructive approach is more open to alteration and expansion than is often assumed.

Good practice in the constructionist sense is likened to good conversations. It is characterised not by logical steps or an action plan but by the components of good conversation: 'simile, memory, metaphor, recounting, irony, analogy and declaration, which take shape in forms that could hardly have been predicted' (Saleebey, 1989, p. 558). Through conversation we explore, evaluate and engage with each other and the qualities with which we imbue this dialogue affect the process. Compassion, respect, affirmation, permission and interest are all likely to increase the chances that the dialogue will realise its creative potential.

As we have argued from the outset, the need to develop theory *for* practice in social work has become particularly pressing and we feel that the approaches we have outlined here can prove not only relevant but capable of further critical refinement and development. We will underline two reasons why we feel this is the case.

The first is simply that such approaches will ensure that in emphasising the importance of talk and language in the process and outcomes of doing social work, it will help clients make sense of and take control of their lives in a way which will open up new possibilities for change. This issue has become of growing significance in more recent years as we have become more and more aware of the socially constructed nature of our lives and the greater uncertainties under which we live. Increasingly individuals and the decisions they make are seen as key to their future but the criteria and rules for making such decisions are more and more fluid, complex and subject to change. Uncertainty is seen as pervasive and a defining characteristic of the 'postmodern' world. Uncertainty is seen to proliferate because as more and more areas of social life are seen to be no longer fixed, inevitable and subject to fate, the more they are seen as being potentially subject to human agency and influence. In the process we no longer assume they are natural and God-given but subject to human choice and responsibility. What is significant about contemporary 'postmodern' or 'post-traditional' times is not that we have to make decisions but that we have to do so in the context of the expectation that we should exercise choice and responsibility. Helping people make sense of their situations and opening up positive possibilities is thus key.

In doing so, however, we cannot fall back on our traditional models of expertise – and this brings us to our second point. Clearly the rational-technical approach to social work so associated with modernity is no longer appropriate. It is to the practical-moral elements we have to look and again there are some discussions related to 'postmodernity' in social theory which are suggestive. In particular, Bauman (1992) has argued that if we are serious about recognising the pluralism of social life and the differences which are not reducible to any single truths, we need to recognise the importance of trying to interpret and mediate across different traditions and cultures rather than emphasise expert interventions to 'resolve' problems as previously. While he is talking primarily of sociology his analysis seems to speak directly to the position that social work finds itself in.

The aim of such interpretation is to illuminate differences, to draw attention to areas of incommensurability, and to attempt to translate between different individuals, groups and communities to facilitate understanding and communication. Rather than burying differences, a serious attempt is made to increase dialogue and hence cultivate greater understanding of both self and other. It is in this sense that we feel the use of constructionism in practice can help make these issues more self-evident and be articulated in ways which mean they can be addressed *with* the various clients with whom social workers are engaged. In the process, however, not only are new possibilities opened up but new solutions found. For as Fleck (1979) has noted, 'a stimulating conversation between two persons soon creates a condition in which each utters thoughts s/he would not have been able to produce by her/himself or in different company' (p. 44).

The *constructive approach* we have outlined is affirmative and reflexive and focuses on dialogue, listening to and talking with the other. It reveals paradox, myth and enigma and persuades by showing, reminding, hinting and evoking rather than applying knowledge and approximating truth. The focus is narrative and different stories, and as a result social work at times may take on the guise of persuasive fiction or poetry.

There are a number of elements which can be seen to characterise the approach. The acknowledgement and use of *uncertainty* is essential and encourages practitioners to respect difference and the client's experience. Practitioners should thus not expect to know in advance what the outcomes of interactions will be, for they can, at best, only trigger an effect. Words are understood by clients according to how they have constructed the reality embodied in the interaction. It is an approach that recognises not only the importance of *dialogue* but that *language* is crucial for constructing the experiences and identity of both the self and the interaction, and which takes seriously the diverse elements of *power* which are involved. It is serious about ideas of *partnership* and *participation* and tries to ensure that the views and interests of service users are prioritised. This is not to say, however, that such issues are straightforward and clear-cut: far from it. A commitment to uncertainty, indeterminacy and unpredictability will reinforce practitioners' continual attempts to consider reflexively what they are doing, why and with what possible outcomes.

It is perhaps the emphasis on language and its intimate relationship with knowledge and power which provides the most distinctive contribution of the approach. A focus on social work as text, narrative and artistry, as opposed to social work as science, moves centre-stage. Whereas science looks for regularities, explanations and causes, we look to *exceptions* and finding accounts that are *meaningful* and which can contribute to *positive change*. Such an approach emphasises *process* and *authorship*. It encourages an open-minded engagement with people's stories and the *possibility* of helping them *re-author* their lives using more helpful stories which can prompt new and more positive *solutions*. A person's own language and metaphors can be incorporated into a less problem-saturated narrative which can tell of triumph, survival and heroism in the face of difficulties. Such an approach provides insights which are novel and creative and which clearly talk to a number of themes which can be seen to characterise social work for much of its history but which have in recent years become marginalised or forgotten. Thus in arguing that constructionist and narrative approaches can make a major contribution to the future of social work practice, we are trying to build on some of the major strengths of its past – something which is very consistent with the philosophy and practice of *constructive social work*.

Appendix 1: Student Strengths Scale (for Children at School)

Part 1

		Not at all	Just a little	Pretty much	Very much
1	I get on well with other students				
2	I get on well at home				
3	I get on well with friends				
4	I get on well with teachers				
5	I get on well with other adults				
6	I cooperate with the ideas of others				
7	I adapt well to new situations				
8	I get on with my school work				
9	I take lessons seriously				
10	I behave well with teachers				
11	I complete what I start				
12	I am considerate towards others				
13	I can pay attention for a whole lesson				
14	I react with a reasonable mood				
15	I follow school rules				
16	I settle disagreements peacefully				
17	I cope with frustration				
18	I respect the rights of others				

		Not at all	Just a little	Pretty much	Very much
19	I respect the rights of teachers				
20	Basically I am happy				
21	I sleep OK				
22	I feel part of my family				
23	I stand up for myself without losing control				
24	I can accept fair criticism				
25	I feel accepted by other students				
26	I show a sense of fair play				
27	I cope well with distractions				
28	I accept blame for my mistakes				
29	I cooperate with authority				
30	I accept praise well				
31	I can think before I act				
32	I can control excitement				
33	I handle stress well				
34	I respect grown ups				
35	I cope with the subjects I have to study				
36	I am honest				
37	I am truthful				
38	I have a good influence on my friends				
39	I can ask for help when I need it				
40	I am accountable for my behaviour				

Part 2

Give yourself points out of 10 for the following: 0 = the pits; 10 = perfect. For example, put 1 if it's really bad but not the pits; or put 9 if it's really good but not perfect.

How happy I am	
How confident I am about improving it	
How determined I am to do something about it	
How well I get on with people	
How confident I am about improving it	
How determined I am to do something about it	
How well my school work is going	
How confident I am about improving it	
How determined I am to do something about it	
How well behaved I am	
How confident I am about improving it	
How determined I am to do something about it	

How well I cope with my biggest problem	
How confident I am about improving it	
How determined I am to do something about it	

(Part 1 of this scale is based, with permission, on Ron Kral's Solution Identification Scale, as published in Durrant, 1993a.)

Appendix 2:
Signs of Safety Scale

NB: It is accepted that a guarantee of absolute safety is never possible in any family and no family can tick 'Very much' all the time.

Tick the box that fits best	Not at all	Just a little	Pretty much	Very much
I have guards for fire, doors and stairs				
Contact by unsafe people is limited or supervised				
I have safe childminding and baby sitting				
I can acknowledge what is unsafe				
I have control of alcohol and drugs (by carer 1)				
Carer 2 also has				
I have control of my temper				
Carer 2 also has				
I have a clear plan for what to do if control is slipping				
Carer 2 also has				
I can recognise danger				
Carer 2 also can				
I have realistic expectations of the child				
Carer 2 also has				
I pay attention to the child				
I make provision for stimulation for the child				
I can give examples of good care				

Tick the box that fits best	Not at all	Just a little	Pretty much	Very much
Family strengths are identifiable				
We have warm family relationships				
My family is clear about its goals				
I am confident about reaching goals				
I am clear about what is useful or needed				
I take steps to get useful help				
Things in the family are just as I want them				
I feel able to make such changes				
Other family members are helpful				
Other family members are confident about my ability to ensure safety				
I am able to discuss worries with my support worker				
I accept responsibility for safety				
The safety plan is clear				
I have some new safety goals to aim for				
Child smiles more at me				
I smile more at child				
I respond to the child more				
I am able to be firm AND friendly at same time				
Child plays				
Child approaches me				
I am confident that a dangerous incident will not happen				
I am willing to make changes if needed				

Other signs of safety:

Mark the 3 most urgent areas with *.
Then list here 3 things you can think of to move those ticks to the right:

Appendix 3: Survival of Poor Parenting Scale

NAME: _____ DATE: _____				
Please answer with a tick	Not at all	Just a little	Pretty much	Very much
1. Able to talk about what happened				
2. Able to talk about other things				
3. Able to grieve about what happened				
4. Able to cope with guilt about what happened				
5. Able to express anger about what happened				
6. Feels part of a new family				
7. Stands up for self				
8. Sleeps OK				
9. Eats well				
10. Keeps smart				
11. Goes to social events				
12. Copes with new situations				
13. Meets new friends				
14. Laughs				
15. Interested in the future				
16. Able to choose supportive relationships				

Please answer with a tick	Not at all	Just a little	Pretty much	Very much
17. Able to relax				
18. Able to tolerate criticism				
19. Able to accept praise				
20. Interested in the future				
21. I like myself				
22. Goes to school				
Other comments:				

Appendix 4: Recovery Scale for Starting a New Life After Abuse

NAME: _____	DATE: _____			
Please answer with a tick	Not at all	Just a little	Pretty much	Very much
1. Able to talk about what happened				
2. Able to talk about other things				
3. Sleeps OK				
4. Feels part of the family				
5. Stands up for self				
6. Keeps smart				
7. Goes to school				
8. Able to leave home				
9. Goes to social events				
10. Cares for relatives				
11. Eats well				
12. Copes with new situations				
13. Meets new friends				
14. Laughs				
15. Able to look male relatives in the eye				

Please answer with a tick	Not at all	Just a little	Pretty much	Very much
16. Able to look male strangers in the eye				
17. Able to shake hands with male relatives				
18. Able to hold hands with male relatives				
19. Kisses male relatives				
20. Interested in the future				
21. Takes safety measures				
22. Chooses supportive relationships				
23. Able to relax				
24. Tolerates criticism				
25. Accepts praise				

Appendix 5: Scale for Reclaiming Life After Drugs

NAME: _____	DATE: _____			
Please answer with a tick	Not at all	Just a little	Pretty much	Very much
1. Talks about his her situation				
2. Talks about other things				
3. Likes him herself				
4. Expresses anger about the past				
5. Makes decisions				
6. Interested in the future				
7. Sleeps OK				
8. Shakes hands with confidence				
9. Takes safety measures				
10. Chooses supportive relationships				
11. Relaxes				
12. Accepts criticism				
13. Accepts praise				
14 Feels part of a family				
15. Stands up for herself				
16. Keeps smart				
17. Goes to work or school				

Please answer with a tick	Not at all	Just a little	Pretty much	Very much
18. Goes to social events				
19. Cares for relatives				
20. Eats well				
21. Copes with situations				
22. Meets new friends				
23. Laughs				
24. Has his her own thoughts				
25. Feels in control				

Further Reading

Below we briefly summarise a number of existing solution-focused and narrative texts and other sources which may be of interest to those working in particular contexts or with more specific client groups and provide clues as to how *constructive social work* ideas are used and might be developed further.

Child-protection work

Insoo Kim Berg (1994) has written on a solution-focused approach in child protection services. She argues that the word 'protection' presents a problem, as it implies 'protection from a carer', usually a family member. Her philosophy is that children are best cared for in strong families and therefore the goal is to strengthen families rather than dismember them. While not being soft on risk of harm, this strengths-focus opens the possibility for a more collaborative relationship between service workers and parents or carers.

Linked to this is the 'signs of safety' approach of Turnell and Edwards (1997). As a result of reading these people's work we have drafted a 'signs of safety scale' (see Appendix 2) and perhaps workers in various settings will wish to develop their own version of this. Definitions of what is safe will vary from culture to culture, community to community, but perhaps there are some 'bottom lines' relating to food, warmth, clothing, and non-abuse. Nothing seems to be threatened – and there may be much to be gained – by starting with an interest in strengths, in safety, in parenting ability and signs of care. This should not preclude seeing signs of danger or neglect too, but at least a more balanced picture emerges when strengths are looked at as well as needs. Turnell and Edwards's (1999) book is *Signs of Safety: A Solution and Safety Oriented Approach to Child Protection Casework* (New York: Norton). Trish Walsh's *Solution-Focused Child Protection* (1997) is also useful.

Children and adolescents

Selekman (1993) has written on work with difficult adolescents, who sometimes have several difficulties, not only personal but in their families and relationships. Difficult children will often be labelled and referred by others who believe in such states or pathologies. It can take time to shift such beliefs. But essentially, the approach seems to work well with young people of all ages. They seem to be particularly versatile in responding to the narrative approach, making the best of their young imaginations and often enjoying outwitting or tricking the problem. They like to talk in metaphors, preferably those of their own making, so it is for workers to join those metaphors and help reshape them. His most recent book is *Solution-Focused Therapy with Children* (Guilford Press, 1997). This contains many useful ideas for work with difficult children.

Freeman, Epston and Lobovits (1997) have collaborated to produce a collection of accounts of playful approaches to serious problems for children. Children in particular respond very well to externalisation; they soon become alienated from the problem and show great creativity in devising ways to defeat it. They seem to enjoy especially 'naughty', deceptive tricks that undermine the problem and lead to it having a 'no good end'. In some cases it may be a matter of taming the problem or changing one's relationship with it. This book has many interesting examples of creative work with children. Of particular interest is their story of Zack.

Couples

Bill O'Hanlon and Pat Hudson (1991) have written of constructive work with couples, 're-writing love stories', as they put it. In this work they place considerable emphasis on storying and re-storying, on 'changing the viewing and the doing', on recognising strengths and exceptions, on talking about when things are better and on telling people stories from their own experience and that of others, that enable the listeners to 'experience possibility' of successful relationships. Michelle Weiner-Davis's (1992) book *Divorce Busting* also offers excellent examples of work with couples and provides a helpful step-by-step approach.

Crime/offenders

Criminal behaviour is a good example of something that does not happen always. Exceptions abound and can be discussed in detail. Rather than trying to stop offending behaviour, one is trying to increase non-offending behaviour. Some offending (or non-offending) may be seen as spontaneous: 'the urge came (or didn't come), and that was that'. *Beyond the Prison – Gathering Dreams of Freedom* edited by David Denborough (1997) (available from BT Press, London) is useful. Also see section on perpetrators below.

Families

We have found Berg's (1992) *Family Preservation* (available from BT Press, London) and her larger book (1994) *Family-Based Services* (New York: Norton) most useful. She has also made an excellent training tape, 'I'd Hear Laughter' (New York: Norton, 1995). A good deal of Michael White's work is with families and will be listed below.

Groups and organisations

In our view, a constructive approach can be used with any group in almost the same way is it can be used with individuals. Sessions will be slower in some ways if all the participants are to have an opportunity to co-construct new behaviours or relationships.

Bill O'Hanlon (*Frozen in Time* training pack) (Omaha: Possibilities, 1996) has described group sessions for victims of abuse, and Michael White (Doncaster conference, 1996) has described group work with people with mental health problems and group work with community health teams. Ben Furman (www.reteaming. com 1998) has produced an illustrated workbook for working in organisations called 'Succeeding Together'. In the UK, Paul Jackson (SFT E-mail List, 1998) uses the solution-focused approach with organisations with a slight change of language.

Gale Miller (SFT E-mail List, 1998) believes that the application of constructivist work to organisations could be an exciting development. He too feels that the overly static language used in organisational theory is an issue. People tend to 'treat organisations as static structures, not as processes and language games'.

Mental illness

There are numerous examples in the literature of work with people who are depressed or who are suffering from schizophrenia. De Shazer (1988, 1991, 1994), O'Hanlon and Beadle (1994), O'Hanlon (1995) and Bertolino and O'Hanlon (1999) have provided case studies of people who are depressed. The process is usually the basic solution-focused approach of listening, validating, asking for exceptions, describing the future when the depression has lifted and using the 'miracle question'. O'Hanlon has added the technique of converting emotions (nouns) into actions (verbs) by talking about how various people 'do' their depression, thereby introducing an element of personal agency and therefore control. For example he tells the story of a woman who worked out ways to 'walk out of depresso-land' – that is, she walked to the library each day and took up reading and new interests. De Shazer works with those suffering from schizophrenia and addresses the problem of voices by discussing exceptions, which are usually spontaneous but which can be increased by prediction tasks. Michael White (White and Epston, 1990) externalises the voices and works with people in groups to talk about how they cope with them and find ways to not let them dominate life.

Older people

Chris Iveson's (1997) *Whose Life? – Community Care of Older People and Their Families* (BT Press) promises to be useful here.

Perpetrators of abuse

Probably the most difficult offenders to deal with are those who commit domestic violence and those who sexually abuse children. Alan Jenkins (1990) uses the Michael White approach to invite such people (usually men) to responsibility. His approach virtually turns the Finkelhor approach upside down – rather than strengthening the blocks that prevent abuse, he seeks to weaken the restraints on responsibility and caring, as he helps to build a story they can be proud of as they take control of themselves.

Residential work with young people

Michael Durrant (1993b) has written the key text for this area of work. As well as showing how solution-focused and narrative ideas can be used in this setting, he does something more important still; he redefines the whole process of residential care. Two grave concerns for some time have been (a) how to deal with the way successful residential workers who manage difficult children well make the families feel all the more inadequate, and (b) how to avoid families saying 'you fix him'. Durrant has shown that the work can be so arranged as to include families in a way that results in *them* taking the credit for progress. He changes the meaning, for workers and residents, of the residential experience; it becomes a 'rite of passage', a time and place in which to practise new states, to experiment with being different even though the situation at home may remain the same. Family members' ideas are valued and used in the process.

School problems

Michael Durrant (1993a) developed a set of creative strategies for school problems. He reproduced Ron Kral's scale (see Appendix 1). It is an attempt to shift the focus from deficits to strengths. In schools, frequently, difficult children get great attention paid to their problems and little if any to their strengths. Many disaffected children feel they are 'bad' or they perceive themselves to be bad; often such children think it is too late to change. The locus of control is a major issue for them; many feel it is external to them – that they and their lives are being controlled or ruled by external forces of various kinds and that the best they can do is to make it difficult for those forces, including school staff. Helping them make the shift to feeling that they have (internal) control of their lives is a key step. Dupper (1998) has published an account of using 'school survival' groups where the central theme is developing an internal 'locus of control'. Dupper ran a series of 10 sessions for 40 to 45 minutes once a week. We have found that a similar programme with a solution-focused approach worked well, using six planned meetings with self-selected pairs of pupils.

Substance abuse

This group of service users tend to be seen as highly resistant, yet they seem to do as well as others when constructive approaches are developed. Berg and Miller (1992) is a classic text. Their 1995 version is called *The Miracle Method: A Radical Approach to Problem Drinking*. We also recommend Berg and Reuss (1997) *Solutions Step by Step; A Substance Abuse Treatment Manual*, also published by Norton. Difficult though this area is, the use of the approach is quite straightforward, so long as one can let go of the disease model of addiction and can hold to the belief that people can control it, that there are always exceptions, and in them lie the seeds for change. People usually do not realise that they can have 'dry' days because they assume that any dry day was an accident.

Surviving abuse

Yvonne Dolan (1991, 1998) has been developing ways of doing solution-focused work with those who have been abused. Work in this area can involve people of all ages and she calls the work 'rekindling hope, love and laughter in therapy and in life' (London conference, 1998). In her view, abused people need to reclaim their life and their pride, rather than continue to explore and relive the abuse itself. Dolan uses the miracle question and scaling questions to 'kindle hope'. She also scales the effects of the problem. She has developed ways of consulting 'the wise, compassionate, sage within', but one of her most helpful technique is to help the person create 'cues' for comfort and safety.

Bibliography

Adams, R., Dominelli, L. and Payne, M. (eds) (1998) *Social Work: Themes, Issues and Critical Debates*. London, Macmillan.

Aldridge, M. (1994) *Making Social Work News*. London, Routledge.

Aldridge, M. (1996) 'Dragged to Market: Being a Profession in the Postmodern World', *British Journal of Social Work*, 26(2), 177–94.

Allen, J. A. (1993) 'The Constructivist Paradigm: Values and Ethics', *Journal of Teaching in Social Work*, 8(1 2), 31–54.

Anderson, H. and Gollishian, H. (1992) 'The Client is the Expert: A Not-Learning Approach to Therapy', in S. McNamee and K. J. Gergen (eds), *Therapy as Social Construction*. London, Sage.

Anderson, T. (1987) 'The Reflecting Team: Dialogue and Meta-Dialogue in Clinical Work', *Family Process*, 26, 415–28.

Atherton, C. R. (1993) 'Empiricists versus Social Constructionists: Time for a Case-Fire', in *Families in Society: Journal of Contemporary Human Services*, Dec., 617–24.

Bailey, R. and Brake, M. (eds) (1975) *Radical Social Work*. London, Edward Arnold.

Baker, M. R. and Steiner, J. R. (1995) 'Solution-Focused Social Work: Metamessages to Students in Higher Education Opportunity Programs', *Social Work*, 40(2), 225–32.

Bandler, R. and Grinder, J. (1979) *Frogs into Princes*. Utah, Real People Press.

Barbu, Z. (1956) *Democracy and Dictatorship*. London, Routledge.

Barnes, S. B. and Law, J. (1976) 'Whatever Should Be Done With Indexical Expressions?', *Theory and Society*, 3, 223–37.

Bartlett, M. (1970) *The Common Base of Social Work Practice*. Washington DC, NASW.

Bateson, G. (1972) 'Form, Substance and Difference', in G. Bateson (ed.), *Steps to an Ecology of Mind*. New York, Ballantine.

Baudrillard, J. (1983) *Simulations*, New York, Semiotext.

Baudrillard, J. (1990) *Fatal Strategies*. London, Semiotext Pluto.

Bauman, Z. (1987) *Legislators and Interpreters: On Modernity, Postmodernity and the Intellectuals*. Oxford, Polity Press.

Bauman, Z. (1992) *Intimations of Postmodernity*. London, Routledge.

Bauman, Z. (1993) *Postmodern Ethics*. Cambridge, Polity Press.

Bauman, Z. (1995) *Life in Fragments*. Oxford, Blackwell.

Bauman, Z. (1997) *Postmodernity and its Discontents*. Cambridge, Polity Press.

208 Bibliography

Bauman, Z. (1998) 'What Prospects of Morality in Times of Uncertainty', *Theory, Culture and Society*, 15(1), 11–22.

Beck, A. T. (1991) *Depression: Clinical Experimental and Theoretical Aspects*. London, Hoeber.

Beck, U. (1992) *Risk Society: Towards a New Modernity*. London, Sage.

Beck, U., Giddens, A. and Lash, S. (eds) (1994) *Reflexive Modernisation: Politics, Tradition and Aesthetics in the Modern Social Order*. Cambridge, Polity Press.

Becker, H. (1963) *Outsiders: Studies in the Sociology of Deviance*. New York, Free Press.

Becker, H. (1964) *The Other Side: Perspectives on Deviance*. New York, Free Press.

Berg, I. K. (1992) *Family Preservation*. London, BT Press.

Berg, I. K. (1994) *Family-Based Services: A Solution-Focused Approach*. New York, Norton.

Berg, I. K. (1995) 'I'd Hear Laughter', Training Tape, New York, Norton.

Berg, I. K. and Miller, S. D. (1992) *Working with the Problem Drinker: A Solution-Focused Approach*. New York, Norton.

Berg, I. K. and Miller, S. D. (1995) *The Miracle Method: A Radical Approach to Problem Drinking*. New York, Norton.

Berg, I. K. and Reuss, N. M. (1997) *Solutions Step by Step: A Substance Abuse Treatment Manual*. New York, Norton.

Berger, P. and Luckman, T. (1967) *The Social Construction of Reality: A Treatise in the Sociology of Knowledge*. New York, Doubleday.

Bertolino, B. and O'Hanlon, B. (1999) *Invitation to Possibilityland: An Intensive Teaching Seminar with Bill O'Hanlon*. Philadelphia, Brunner/Mazel.

Besa, D. (1994) 'Evaluating Narrative Therapy Using Single-System Research Designs', *Research on Social Work Practice*, 4(3), 309–25.

Beyebach, M., Morejon, A. R., Palenzuela, D. L. and Rodriguez-Aries, J. L. (1996) 'Research on the Process of Solution-Focused Brief Therapy' in Miller, Happle and Duncan (eds) *Handbook of Solution-Focused Brief Therapy*. San Francisco, Jossey-Bass.

Bhaskar, R. (1979) *The Possibility of Naturalism: A Critique of Contemporary Human Sciences*. Brighton, Harvester Press.

Biestek, F. (1961) *The Casework Relationship*. London, Allen & Unwin.

Billig, M. (1987) *Arguing and Thinking: A Rhetorical Approach to Social Psychology*. Cambridge, Cambridge University Press.

Blumer, H. (1971) 'Social Problems as Collective Behaviour', *Social Problems*, 18(3), 310–26.

Bowlby, J. (1951a) *Child Care and the Growth of Love*. Geneva, World Health Organisation.

Bowlby, J. (1951b) *Maternal Care and Mental Health*. London, HMSO.

Brandon, D. and Jordan, B. (eds) (1979) *Creative Social Work*. Oxford, Blackwell.

Bruner, E. (1986) 'Ethnography as Narrative', in V. Turner and E. Bruner (eds), *The Autobiography of Experience*. Chicago, University of Illinois University Press.

Bruner, J. (1986a) *Actual Minds, Possible Worlds*. Cambridge MA, Harvard University Press.

Bruner, J. (1986b) *Acts of Living*. Cambridge MA, Harvard University Press.

Burke, K. (1937) *Attitudes Towards History*, 2 vols. New York, The New Republic.

Burnham, J. (1997) Leeds University Workshop on Reflexivity.

Burr, V. (1995) *An Introduction to Social Constructionism*. London, Routledge.

Burr, W. (1993) 'Evaluation of the use of brief therapy in a practice for children and youths'. *Families dynamite*, 18, 11–21 (Translated from the German).

Butler, J. and Scott, J. W. (eds) (1992) *Feminists Theorise the Political*. London, Routledge.

Cade, B. (1992) 'I am an unashamed expert', *Context*, 11, 30–1.

Campbell, J. and Pinkerton, J. (1997) 'Embracing Change as Opportunity: Reflections on Social Work from a Northern Ireland Perspective', in B. Lesnik (ed.), *Change in Social Work*. Aldershot, Arena.

Carr, A. (1990) 'From Problem to Solution', *Context*, , 6., p. 12.

Cecchin, G. (1987) 'Hypothesising, Circularity and Neutrality Revisited.' *Family Process* 26(4), 405–413.

Cecchin, G. (1992) 'Constructing Therapeutic Possibilities', in S. McNamee and K. J. Gergen (eds), *Therapy as Social Construction*. London, Sage.

Chambon, A. and Irving, A. (eds) (1994) *Essays on Postmodernism and Social Work*. Toronto, Canadian Scholars' Press.

Clarke, J. (ed.) (1993) *A Crisis in Care? Challenges to Social Work*. London, Sage.

Clegg, S. R. (1993) 'Narrative Power and Social Theory', in D. K. Mumby (ed.), *Narrative and Social Control*. Newbury Park CA and London, Sage.

Cohen, S. (1985) *Visions of Social Control: Crime, Punishment and Classification*. Cambridge, Polity Press.

Collins, M. (1983) 'An Empirical Relativist Programme in Sociology of Scientific Knowledge', in K. D. Knorr-Cetina and M. Mulkay (eds), *Science Observed: Perspectives in the Social Study of Science*, 85–113. Beverly Hills CA, Sage.

Craib, I. (1997) 'Social Constructionism as a Social Psychosis', *Sociology*, 31(1), 1.15.

Cushman, P. (1995) *Constructing the Self, Constructing America: A Cultural History of Psychotherapy*. Reading MA, Addison-Wesley.

Dean, R. (1993) 'Constructivism: An Approach to Clinical Practice', *Smith College Studies in Social Work*, 63(2), 127–46.

De Jong, P. and Berg, I. K. (1997) *Interviewing for Solutions*. New York, Brooks Cole.

De Jong, P. and Miller, S. D. (1995) 'How to Interview for Client Strengths', *Social Work*, 40(6), 729–36.

Denborough, D. (1997) (ed.) *Beyond the Prison – Gathering Dreams of Freedom*. London, BT Press.

Department of Health (1998) *Modernising Social Services: Promoting Independence; Improving Protection; Raising Standards*, Cm. 4169. London, The Stationery Office.

Dermer, S. B., Hemesath, C. W. and Russell, C. S. (1998) 'A Feminist Critique of Solution-Focused Therapy', *American Journal of Family Therapy*, 26, 239–50.

Derrida, J. (1978) *Writing and Difference*. Chicago, University of Chicago Press.

De Shazer, S. (1982) *Patterns of Brief Family Therapy*. New York, Guilford.

De Shazer, S. (1984) 'The Death of Resistance', *Family Process*, 23, 11–21.

De Shazer, S. (1985) *Keys to Solutions in Brief Therapy*. New York and London, Norton.

De Shazer, S. (1988) *Clues: Investigating Solutions in Brief Therapy*. New York and London, Norton.

De Shazer, S. (1991) *Putting Difference to Work*. New York and London, Norton.

De Shazer, S. (1993a) '*Vive la Différence*', in S. Gilligan and R. Price (eds), *Therapeutic Conversations*. New York and London, Norton.

De Shazer, S. (1993b) 'Creative Misunderstanding: There Is No Escape From Language', in S. Gilligan and R. Price (eds), *Therapeutic Conversations*. New York and London, Norton.

De Shazer, S. (1994) *Words Were Originally Magic*. New York and London, Norton.

De Shazer, S. (1997) '*Staying Brief*'. Glasgow Conference, verbal report.

De Shazer, S. and Berg, I. K. (1997) 'What Works?', *Journal of Family Therapy*, 19(2), 1221–5.

De Shazer, S., Berg, I. K., Lipchic, E., Nunnally, E., Molnar, E., Gingerich, W. and Weiner-Davis, M. (1986) 'Brief Therapy: Focused Solution Development', *Family Process*, 25, 207–15.

Deutscher, M. (1983) *Subjecting and Objecting*. St Lucia, University of Queensland Press.

Dingwall, R. and Eekelaar, J. (1988) 'Families and the State: An Historical Perspective on the Public Regulation of Private Conduct', *Law and Policy*, 10(4), 341–61.

Dingwall, R., Eekelaar, J. and Murray, T. (1983) *The Protection of Children: State Intervention and Family Life*. Oxford, Basil Blackwell.

Dolan, Y. (1991) *Resolving Sexual Abuse*. New York, Norton.

Dolan, Y. (1998) *One Small Step*. Waterville CA, Papier-Mâché Press.

Dominelli, L. (1996) 'Deprofessionalising Social Work: Anti-Oppressive Practice, Competencies and Post-Modernism', *British Journal of Social Work*, 26(2), 153–75.

Donzelot, J. (1980) *The Policing of Families: Welfare versus the State*. London, Hutchinson.

Donzelot, J. (1988) 'The Promotion of the Social', *Economy and Society*, 17(3), 395–427.

Driver, S. and Martell, L. (1998) *New Labour: Politics after Thatcherism*. Cambridge, Polity Press.

Dupper, D. R. (1998) 'An Alternative to Suspension for Middle School Youths with Behavioural Problems; Findings from a School Survival Group', *Research on Social Work Practice*, 8(3), 354–66.

Durrant, M. (1993a) *Creative Strategies for School Problems*. Epping, NSW, Australia, Eastwood Family Therapy Centre.

Durrant, M. (1993b) *Residential Treatment: A Cooperative Competency Approach to Therapy and Programme Design*. New York, Norton.

Durrant, M. and Kowakski, K. (1990) 'Overcoming Effects of Sexual Abuse: Developing a Self-Perception of Competence', in M. Durrant and C. White (eds), *Ideas for Therapy with Sexual Abuse*. Adelaide, Dulwich Centre Publications.

Eakes, G., Walsh, S., Markowski, M., Cain, H. and Swanson, M. (1997) 'Family-Centred Brief Solution-Focused Therapy with Chronic Schizophrenia: A Pilot Study', *Journal of Family Therapy*, 19, 145–58.

Efran, J. S. and Clarfield, L. E. (1992) 'Constructing Therapy: Sense and Nonsense', in S. McNamee and K. J. Gergen (eds), *Therapy as Social Construction*. London, Sage.

Ellis, A. (1962) *Reason and Emotion in Psychotherapy*. New York, Lyle Stuart.

England, H. (1986) *Social Work as Art: Making Sense of Good Practice*. London, Allen & Unwin.

Epston, D. and White, M. (1991) *Experience, Contradiction, Narrative and Imagination*. Adelaide, Dulwich Centre.

Farmer, E. and Owen, M. (1995) *Child Protection Practice: Private Risks and Public Remedies*. London, HMSO.

Fawcett, B. Featherstone, B. Fook, J, and Rossiter, A. (eds) (2000) *Practice Research in Social Work: Postmodern Feminist Perspectives*, London, Routledge.

Fazio, R. H., Effrein, E. A. and Falender, V. J. (1981) 'Self-Perceptions Following Social Interactions', *Journal of Personality and Social Psychology*, 41(2), 232–42.

Featherstone, B. and Fawcett, B. (1995) 'Oh No! Not More Isms: Feminism, Postmodernism, Poststructuralism and Social Work Education', *Social Work Education*, 14(3), pp. 25–43.

Featherstone, M. (1988) 'In Pursuit of the Postmodern: An Introduction', *Theory, Culture and Society*, 5(2–3), 195–216.

Finkelhor, D. A. (1986) *A Source Book of Child Sexual Abuse*. New York, Sage.

Fisher, D. J., Himle, J. A. and Hanna, G. L. (1998) 'Group Behavioural Therapy for Adolescents with Obsessive-Compulsive Disorder', *Research on Social Work Practice*, 8(6), 629–636.

Fisher, M. (ed.) (1983) *Speaking of Clients*, Social Services Monographs: Research in Practice. University of Sheffield, Joint Unit for Social Services Research Community Care.

Flaskas, C. (1997) 'Reclaiming the Idea of Truth: Some Thoughts on Theory in Response to Practice', *Journal of Family Therapy*, 19(1), 1–20.

Fleck, L. (1979) *Genesis and Development of a Scientific Fact*. Chicago, University of Chicago Press.

Fook, J. (ed.) (1996) *The Reflective Researcher: Social Workers' Theories of Practice Research*. Australia, Allen & Unwin.

Fook, J. (2000) 'Deconstructing and Reconstructing Professional Expertise' in B. Fawcett, B. Featherstone, J. Fook and A. Rossiter (eds), *Practice Research in Social Work: Postmodern Feminist Perspectives*, London, Routledge.

Fook, J., Ryan, M. and Hawkins, L. (1997) 'Towards a Theory of Social Work Expertise', *British Journal of Social Work*, 27(3), 300–417.

Foucault, M. (1973) *The Birth of the Clinic*. London, Tavistock.

Foucault, M. (1977) *Discipline and Punish: The Birth of the Prison* (trans. A. Sheridan). Harmondsworth, Allen Lane.

Foucault, M. (1980) *Power (Knowledge)*. New York, Pantheon.

Foucault, M. (1984) *Space, Knowledge and Power*. New York, Pantheon.

Foucault, M. (1988) 'Technologies of the Self', in L. Martin, H. Gutman and P. Hutton (eds), *Technologies of the Self*. Amherst, University of Massachusetts Press.

Foucault, M. (1989) *Foucault Live*. New York, Semiotext.

Franklin, B. (1998) *Hard Pressed: National Newspaper Reporting of Social Work and Social Services*. Sutton, Community Care.

Franklin, B. and Parton, N. (eds) (1991) *Social Work, the Media and Public Relations*. London, Routledge.

Franklin, C. (1995) 'Expanding the Vision of the Social Constructionist Debates: Creating Relevance for Practitioners', *Families in Society: Journal of Contemporary Human Services*, September, 395–407.

Freeman, J., Epston, D. and Lobovits, D. (1997) *Playful Approaches to Serious Problems*. New York, Norton.

Fuchs, S. and Ward, S. (1994) 'What is Deconstruction and Where and When Does it Take Place?: Making Facts in Science, Building Cases in Law', *American Sociological Review*, 54(4), 481–500.

Fuller, R. C. and Myers, R. D. (1941) 'The Natural History of a Social Problem', *American Sociological Review*, 6(6), 318–28.

Furman, B. (1998) 'Kids n' Skills. A Cooperative Educational Programme for Helping Children with Behavioural Problems', Personal website.

Furman, B. and Ahola, T. (1992) *Solution Talk*. New York, Norton.

Garland, D. (1985) *Punishment and Welfare: A History of Penal Strategies*. Aldershot, Gower.

George, E., Iveson, C. and Ratner, H. (1990) *Problem to Solution*. London, BT Press.

Gergen, K. J. (1990) 'Therapeutic Professions and the Diffusion of Deficit', *Journal of Mind and Behaviour*, 11, 353–68.

Gergen, K. J. and Gergen, M. J. (1986) 'Narrative Form and the Construction of Psychological Science', in T. R. Sarbin (ed.), *The Storied Nature of Human Conduct*. New York, Praeger.

Gergen, K. J. and Kaye, J. (1992) 'Beyond Narrative in the Negotiation of Therapeutic', in S. McNamee and K. J. Gergen (eds), *Therapy as Social Construction*. London, Sage.

Gibson, J. J. (1979) *The Ecological Approach to Visual Perception*. Boston, Houghton Mifflin.

Gilligan, S. and Price, R. (eds) (1993) *Therapeutic Conversations*. New York, Norton.

Gingrich, W., De Shazer, S. and Weiner-Davis, M. (1988) 'Constructing Change: A Research View of Interviewing', in E. Lipchik (ed.), *Interviewing*. Rockville MD, Aspen.

Goffman, E. (1968a) *Stigma: Notes on the Management of Spoiled Identity*. Harmondsworth, Penguin.

Goffman, E. (1968b) *Asylums: Essays on the Social Situation of Mental Patients and Other Inmates*. Harmondsworth, Penguin.

Goffman, E. (1971) *The Presentation of the Self in Everyday Life*. Harmondsworth, Penguin.

Goffman, E. (1974) *Frame Analysis*. New York, Harper.

Goldstein, H. (1990) 'The Knowledge Base of Social Work Practice: Theory, Wisdom, Analogue or Art', *Families in Society*, 71(1), 32–42.

Goldstein, H. (1992) 'If Social Work Hasn't Made Progress as a Science, Might It Be an Art?', *Families in Society*, 73(1), 48–55.

Good, J. and Velody, I. (eds) (1998) *The Politics of Postmodernity*. Cambridge, Cambridge University Press.

Gorey, K. M., Thyer, B. A. and Pawluch, D. E. (1998) 'Differential Effectiveness of Prevalent Social Work Practice Models: A Meta-Analysis', *Social Work*, 43(3), 269–79.

Gorman, J. (1993) 'Postmodernism and the Conduct of Inquiry in Social Work', *Affilia*, 8(3), 247–64.

Gray, M. (1995) 'The Ethical Implications of Current Theoretical Developments in Social Work', *British Journal of Social Work*, 25(1), 55–70.

Green, G. J., Jensen, C. and Jones, D. H. (1996) 'A Constructivist Perspective on Clinical Social Work Practice with Ethnically Diverse Clients', *Social Work*, 41(2), 172–80.

Hacking, I. (1999) *The Social Construction of What?*. London and Cambridge, Mass, Harvard University Press.

Hall, C. (1997) *Social Work as Narrative: Storytelling and Persuasion in Professional Texts*. Aldershot, Ashgate.

Hammersley, M. (1992) *What's Wrong with Ethnography: Methodological Explorations*. London, Routledge.

Hare-Mustin, R. T. (1978) 'A Feminist Approach to Family Therapy', *Family Process*, 17, 181–94.

Hare-Mustin, R. T. (1987) 'The Problem of Gender in Family Therapy Theory', *Family Process*, 26, 15–27.

Healy, K. (1999) *Social Work Practices: Contemporary Perspectives on Change*. London, Sage.

Held, B. S. (1995) *Back to Reality: A Critique of Postmodern Theory in Psychotherapy*. New York and London, Norton.

Hirst, P. (1981) 'The Genesis of the Social', *Politics and Power*, 3, 67–82.

Hoffman, L. (1990) 'Constructing Realities: An Art of Lenses', *Family Process*, 29(1), 1–12.

Hoffman, L. (1993) *Exchanging Voices: A Collaborative Approach to Family Therapy*. New York and London, Karnac.

Hollis, M. (1985) 'On Masks and Men', in M. Carrithers, S. Collins and S. Lukes (eds), *The Category of the Person: Anthropology, Philosophy, History*. Cambridge, Cambridge University Press.

Holstein, J. A. and Miller, G. (eds) (1993) *Reconsidering Social Construction: Debates in Social Problems Theory*. New York, Aldine de Gruyter.

Holstein, J. A. and Miller, G. (eds) (1997) *Social Problems in Everyday Life: Studies of Social Problems Work*. Greenwich, Jai Press.

Home Office (1995) *National Standards for the Supervision of Offenders in the Community*. London, Home Office.

Horne, M. (1987) *Values in Social Work*. London, Wildwood House.

Howe, D. (1987) *An Introduction to Social work Theory: Making Sense in Practice.* Aldershot, Wildwood House.

Howe, D. (1992) 'Child Abuse and the Bureaucratisation of Social Work', *The Sociological Review*, 40(3), 491–508.

Howe, D. (1993) *On Being a Client: Understanding the Process of Counselling and Psychotherapy.* London, Sage.

Howe, D. (1994) 'Modernity, Postmodernity and Social Work', *British Journal of Social Work*, 24(5), 513–32.

Howe, D. (1995a) *Attachment Theory for Social Work Practice.* London, Macmillan.

Howe, D. (1995b) *Social Work and the University.* Department of Social Studies Occasional Paper No.4. Dublin, University of Dublin, Trinity College.

Howe, D. (1996) 'Surface and Depth in Social Work Practice', in N. Parton (ed.), *Social Theory, Social Change and Social Work.* London, Routledge.

Howe, D. (1997) 'Psychosocial and Relationship-Based Theories for Child and Family Social Work: Political Philosophy, Psychology and Welfare Practice', *Child and Family Social Work*, 2(3), 161–9.

Howe, D. (1998) 'Relationship-Based Thinking and Practice in Social Work', *Journal of Social Work Practice*, 12(1), 45–56.

Howe, D. and Hinings, D. (1995) 'Reason and Emotion in Social Work Practice: Managing Relationships with Difficult Clients', *Journal of Social Work Practice*, 9(3), 5–14.

Howe, D., Brandon, M., Hinings, D. and Schofield, D. (1999) *Attachment Theory, Child Maltreatment and Family Support: A Practice and Assessment Model.* London, Macmillan.

Husserl, E. (1975) *Ideas.* New York, Macmillan.

Ingleby, D. (1985) 'Professionals as Socialisers: The "Psy Complex"', in A. Scully and S. Spitzer (eds), *Research in Law, Deviance and Social Control*, 7. New York, Jai Press.

Iveson, C. (1990) 'Reluctant Clients', *Context*, 17, p. 19.

Iveson, C. (1997) *Whose Life? – Community Care of Older People and their Families.* London, BT Press.

Jenkins, A. (1990) *Invitations to Responsibility.* Adelaide, Dulwich Centre.

Jokinen, A., Juhila, K. and Pösö, T. (eds) (1999) *Constructing Social Work Practices.* Aldershot, Ashgate.

Jong, P. and Hopwood, L. E. (1996) 'Outcome Research on Treatment Conducted at a Brief Family Therapy Centre', in Miller, Happle and Duncan (eds), *Handbook of Solution-focused Brief Therapy.* San Francisco, Jossey-Bass.

Jordan, W. (B.) (1970) *Client Worker Transactions.* London, Routledge & Kegan Paul.

Jordan, W. (B.) (1972) *The Social Worker in Family Situations.* London, Routledge & Kegan Paul.

Jordan, W. (B.) (1978) 'A Comment on "Theory and Practice in Social Work"', *British Journal of Social Work*, 8(11), 23–5.

Jordan, B. (1979) *Helping in Social Work*. London, Routledge & Kegan Paul.

Jordan, B. (1984) *Invitation to Social Work*. Oxford, Robertson.

Jordan, B. (1987) 'Counselling, Advocacy and Negotiation', *British Journal of Social Work*, 17(2), 135–46.

Jordan, B. (1990) *Social Work in an Unjust Society*. Hemel Hempstead, Harvester Wheatsheaf.

Jordan, B. (1998a) *The New Politics of Welfare*. London, Sage.

Jordan, B. (1998b) Personal communication.

Jordan, B. and Parton, N. (eds) (1983) *The Political Dimensions of Social Work*. Oxford, Basil Blackwell.

Kahnemann, D. and Tversky, A. (1979) 'Prospect Theory, an Analysis of Decision Making under Risk', *Econometrician*, 47, 263–91.

Karvinen, S., Pösö, T. and Satka, M. (eds) (1999) *Reconstructing Social Work Research*. Finland, University of Jyväskylä.

Keeney, B. (1985) *Aesthetics of Change*. New York, Guilford Press.

Kelly, L. (1988) *Surviving Sexual Violence*. Cambridge, Polity Press.

Kemshall, H., Parton, N., Walsh, M. and Waterson, J. (1997) 'Concepts of Risk in Relation Organizational Structures and Functioning within the Personal Social Services and Probation', *Social Policy and Administration*, 31(3), 213–32.

Lacan, J. (1981) *Speed and Language in Psychoanalysis*. Baltimore, Johns Hopkins University Press.

Laing, R. D. (1965) *The Divided Self: An Existential Study in Sanity and Madness*. Harmondsworth, Penguin.

Laing, R. D. (1971) *Self and Others*, 2nd edn. Harmondsworth, Penguin.

Laing, R. D. and Esterson, A. (1970) *Sanity, Madness and the Family*. Harmondsworth, Penguin.

Laird, J. (ed.) (1993) *Revisioning Social Work Education: A Social Constructionist Approach*. New York, The Haworth Press. Published simultaneously as the *Journal of Teaching in Social Work*, 8(1/2).

Laird, J. (1995) 'Family-Centred Practice in the Postmodern Era', *Families in Society: The Journal on Contemporary Human Services*, March, 150–62.

Langellier, K. M. and Peterson, E. E. (1993) 'Family Story-Telling as a Strategy', in D. K. Mumby (ed.), *Narrative and Social Control*. Newbury Park CA and London, Sage.

Lash, S., Szerszynski, B. and Wynne, B. (eds) (1996) *Risk, Environment and Modernity: Towards a New Ecology*. London, Sage.

Lee, M. Y. (1997) 'A Study of Solution-Focused Brief Family Therapy: outcomes and issues', *American Journal of Family Therapy*, 25, 3–17.

Lees, S. (1997) *Ruling Passions, Sexual Violence, Reputation and the Law*. Buckingham, Open University Press.

Lentricchia, F. (1983) *Criticism and Social Change*. Chicago, IL, University of Chicago Press.

Leonard, P. (1994) 'Knowledge Power and Postmodernism: Implications for the Practice of a Critical Social Work Education', *Canadian Social Work Review*, 11(1), 11–26.

Leonard, P. (1995) 'Postmodernism, Socialism and Social Welfare', *Journal of Progressive Human Services*, 6(2), 3–19.

Leonard, P. (1996) 'Three Discourses on Practice: A Postmodern Reappraisal', *Journal of Sociology and Social Welfare*, 23(2), 7–26.

Leonard, P. (1997) *Postmodern Welfare*. London, Sage.

Lerner, H. G. (1987) 'Is Family Systems Theory Really Systemic? A Feminist Communication', *Journal of Psycho-therapy and the Family*, 3(4), 47–63.

Lethem, J. (1994) *Moved to Tears, Moved to Action. Solution Focused Brief Therapy with Woman and Children*. London, BT Press.

Leupnitz, D. A. (1988) *The Family Interpreted: Psychoanalysis, Feminism and Family Therapy*. New York, Basic Books.

Levitas, R. (ed.) (1986) *The Ideology of the New Right*. Cambridge, Polity Press.

Lewis, G. (1996) 'Situated Voices: Black Women's Experience and Social Work', *Feminist Review*, 53 (Summer), 24–56.

Lindfoss, L. and Magnusson, D. (1997) 'Solution-Focused Therapy in Prison', *Contemporary Family Therapy*, 19, 89–104.

Lloyd, L. (1998) 'The Post- and the Ante-: Analysing Change and Changing Analyses in Social Work', *British Journal of Social Work*, 28(5), 709–727.

Lukes, S. (1974) *Power: A Radical View*. London, Macmillan.

Lynch, G. (1997) 'Therapeutic Theory and Social Context: A Social Constructionist Perspective', *British Journal of Guidance and Counselling*, 25(1), 5–15.

Lynch, M. (1998) 'Towards a Constructivist Genealogy of Social Constructionism', in I. Velody and R. Williams (eds), *The Politics of Constructionism*. London, Sage.

Lyotard, J. (1984) *The Postmodern Condition: A Report on Knowledge*. Manchester, Manchester University Press.

Macdonald, A. (1994) 'Brief Therapy in Adult Psychiatry', *Journal of Family Therapy*, 16, 415–526.

Macdonald, A. (1997) 'Brief Therapy in Adult Psychiatry: Further Outcomes', *Journal of Family Therapy*, 19, 213–22.

MacIntyre, A. (1984) *After Virtue*. London, Duckworth.

MacMurray, J. (1961) *Persons in Relation*. London, Faber.

Madge, N. (1997) *Abuse and Survival. A Fact File*. London, The Prince's Trust (in association with NCB).

Mahoney, M. J. (1991) *Human Change Processes*. New York, Basic Books.

Martinez-Brawley, E. E. and Zorita P, M. B. (1998) 'At the Edge of the Frame: Beyond Science and Art in Social Work', *British Journal of Social Work*, 28(2), 197–212.

Maturana, H. (1988) 'Reality: The Search for Objectivity or the Request for a Compelling Argument', *Irish Journal of Psychology*, 9, 25–82.

McBeath, G. B. and Webb, S. A. (1991) 'Social Work, Modernity and Postmodernity', *Sociological Review*, 39 4, 171–92.

McLeod, J. (1997) *Narrative and Psychotherapy*. London, Sage.

McNamee, S. (1992) 'Re-constructing Identity – the Command Construction of Crisis', in S. McNamee & K. J. Gergen, *Therapy as Social Construction*. London, Sage.

McNamee, S. and Gergen, K. J. (eds) (1992) *Therapy as Social Construction*. London, Sage.

Meinert, R. G., Pardeck, J. T. and Murphy, J. W. (eds) *Postmodernism, Religion and the Future of Social Work*. Binghamton, NY, Haworth Press (published simultaneously as *Social Thought*, 18(3), 1998.)

Meyer, C. (1993) *Assessments in Social Work*. New York, Columbia University Press.

Miller, G. (1987) *Becoming Miracle Workers: Language and Meaning in Brief Therapy*. New York, Aldine de Gruyter.

Miller, G. (1992) 'Human Service Practice as Social Problems Work', *Current Research on Occupations and Professions*, 7, 3–21.

Miller, G. and de Shazer, S. (1998) 'Have You Heard the Latest Rumour about ...? Solution-Focused Therapy as a Rumour', *Family Process*, 37(3), 363–77.

Miller, G. and Holstein, J. A. (eds) (1993) *Constructionist Controversies: Issues in Social Problems Theory*. Hawthorne, NY, Aldine de Gruyter.

Miller, J. and Rodwell, M. K. (1997) 'The Context of Constructivism for Social Work Practice and Research: The Clinician-Research Dialogue', paper for the Constructing Social Work Practice Symposium. Tampere, Finland.

Milner, J. (2000) *Women and Social Work: Narrative Approaches*. London, Macmillan.

Milner, J. and O'Byrne, P. (1998) *Assessment in Social Work*. Basingstoke and London, Macmillan.

Mumby, D. K. (1993) 'Introduction', in D. K. Mumby (ed.), *Narrative and Social Control*. Newbury Park CA and London.

Munro, E. (1998) *Understanding Social Work: An Empirical Approach*. London, The Athlone Press.

Murphy, J. W. and Pardeck, J. T. (1998) 'Renewing Social Work through a Postmodern Perspective', *Social Thought*, 18(3), p. 5.

Neimeyer, G. J. (ed.) (1993) *Constructivist Assessment*. New York, Sage.

Newton, C. and Marsh, P. (1993) *Training in Partnership – Translating Interventions into Practice in Social Services*. York, Joseph Rowntree Foundation.

Noaparast, K. (1995) 'Toward a More Realistic Constructivism', in R. A. Neimeyer and G. J. Neimeyer (eds), *Advances in Personal Construct Psychology*. Greenwich, CT, Jai Press.

Noble, W. (1991) 'Ecological Realism and the Fallacy of "Objectification"', in A. Still and A. Costall (eds), *Against Cognitivism: Alternative Foundations for Cognitive Psychology*. New York, Harvester Wheatsheaf.

Norman, A. P. (1991) 'Tell It As It Was: Historical Narratives on Their Own Terms', *History and Theory*, 30(2), 119–35.

Norris, C. (1990) *What's Wrong with Postmodernism?* London, Harvester Wheatsheaf.

O'Hanlon, B. (1993) 'Possibility Theory', in S. Gilligan and R. Price (eds), *Therapeutic Conversations*. New York, Norton.

O'Hanlon, B. (1995) 'Breaking the Bad Trance', London Conference.

O'Hanlon, B. (1996) *Frozen in Time*. Pack of training tapes. Omaha, Possibilities.

O'Hanlon, B. and Beadle, S. (1994) *A Field Guide to Possibilityland*. Omaha, Possibility Press.

O'Hanlon, B. and Hudson, P. (1991) *Re-writing Love Stories*. New York, Norton.

O'Hanlon, B. and Weiner-Davis, M. (1989) *In Search of Solutions*. New York, Norton.

O'Leary, D. (1998) *Passion for the Possible*. Dublin, Columban Press.

Omer, H. (1993) 'Quasi-Literal Elements in Psychotherapy', *Psychotherapy*, 30, 59–66.

Omer, H. (1994) *Critical Intervention in Psychotherapy: From Impasse to Turning Point*. New York, Norton.

O'Neill, J. (1995) *The Poverty of Postmodernism*. London, Routledge.

Pardeck, J. T., Murphy, J. W. and Choi, J. M. (1994) 'Some Implications of Postmodernism for Social Work Practice', *Social Work*, 39(4), 243–6.

Pardeck, J. T., Murphy, J. W. and Chung, W. S. (1994) 'Social Work and Postmodernism', *Social Work and Social Sciences Review*, 5(2), 113–23.

Parker, I. (1992) *Discourse Dynamics: Critical Analysis of Social and Individual Psychology*. London, Routledge.

Parton, N. (1985) *The Politics of Child Abuse*. London, Macmillan.

Parton, N. (1994a) 'The Nature of Social Work under Conditions of (Post)Modernity', *Social Work and Social Sciences Review*, 5(2), 93–112.

Parton, N. (1994b) 'Problematics of Government, (Post)Modernity and Social Work', *British Journal of Social Work*, 24(1), 9–32.

Parton, N. (ed.) (1996) *Social Theory, Social Change and Social Work.* London, Routledge.

Parton, N. (1998a) 'Advanced Liberalism, (Post)Modernity and Social Work: Some Emerging Social Configurations', *Social Thought*, 18(3), 71–88. Reprinted in Meinert, R. G., Pardeck, J. T. and Murphy, J. W. (1998) *Postmodernism, Religion and the Future of Social Work.* New York, The Haworth Press.

Parton, N. (1998b) 'Risk, Advanced Liberalism and Child Welfare: The Need to Rediscover Uncertainty and Ambiguity', *British Journal of Social Work*, 28(1), 5–27.

Parton, N. and Marshall, W. (1998) 'Postmodernism and Discourse Approaches to Social Work', in R. Adams, L. Dominelli and M. Payne (eds), *Social Work: Themes, Issues and Critical Debates.* London, Macmillan.

Parton, N., Thorpe, D. and Wattam, C. (1997) *Child Protection: Risk and the Moral Order.* London, Macmillan.

Payne, M. (1991) *Modern Social Work Theory.* London, Macmillan.

Payne, M. (1992) 'Psychodynamic Theory within the Politics of Social Work Theory', *Journal of Social Work Practice*, 6(2), 141–9.

Payne, M. (1996) *What is Professional Social Work?* Birmingham, Venture Press.

Payne, M. (1997) *Modern Social Work Theory.* 2nd edn. London, Macmillan.

Pearson, G., Treseder, J. and Yelloly, M. (eds) (1988) *Social Work and the Legacy of Freud.* London, Macmillan.

Pease, B. and Fook, J. (eds) (1999) *Transforming Social Work Practice: Postmodern Critical Perspectives*, London, Routledge.

Peile, C. and MacCourt, M. (1997) 'The Rise of Relativism: The Future of Theory and Knowledge Development in Social Work', *British Journal of Social Work*, 27(3), 343–60.

Philp, M. (1979) 'Notes on the Form of Knowledge in Social Work', *Sociological Review*, 27(1), 83–111.

Pietroni, M. (1995) 'The Nature and Aims of Professional Education for Social Workers: A Postmodern Perspective', in M. Yelloly and M. Henkel (eds), *Learning and Teaching in Social Work: Towards Reflective Practice.* London, Jessica Kingsley.

Pincus, A. and Minahan, A. (1973) *Social Work Practice: Model and Method.* Itasca, IL, Peacock.

Pithouse, A. (1998) *Social Work: The Social Organisation of an Invisible Trade*, 2nd edn. Aldershot, Ashgate.

Potter, J. and Wetherell, M. (1987) *Discourse and Social Psychology: Beyond Attitudes and Behaviour.* London, Sage.

Pozatek, E. (1994) 'The Problem of Certainty: Clinical Social Work in the Postmodern Era', *Social Work*, 39(4), 396–403.

Pugh, R. (1997) 'Change in British Social Work', in B. Lesnik (ed.), *Change in Social Work*. Aldershot, Arena.

Ratner, H. (1989) 'Introducing Steve de Shazer', *Context*, 3, p. 17.

Rees, S. and Wallace, A. (1982) *Verdicts on Social Work*. London, Edward Arnold.

Reid, W. J. (1978) *The Task Centred System*. New York, Columbia University Press.

Reid, W. J. and Epstein, L. (1977) *Task Centred Practice*. New York, Columbia University Press.

Rodwell, M. K. (1990) 'Person Environment Construct: Positivist versus Naturalist; Dilemma or Opportunity for Health Social Work Research and Practice?', *Social Science and Medicine*, 31(1), 27–34.

Rodwell, M. K. (1998) *Social Work Constructivist Research*. New York and London, Garland Publishing Inc.

Rodwell, M. K. and Wood, D. (1994) 'Constructivist Evaluation: The Policy Practice Context', in E. Sherman and W. J. Reid (eds), *Qualitative Research in Social Work*. New York, Columbia University Press.

Rojek, C., Peacock, G. and Collins, S. (1988) *Social Work and Received Ideas*. London, Routledge.

Rorty, R. (1979) *Philosophy and the Mirror or Nature*. Princeton NJ, Princeton University Press.

Rorty, R. (1980) 'Pragmatism, Relativism and Irrationalism', *Proceedings and Addresses of the American Philosophical Association*, 53, 719–38.

Rose, N. (1985) *The Psychological Complex: Psychology, Politics and Society in England, 1869–1939*. London, Routledge & Kegan Paul.

Rose, N. (1989) *Governing the Soul: The Shaping of the Private Self*. London, Routledge.

Rose, N. (1996) 'The Death of the Social: Re-figuring the Territory of Government', *Economy and Society*, 25(3), 327–50.

Rose, N. and Miller, P. (1992) 'Political Power Beyond the State: Problematics of Government', *British Journal of Sociology*, 43(2), 173–205.

Rosenau, P. M. (1992) *Post-Modernism and the Social Sciences: Insights, Inroads and Intrusions*. Princeton, NJ, Princeton University Press.

Saleebey, D. (1989) 'The Estrangement of Knowing and Doing: Professions in Crisis', *Social Casework*, 70, 556–663.

Sands, R. G. and Nuccio, K. (1992) 'Postmodern Feminist Theory and Social Work', *Social Work*, 37(6), 489–94.

Sarbin, T. R. (1986) 'The Narrative as Root Metaphor for Psychology', in T. R. Sarbin (ed.), *The Storied Nature of Human Conduct*. New York, Praeger.

Sarbin, T. R. and Kitsuse, J. I. (1994) 'A Prologue to Constructing the Social', in T. R. Sarbin and J. I. Kitsuse (eds), *Constructing the Social*. London, Sage.

222 *Bibliography*

Saunders, T. R. (1996) 'Solution-Focused Therapy in Practice: A Personal Experience', *Counselling*, November, 312–16.

Schön, D. A. (1983) *The Reflective Practitioner: How Professionals Think in Action.* New York, Basic Books.

Schön, D. A. (1987) *Educating the Reflective Practitioner.* San Francisco, CA, Jossey-Bass.

Schutz, A. (1962–6) *Collected Papers*, 3 vols. The Hague, Martinus Nijhoff.

Seidman, S. (1998) *Contested Knowledge: Social Theory in the Postmodern Era.* 2nd edn. Oxford, Blackwell.

Selekman, M. D. (1991) 'The Solution-Orientated Parenting Group: A Group Alternative that Works', *Journal of Strategic and Systemic Therapies*, 10(1), 37–50.

Selekman, M. D. (1993) *Pathways to Change.* New York, Guilford.

Selekman, M. D. (1997) *Solution-Focused Therapy with Children.* New York, Guilford Press.

Seligman M. E. P. (1995) 'The Effectiveness of Psychotherapy: The Consumer Reports Study', *American Psychologist*, 50, 965–74.

Sheldon, B. (1978) 'Theory and Practice in Social Work: A Re-examination of a Tenuous Relationship', *British Journal of Social Work*, 8(1), 1–22.

Sheppard, M. (1995a) *Care Management and the New Social Work: A Critical Analysis.* London, Whiting & Birch.

Sheppard, M. (1995b) 'Social Work, Social Science and Practice Wisdom', *British Journal of Social Work*, 25(3), 265–94.

Sheppard, M. (1998) 'Practice Validity, Reflexivity and Knowledge for Social Work', *British Journal of Social Work*, 28(5), 763–81.

Shotter, J. (1993) *Conversational Realities: Constructing Life through Language.* London, Sage.

Simons, J. W. and Billig, M. (eds) (1994) *After Postmodernism: Reconstructing Ideology Critique.* London, Sage.

Smale, G., Tuson, G., Behal, N. and Marsh, P. (1993) *Empowerment, Assessment, Care Management and the Skilled Worker.* London, NISW.

Smart, B. (1999) *Facing Modernity: Ambivalence, Reflexivity and Morality.* London, Sage.

Smith, B. H. (1997) *Belief and Resistance: Dynamics of Contemporary Intellectual Controversy.* London, Harvard University Press.

Smith, C. and White, S. (1997) 'Parton, Howe and Postmodernity: A Critical Comment on Mistaken Identity', *British Journal of Social Work*, 27(2), 272–96.

Smith, G., Cox, D. and Saradjian, J. (1998) *Women and Self-Harm.* London, The Women's Press.

Snyder, M. (1984) 'When Belief Creates Reality', *Advances in Experimental Social Psychology*, 18, 247–300.

Specht, H. and Vickery, A. (eds) (1977) *Integrating Social Work Methods.* London, Allen & Unwin.

Spector, M. and Kitsuse, J. I. (1973) 'Towards a Sociology of Social Problems: Social Conditions, Value Judgements and Social Problems', *Social Problems*, 20(4), 380–95.

Spector, M. and Kitsuse, J. (1987) *Constructing Social Problems.* Hawthorne, NY, Aldine de Gruyter.

Spence, D. P. (1982) *Narrative Truth and Historical Truth: Meaning and Interpretation in Psychoanalysis.* New York, Norton.

Staten, H. (1984) *Wittgenstein and Derrida.* Lincoln, University of Nebraska Press.

Stenson, K. (1993) 'Social Work Discourse and the Social Work Interview', *Economy and Society*, 22(1), 42–76.

Stevenson, O. (1998a) 'It Was More Difficult Than We Thought: A Reflection on 50 Years of Child Welfare Practice', *Child and Family Social Work*, 3(3), 153–61.

Stevenson, O. (1998b) 'Social work with children and families', in O. Stevenson (ed.) *Child Welfare in the UK.* Oxford, Blackwell Science.

Stone, E. (1988) *Black Sheep and Kissing Cousins: How Our Family Stories Shape Us.* New York, Time Books.

Stubbs, M. (1980) *Language and Literacy.* London, Routledge & Kegan Paul.

Sundman, P. (1997) 'Solution-Focused Ideas in Social Work', *Journal of Family Therapy*, 19, 159–72.

Swann, W. B., Giuliano, T. and Wegner, D. M. (1982) 'Where Leading Questions Can Lead', *Journal of Personality and Social Psychology*, 24(6), 1025–35.

Teubner, G. (1989) 'How the Law Works: Towards a Constructivist Epistemology of Law', *Law and Society Review*, 23(5), 727–56.

Thompson, N. (1997) *Anti-Discriminatory Practice*, 2nd edn. London, Macmillan.

Thompson, N. (1998) *Promoting Equality: Challenging Discrimination and Oppression in the Human Services.* London, Macmillan.

Thyer, B. A. (1994) 'Empiricists versus Social Constructionists: More Fuel on the Flames', *Families in Society: Journal of Contemporary Human Services*, May, 308–12.

Timms, N. (1968) *The Language of Social Casework.* London, Routledge & Kegan Paul.

Tomm, K. (1987) 'Interventive Interviewing', *Family Process*, 26, 167–83.

Townsend, P. (1970) *The Fifth Social Service.* London, Fabian Society.

Turnell, A. and Edwards, S. (1997) 'Aspiring to Partnership: The Signs of Safety Approach to Child Protection', *Child Abuse Review*, 6, 179–90.

Turnell, A. and Edwards, S. (1999) *Signs of Safety: A Solution and Safety Oriented Approach to Child Protection Casework.* New York, Norton.

Turner, B. S. (1990) *Theories of Modernity and Postmodernity*. London, Sage.

Varella, F. (1989) 'Reflections on the Circulation of Concepts between the Biology of Cognition and Systemic Family Therapy', *Child Process*, 28, 15–24.

Vaughan, K., Young, B. C., Webster, D. C. and Thomas, M. R. (1996) 'A continuum-of-cake Model for Inpatient Psychiatric Treatment', in Miller, Happle and Duncan (eds) *Handbook of Solution-Focused Brief Therapy*. San Francisco, Jossley-Bass.

Velody, I. and Williams, R. (eds) (1998) *The Politics of Constructionism*. London, Sage.

Wagner, P. (1994) *A Sociology of Modernity: Liberty and Discipline*. London, Routledge.

Walker, A. (1983) *In Search of Our Mothers' Gardens*. London, The Women's Press.

Waller, W. (1936) 'Social Problems and Mores', *American Sociological Review*, 1, 922–33.

Walsh, T. (1997) *Solution-Focused Child Protection – Towards a Positive Frame for Social Work Practice*. Dublin, Trinity College.

Walter, J. L. and Peller, J. E. (1992) *Becoming Solution-Focused in Brief Therapy*. New York, Bruner/Mazel.

Warren, W. G. (1994) 'Subjecting and Objecting in Personal Construct Psychology', in A. Thompson and P. Cummings (eds), *European Perspecives in PCP: Selected Papers from the Inaugural Conference of European Personal Construct Association, York, England, 1992*. Lincoln, European Personal Construct Association.

Warren, W. G. (1998) *Philosophical Dimensions of Personal Construct Psychology*. London, Routledge.

Watzlawick, P. (1984) *The Invented Reality*. New York, Norton.

Weakland, J. H., Fisch, R., Watzlawick, P. and Bodin, A. (1974) 'Brief Therapy: Focused Problem Solution', *Family Process*, 13, 141–68.

Weakland, J. H. and Jordan, L. (1992) 'Working Briefly with Reluctant Clients: Child Protective Services as an Example', *Journal of Family Therapy*, 14, 231–54.

Weick, A. and Saleebey, D. (1998) 'Postmodern Perspectives for Social Work', *Social Thought*, 18(3), 21–40. Reprinted in R. G. Meinert, J. T. Pardeck and J. W. Murphy (eds), *Postmodernism, Religion and the Future of Social Work*. New York, Haworth Press.

Weiner-Davis, M. (1992) *Divorce Busting*. New York, Fireside.

Weiner-Davis, M. (1993) 'Pro-constructed Realities', in S. Gilligan and R. Price (eds), *Therapeutic Conversations*. New York, Norton.

Weingarten, K. (1998) 'The Small and the Ordinary: The Daily Practice of a Postmodern Therapy', *Family Process*, 37, Spring, 3–15.

Wheeler, J. (1995) 'Believing in Miracles', *ACPP Reviews and Newsletter*, 17, 255–61.

White, M. (1984) 'Pseudo-Encopresis: From Avalanche to Victory', *Family Systems Medicine*, 2(2), 150–60.

White, M. (1989) *Selected Papers*. Adelaide, Dulwich Centre.

White, M. (1990) *Re-authoring Lives: Interviews and Essays*. Adelaide, Dulwich Centre.

White, M. (1993) 'Deconstruction and Therapy', in S. Gilligan and R. Price (eds), *Therapeutic Conversations*. New York, Norton.

White, M. (1996) Doncaster 2-day Training Conference.

White, M. and Epston, D. (1990) *Narrative Means to Therapeutic Ends*. New York, Norton.

White, S. (1997) 'Beyond Retroduction? – Hermeneutics, Reflexivity and Social Work Practice', *British Journal of Social Work*, 27(5), 739–53.

White, S. (1998) 'Analysing the Content of Social Work: Applying the Lessons from Qualitative Research', in J. Cheetham and M. Kazi (eds), *The Working of Social Work*. London, Jessica Kingsley.

Wilgosh, R., Hawkes, D. and Marsh, I. (1993) 'Session Two and Beyond – or what do you say after you say hello again?', *Context*, 17, 31–3.

Wilkes, R. (1981) *Social Work with Undervalued Groups*. London, Tavistock.

Williams, F. (1996) 'Postmodernism, Feminism and the Question of Difference', in N. Parton (ed.), *Social Theory, Social Change and Social Work*. London, Routledge.

Winnicott, D. W. (1953) 'Transitional Objects and Transitional Phenomena', *Journal of Psycho Analysis*, vol. xxxiv. Reprinted in *Collected Papers* (1958), London, Tavistock Publications, 229–42.

Witkin, S. L. (1991) 'The Implications of Social Constructionism for Social Work', *Journal of Teaching in Social Work*, 4(1), 37–48.

Witten, M. (1993) 'Narrative and Obedience in the Workplace', in D. K. Mumby (ed.), *Narrative and Social Control*. Newbury Park CS and London, Sage.

Wittgenstein, L. (1963) *Philosophical Investigations*. Oxford, Blackwell.

Wittgenstein, L. (1968) *Philosophical Investigations*, 3rd edn. New York, Macmillan.

Wittgenstein, L. (1972) *Lectures and Conversations on Aesthetics, Psychology and Religious Belief*. Berkeley, University of California Press.

Zimmerman, T. S., Prest, L. A. and Wetzel, B. E. (1997) 'Solution-Focused Couples Therapy Groups: An Empirical Study', *Journal of Family Therapy*, 19, 125–44.

Index